Swami Muktananda Paramahansa

# THE PLAY
# OF CONSCIOUSNESS

## (CHITSHAKTI VILAS)

### SWAMI MUKTANANDA PARAMAHANSA

Shree Gurudev Siddha Yoga Ashram

*California*

ISBN 0-914602-26-8
An abridged version of this book was published in hardback under the title
*Guru* by Harper & Row, New York.

# INTRODUCTION
Ram Dass

In 1970 I had the opportunity to travel halfway around the world on an extended tour with Swami Muktananda. In 1971 he invited me to accompany him and his devotees on a pilgrimage of Shiva temples in South India. Later in 1971, again at his invitation, I participated in ceremonies honoring his Guru, Swami Nityananda at Ganeshpuri. For me, all of these opportunities to be in the presence of Babaji (Swami Muktananda) were experienced as palpable grace. The combination of his wisdom, compassion, power, unpredictability and love create for those about him an intense fire of purification. The moments shared with Babaji I number amoung the most profound spiritual teachings I have been blessed to receive.

There are several reasons why this volume is of significance to the sadhaka or spiritual seeker:

1. It is extremely rare that an individual of the level of conscious evolution of Swami Muktananda offers to us such an explicit autobiographical statement. Many of us have noted in the course of our own work on ourselves that at each successive stage of awakening, we re-view our past experiences in a new and liberating perspective. Often, however, we have very little understanding of the experiences correlated with our present level of consciousness because we are too close and cannot see the forest for the trees. To have the many stages of sadhana depicted by one who has gone beyond them helps us to gain a perspective which can only facilitate our journey.

2. Most of the literature depicts the spiritual journey in terms of abstract philosophical terminology which is difficult to use in relation to our own immediate predicaments. How much more relevant is the intimate experiential chronology of spiritual autobiography. Although we recognize

that experiences along the path are but forms of spiritual materialism, yet we can honor them as signposts which guide us and which we will ultimately leave behind.

3. In the history of the human journey into consciousness there are a number of lineages, or strategies, or rays or forms of yoga, all of which have the potentiality for bringing about enlightenment. Of all these paths, among the least understood are those which work primarily through energy and through the Guru. In the West, most of our conceptualizing of energy is in worldly rather than spiritual terms; our understanding of the relation between Guru and disciple is often only conceived of in terms of interpersonal power, surrender and dependency.

It is the combination of the Yoga of Kundalini (spiritual energy) and Gurukripa (grace of the Guru) which would seem to best characterize the lineage of Swami Muktananda. To have these esoteric traditions spelled out for us as he has done in such a subtle and explicit manner, gives us a spiritually productive way of viewing energy and Guru. This is a significant enrichment of our appreciation of the diverse vehicles for approaching enlightenment.

Now, when there is apparently a spiritual renaissance occurring in the West, we are indeed fortunate to be the beneficiaries of the teachings of the living spiritual guides of the East. I honor Swami Muktananda and the rich treasure he is sharing with us.

July 22, 1974

Shanti,

*Ram Dass*

# CONTENTS

## Book I

## THE PATH OF THE SIDDHAS

### 1. THE IMPORTANCE OF GOD-REALISATION

## 2. MY SPIRITUAL EXPERIENCES

# Book II

# TEACHING OF THE SIDDHAS

# Appendix

# SOME EXPERIENCES OF SIDDHA STUDENTS

# INTRODUCTION

Last summer, I had the good fortune of accompanying Gurudev Muktananda Baba to the sacred, beautiful hill resort of Mahableshwar. Before we left the Ashram, Gurudev said, "Amma, take some sheets of blank paper as I would like to complete the second part of *Mukteshwari** there." We had been in Mahableshwar for barely three days when a message was received from the Ashram secretary, Shri K. S. Desai, requesting us to persuade Gurudev to write something for the Special Issue of the monthly journal *Deeplakshmi,* entitled *Swami Muktananda Paramahansa.* Gurudev agreed to our request. As a result, the paper meant for *Mukteshwari* turned into the manuscript of this unique volume. Starting as a small article, it eventually took the shape of this book. In such favourable circumstances—the ancient joyful resort of Lord Shiva, the calm environment, the cool air, the respite from the usual throng of devotees and concern about Ashram management, Sri Gurudev's pen gathered momentum and this exceptional book was completed in just twenty-two days. Gurudev has always been like that. Once the inspiration comes, he acts with great speed as long as it lasts.

In the mornings, before sunrise, Gurudev used to go out for about an hour to enjoy cool air in the forest. He would sit in the clouds for a while, come back with fresh inspiration and start writing. He wrote for six or seven hours every day. Visitors were allowed only half an hour for satsang in the evening. At midday, after lunch, Professor Jain would read out what Gurudev had written. The devotees eagerly waited for this hour. Everyone's mind was occupied with the mysteries of Siddha Yoga. Hearing about the divine experiences of Gurudev, they would talk about them with wonder and growing deeply

*A compilation of 501 aphorisms by Swami Muktananda.

absorbed in the subject, they became one with him, as it were. Thus, Shri Yogendra (Papa) Trivedi's insistance on taking Gurudev to Mahableshwar, away from the heat of Ganeshpuri, bore fruit in the form of this work.

Gurudev had never granted our earlier requests to write about his sadhana. This time, however, out of compassion for seekers, he expounded Siddha Yoga through his own experiences. Very few people are familiar with Siddha Yoga in the present age. Even so, this yoga still survives and will endure forever. Its tradition goes back to times unknown. Only its initiates know its secret. This is the path of the Siddhas. Siddha Gurus and their followers are reluctant to reveal it to everyone. This yoga requires a Siddha Guru who can initiate by Shaktipat and a disciple who is worthy of his grace.

One may have a theoretical knowledge of Siddha Yoga, but its real understanding is not possible without direct experience. This is because the experiences are so extra-ordinary and miraculous that one neither finds them in books nor hears about them; also, one does not easily meet a yogi or a student who knows this yoga truly. However, we have had yogis in the past who knew and experienced Shaktipat through the Guru's grace, we have them today and we will have them in the future. Seekers have always benefited from them and will continue to do so. In fact, the tradition of Siddha Yoga remains un-broken.

There are obvious as well as veiled references to the nature and experiences of Shaktipat in the poetry of such saints as Sri Jnaneshwar, Sant Tukaram, Yogi Mukund Rai, Kabir Sahib and Sri Shankaracharya. References to and some explanations of this yoga are found in such ancient books as *Yoga Vasishtha*, *Vayaviya Samhita* (of *Shiva Mahapurana*), *Yogashikhopanishad*, *Jnaneshwari*, *Eknathi Bhagavat*, *Devi Bhagavat*, *Tantraloka* and *Kular-nava Tantra*. There are also a few books by some yogis of recent times who knew and experienced it, such as *Mahayoga Vijnana* by Yogendra Vijnani, *Yogavani* by Swami Shankar Purushottam Tirth, and *Devatma Shakti* (in English) by Swami Vishnu Tirth. As it is fundamentally a matter of direct experience, Siddha Yoga becomes nothing more than a topic for mere discussion if one does not meet a Sadguru who can transmit his grace. That is why there is neither much traditional literature nor many works exclusively on this subject.

The path of Siddha Yoga is one in which the Guru awakens the disciple's inner Shakti, Kundalini, through the yogic process of Shaktipat. As a result the seeker undergoes various spiritual experiences and ultimately attains the goal of God-realisation while practising spiritual disciplines with implicit faith in the Guru. Experiences somewhat similar to those of Shaktipat are known to occur through other disciplines as well. The mantra or mode of worship or exercise given by a Guru does bring some experiences. Shaktipat or Kundalini awakening may occur even without a Guru. For instance, the inner Shakti or Kundalini can also become activated through austerities, mantra recitation, intense devotion or special worship, by the influences of Guru's grace received in a previous life or as a result of an incompleted sadhana of a past birth. Sometimes one receives initiation from a saint or deity in a dream. In such cases of Kundalini awakening, if the person has no knowledge of this subject or his Guru is not perfect in this Yoga, he will not understand the significance of his experiences nor will he know how to make further progress through these experiences. As a result he will not derive inner satisfaction.

Many such seekers come to our Gurudev. Someone says that he hears a sound in his ears, another says he feels a burning sensation in the body. Someone has a vision of the sun, moon and stars; another feels electric shocks. One seems to have gone quite blank, another is overwhelmed by an urge to run away from the world. One sees his own double, another hears a voice within himself. One is carried away by rage and feels like breaking everything, another bursts into song or dance. One sees snakes all around, another sees his own death. Not knowing the true significance of these experiences, some attribute them to ghosts, evil spirits or mental illness, and become miserable. Some give up their sadhana thinking they have strayed from the right path. Some try another path, whereby they suffer even more. Some are discouraged and even deluded by other equally ignorant seekers who tell them that their sadhana has taken a wrong turn. Thus, in spite of the Kundalini having been awakened in one form or another, one does not reach the divine goal because of ignorance. One throws away a gem which has somehow come one's way, thinking it to be a pebble.

Thus, in each path, discipline or mode of worship, some signs of the awakening of Kundalini are seen. By whatever means it be awakened, a Siddha Guru's grace is essential for final attainment and Siddha Yoga is unique in that it is entirely dependent on the Guru's grace. In it, immediately after receiving Shaktipat from the Guru, the disciple starts having experiences. As his Kundalini becomes fully awakened, he acquires a new vision and sees a new world. The special feature of Siddha Yoga is that only what is necessary for the individual seeker occurs, without any effort on his part. He progresses in the manner which is best suited to him and begins to acquire knowledge spontaneously. Therefore, he feels completely satisfied. The all-knowing Shakti acts within him, taking into account the sadhana he has already practised, the degree of his purity, his capacity and aptitude. When the Kundalini is aroused, the seeker immediately becomes aware of the freedom of Her will. She takes charge of his body, prana, mind and intellect. As a result, he has physical, mental and intellectual experiences such as yogic movements, a changed outlook and a more refined perception of spiritual matters.

Although the Guru transmits the same spiritual power, it manifests itself differently in different disciples according to their respective capacities and dispositions. The Guru grants Shaktipat by touch, word, look or thought. Whatever the method, the Shaktipat initiation is one and the same. As its effects vary with different persons, the initiation has been given various names in the scriptures, such as *kriyavati, kalavati, varnamayi, vedhamayi* or *jnanamayi*. In *kriyavati* the disciple starts automatically performing yogic postures, *mudras*, *bandhas* and *prana-yama*. In *kalavati* he has visions of various lights, gods and goddesses, and perceives divine touch, sounds, smells, tastes and forms. In *varnamayi* he is inspired to compose poetry or chant mantras. In *vedhamayi* he experiences the piercing of the *chakras* in the *sushumna* nerve. In *jnanamayi* instantaneous enlightenment takes place. Many seekers have several of these experiences together, but in all of them only the experiences vary, not the initiation.

Sometimes Shaktipat takes place even without a thought on the part of the Guru. Gurudev considers this to be the best initiation. The atmosphere around Siddhas is always saturated with Chiti. In their dwellings their Shakti spreads all around and passes into everything— birds and animals, trees and creepers, flowers and fruit and even inanimate things. It may automatically enter a seeker at any time. For this reason the scriptures have emphasised the importance of the company of saints and their dwellings. Gurudev often says: "I don't do any-thing. Although I haven't thought about it, some seekers receive Shaktipat through me. Like radar—when I feel vibrations within me I realise that somebody has received Shakti, and as soon as I see him I recognise him." Each one receives according to his capacity. Therefore Gurudev says to those who want to be initiated, "Stay in any corner of the Ashram and relax completely. Live and meditate with the other seekers. Hold satsang with them. The omniscient Shakti will catch you at any time."

The word *pat* which means 'descent' in the word 'Shaktipat' should not be taken to indicate that any force is being instilled from outside, for the Shakti does lie latent in each person's *muladhar*. By his grace the Guru simply awakens the dormant force and makes it active. Since grace comes from 'outside' the word *pat* is used. In fact, 'Gurukripa' is the more appropriate expression. One candle is being lighted from another—this is a good analogy to understand this process.

On receiving the divine spark from the Guru, the disciple begins to have experiences according to his disposition. If he is an intellectual type, his intellect will be so sharpened as to understand subtler subjects and find satisfactory answers to questions which have been baffling him. If devotional, he will experience the eight *sattvic* states, *bhava-samadhi* and sublime love. Those who must see lights and hear sounds will experience them; their minds will become absorbed in them and achieve one-pointedness. Others whose bodies need purification will begin to be purified through automatic yogic movements. Cravings may get stronger for a while, but will eventually disappear. Chronic or dormant diseases may erupt but will be finally expelled from the system forever. Thus the awakened Shakti securely sets the seeker on the path to spiritual progress. Once the Guru's Shakti passes into the disciple, the Guru's duty is only to watch him until he attains perfection. If on the way he meets obstacles, the Guru helps him to overcome them and also regulates the intensity of the Shakti as necessary. It is believed that Shakti is identical with the Guru. Therefore, by having full faith in the experiences of his sadhana and steadfast devotion to the Guru, the disciple automatically progresses on the spiritual path. Doubt or lack of faith will only impede his development. For this reason the Guru and devotion to him are considered very important in Siddha Yoga.

Nowadays it is argued that since the divine power is all-pervasive and dwells in every man, there is no need for a Guru; we can safely rely on God to guide us from within. It is true that God is present in everyone's heart, but being covered by thick layers of ignorance, He is scarcely perceptible. Seated in the heart He keeps man bound to the wheel of time according to the laws of destiny— भ्रामयन् सर्वभूतानि यन्त्रारूढानि मायया (*Gita,* XVIII-61). Man cannot therefore hope to be redeemed by this Power, which is inaccessible to him. It is only when, by the grace of the Guru in whom God has been fully manifested, the veil is removed, that God hidden within reveals Himself and ensures the seeker's ultimate welfare. The tradition of such Gurukripa goes back to time immemorial, but in the present materialistic age it is dis-

missed as 'gurudom,' and that is why most people are
unfamiliar with this spiritual science and its practic-
ability.

When our compassionate Gurudev saw the young
school and college boys and girls who had accompanied
us to Mahableshwar meditating so earnestly, he was
moved to write this work on Siddha Vidya, the Science
of the Perfected Ones. His purpose was to encourage and
help them to progress and feel satisfied with their
sadhana and to promote their true happiness and welfare.
This book is chiefly meant for all those seekers, young
and old, who follow the Siddha path. They are coming
to our Ashram in ever-increasing numbers and every
morning and evening one can see them sitting in the
Meditation Hall absorbed in meditation. Some may break
into the melodious chanting of such mantras as *Om
Namah Shivaya* or *Guru Om*, while others may be performing charming *mudras*. Some may be dancing in
classical styles, while others may be shedding involuntary
tears of joy. One performs yogic postures while another
does violent *bhasrika*. One is merrily rolling on the
ground, while another is engrossed in the *tandra* state,
as if travelling through various worlds.

As the seeker advances in sadhana after receiving the
Guru's grace, he has to become his own Guru by understanding his own progress, remaining witness to his inner
processes while surrendering himself to the awakened
Shakti. Even then he may feel curious about the nature
of the experiences he has had, about those he will have
later and their sequence, about the present level of his
progress and what he should do to advance further.
Sometimes seekers have such strange and unheard of
experiences that they become anxious and frightened.
Those who have been initiated by Gurudev frequently
come to him to ask about Siddha Yoga in general and
their own experiences in particular. He assures them,
"Whatever is happening is for your good. Do not be
afraid. I went through the same. I too had strange
movements. Every now and then I had my share of restlessness, anger, dejection, apathy, sensuality and blank-

ness which are generally considered to be *tamasic* tendencies, but I suffered no harm from them. On the contrary, I realised the Divine. So do not worry. Let whatever is happening run its course. In reality your nerves are being purified and the accumulated impressions of the past are being wiped out. You will eventually experience such divine bliss as will keep you continually bright and cheerful."

It is for the guidance of such Siddha students that *Chitshakti Vilas* has been written. It is divided into two books. In Book One Sri Gurudev presents Gurukripa as the best means of God-realisation. Then he demonstrates the validity of Siddha Yoga by describing his own experiences following his initiation through Shaktipat. According to him, forgetfulness of one's own true nature is the real cause of all one's misery and suffering. This has also been called ignorance, nescience or *maya*. Self-realisation or Self-knowledge, which follows the awakening of the inner Shakti, is the means of deliverance from its clutches. For this, one has to surrender to the true Guru and become worthy of his grace. The true Guru makes his disciple renounce not the world but his limited self; he takes away not his wealth and possessions but his sins and anxieties; he enables him to experience the silence of a cave and the peace of solitude in his own home and transforms his daily life into a spiritual sadhana.

In describing the greatness of his own Guru, Bhagawan Nityananda, Gurudev brings out the divinity of the Guru. The Guru is the supreme deity. He endows a mantra with living, conscious force. He is the divine power of grace. He is the highest consciousness which manifests itself in ever-new ways; indeed, he is Parashakti Chiti or Mother Kundalini Herself. It is indeed good fortune to receive initiation from such a perfected Master. Meditation on the Guru is the noblest means of receiving his grace. The Guru imparts the mantra, teaches the technique of repeating it and awakens the inner Shakti in you—so then meditation on him leads to the highest goal. Sri Gurudev has also discussed a unique method of meditation on the Guru. Joyful contemplation of the Guru is the very essence of Siddha Yoga, the sadhana of Shaktipat and the secret of God-realisation. As the disciple constantly remembers his divine Guru, the Guru begins to work within him as Chitshakti, washing away all his impurities and raising his finite being to infinite Godhood. Therefore the disciple's paramount duty is to seek the Guru's company and to serve and obey him. This is Siddha Yoga, the Path of the Perfected Ones.

Sri Gurudev has given an account of the marvellous workings of the inner Shakti by relating his own experiences* such as Shaktipat initiation, the yogic movements caused by the awakened Kundalini, the frightful visions, the confused state of the mind, the visions of lights, gods and goddesses and different worlds, the divine sounds, the vision of his own double, the fear of death, piercing of the ear-*chakra* and the ocular *bindu*, the tasting of ambrosia, the upsurge of love, the awareness of oneness with the Absolute and the experience of identification with the Guru. He has depicted in full detail the four lights (red, white, black and blue) and their sizes (physical body, thumb, finger-tip and lentil-size) which appear in meditation and represent the four bodies (gross, subtle, causal and supracausal) and the four states (waking, dream, deep sleep and transcendent) described in Vedanta. These lights appear one within the other. The sequence of the visions of the lights indicates the different stages of the spiritual journey. Sri Gurudev explains how a seeker gradually rises above body-consciousness and the sense of duality until he attains the Witness-consciousness and spontaneously feels: *aham brahmasmi*, I am the Absolute.' The greatness of Siddha Yoga is that it positively affirms the Ultimate Reality as *idam iti* 'This is It' or *ayam asmi* 'I am It,' which is negatively indicated in Vedanta by *neti neti* 'not this, not this' and testifies to Its existence by direct experience. Vedanta is lame without yoga. Knowledge without experience is merely a subject for learned discourse. In fact Siddha Yoga com-

---

* There is a short account of the same in the biography of Swami Muktananda, published in 1969 in English.

plements Vedanta: perfect realisation is attained when
the two are united. Sri Gurudev has also quoted the
poetic passages of different saints which allude to the red,
white, black and blue lights—particularly the relevant
verses of Sant Jnaneshwar and Sant Tukaram.

Sri Gurudev has especially sung the praises of the
radiant, shimmering Blue Pearl and its sparkling blue
light. He calls it Neeleshwari, the Blue Goddess, who is
all in all—Chiti, Kundalini, Parashakti, the Absolute, God,
the Guru, Soul, the Abode of Supreme Peace. She is the
self-luminous Chitshakti, playing in the form of the
universe. Only the pure can see this Blue Pearl. Here
Sri Gurudev has revealed a new and miraculous pheno-
menon, the vision of the Divine Being within the Blue
Pearl, described in the *Vedas* as *sahasraksah sahasrapat*,
the One with a thousand eyes and a thousand feet.

Furthermore, he has disclosed the ultimate vision
through his marvellous description of the finale of his
sadhana. He says that towards the very end of his
sadhana of meditation, as his eyes were drawn up towards *sahasrar*, the Blue Pearl began to sparkle, radiating
its conscious blue light on all sides. Within this sphere
of light he had the beatific vision first of his Gurudev,
Bhagawan Nityananda, then of supreme Shiva and finally
of his own form. Afterwards the process reversed—
everything was merged in the Blue Pearl which still
retained its identity. In other words, he now constantly
sees the blue radiance everywhere. This is the supreme
attainment, in which the realised one sees the entire
universe as a luminous sport of Chitshakti. He acquires
the divine vision by which he sees the blue light of Chiti
in everyone. He now perceives the immanence of Parashiva everywhere. He realises the Vedantic truth that
nothing but the all-pervasive God exists. "The universe
is mine, I belong to the universe"—such a vision of unity
inspires him to embrace the entire cosmos. The world,
which according to philosophers is joyless, false and
illusory and which a seeker shuns during his sadhana
because he does not understand its true nature, is now
seen as his own Self. The same world which earlier had

appeared full of misery now becomes the joyful abode of
God. This knowledge, this realisation comes as a gift of
the Guru's grace: it is the boon of Siddha Yoga.

Sri Gurudev has frankly related his experiences in the
tone of an ordinary seeker. He is not in favour of concealing one's spiritual experiences and therefore also
allows Siddha students to disclose theirs. This helps to
bring out the importance, utility and true nature of Siddha
Yoga, which may guide and encourage other seekers.
Gurudev repeats quite often that Siddha Yoga is an easy
means to God-realisation. By revealing his own experiences he seems to say, "If I have attained, you also can.
You can reach the same goal by following the path which
I have followed. It is not at all difficult. I have already
tested what I am telling you." This path is meant for
everyone, young and old, men and women, literate and
illiterate, householders and renunciants. Sri Gurudev
has set many on the Siddha path by transmitting to them
the knowledge and experience he himself has received.

Gurudev loves Siddha students as his own Self and
they are worthy of his love. Some have acquired such
ability that those who sit near them for meditation are
automatically initiated. If anyone happens to be touched
by a student who is deep in a meditative state, he feels
an electric shock and he either begins to perform yogic
movements or goes into deep meditation. Some Siddha
students develop an extraordinary knowledge of past,
present and future events, or receive warnings of forth-
coming mishaps. They talk to and receive instructions
from gods and goddesses. They obtain insight into
spiritual matters and readily find solutions to problems.
They also acquire the ability to guide others in their
sadhana.*

In Book Two Gurudev has prescribed a discipline for
these Siddha students so that their progress may be
smooth and they may achieve the final goal quickly. This
teaching is embodied in seven articles in which Gurudev
directs his beloved Siddha students to put complete trust

* Interested readers can find accounts of these experiences in
the Ashram Annual publication, *Shree Gurudev-Vani.*

in the Guru, to keep their conduct pure, to talk less, to
remain chaste, to have noble thoughts, to love solitude,
and to seek the company of saints and good people, so
that they may be able to conserve the Shakti aroused by
the Guru's grace. He urges them to remember that on
receiving the Guru's grace they belong to the Siddha
tradition. They should live in accordance with it because
they themselves are going to become Siddhas. Their
reward will be quicker if they obey and serve the Guru
and follow the path shown by him in faith, love and
surrender. In fact, their highest attainment lies in
pleasing the Guru. Their sadhana will be weakened if
the Guru is displeased. Siddha students should remain
alert and vigilant in this matter. Their gains will vary
in direct proportion to their devotion to the Guru. The
greater a disciple considers his Guru to be, the greater
he himself becomes. The completion and fruit of sadhana
depend entirely on his attitude to his Guru. If the Guru
is fully pleased it will not take the disciple long to
achieve perfection. The Guru has the power to fill his
disciple's world with Chiti so that he remains constantly
aware of Chiti, the divine Self, in each aspect of his daily
life, and dwells in supreme bliss. In this manner the
disciple lives his life playfully and self-contented. Being
desireless he rises above both possession and renunciation.
He becomes united with Chiti and enjoys imperishable
happiness. His state of inner calm is not disturbed while
he attends to the various demands of his life in the
world. This is the stage of equanimity, the state of
spontaneity, which is the final reward of sadhana.

Sri Gurudev warns his students against any pretence
at meditation if they wish to attain the Siddha state.
They should not be hypocrites and imitate others simply
for praise like a heron affecting meditation only to catch
fish. Their devotion to the Guru, meditation and spiritual
seeking should be genuine. They should not forget that
they will be tested and that their reward will depend
upon their motive. Gurudev says that instead of hankering after worldly benefits, one should desire internal
gain.

Sri Gurudev has explained the true meaning of renunciation in Siddha Yoga. Renunciation is necessary in yoga, but to give up one's home, children, food or society and to retire to the solitude of a forest is not true renunciation; it brings only delusions and not peace. Renunciation should always be accompanied by discrimination. What is there to discard in a world which is pervaded by Chiti or God? For him the world becomes a help and not a hindrance. Therefore one should give up not home but the egoistic notion of 'I and mine,' the sense of a separate existence, the identification of the Self with the body. This attitude alone will lead to the vision of equality.

Sri Gurudev says that if a Siddha student wishes to realise God, who is Love, he must first love himself. He should not consider himself to be wretched, sinful and worthless. Nor should he torture or pamper his body because the body is endowed with consciousness and is a temple of God. God is attained within it. A seeker should feel grateful to his body and keep it pure, clean and healthy. Nor should he punish the mind thinking that it is impure, restless and unstable. It is the mind's restlessness which has led him to the path of yoga. The fact is that the mind is always seeking a suitable place to rest, and if it is lovingly led to a proper place, that is when it is allowed to rest in the Self, it becomes tranquil. Thus the body and the mind are great benefactors and should be treated with love and respect. Gurudev asks how a person can love the world when he despises himself. To be filled with love, a seeker has to expand his self-love to embrace everyone and everything.

The book concludes with Gurudev's blessings on Siddha students, all of whom are very dear to him. He wishes them well; that they may always be protected by the grace of the Siddhas; that they may obtain perfection in Siddha Yoga; that they may ever repose in Chiti and enjoy everlasting bliss.

*Chitshakti Vilas* is indeed a sport of Chitshakti which continually revels in Sri Gurudev. It is inspired by Chiti and dictated by Her. Quite often while writing Gurudev

would pass into meditation for sometime and would say
that he was reliving the experiences of his sadhana,
vividly recollecting and even seeing the same brilliant
lights. It appeared as if the book were writing itself.
While describing his vision of the Divine Being, Gurudev
says, "At this time I am unable to write about this extraordinary miracle. My hand does not move, my pen has
stopped. It is difficult even to keep my eyes open. Only
my lips and tongue are moving. Perhaps Nityananda is
moving them by force." This book is a vibration of the
supremely free Goddess Chiti, who is embodied in the
form of the Guru. It is a gift of Her grace. Therefore
it has been named *Chitshakti Vilas,* the Play of Consciousness. It is pervaded by Chiti and dedicated to
Chitshakti, the Supreme Mother.

This book will have a unique place in the literature of
spiritual sadhana. Such a detailed and lucid account of
Siddha Yoga based on the writer's own experience is rare.
Here Gurudev has revealed the mysteries of travelling to
different worlds in the Blue Star, the vision of the Divine
Being, varied inner lights and their significance, the
process of becoming an *urdhvareta* and its meaning, and
the final realisation. The secrets of Maha Yoga, which
until now had been handed down in the Siddha tradition
from Guru to disciple in strictest secrecy, have been disclosed here so that seekers may become familiar with
this profound science of perfection.

We are sure that earnest seekers will read this book
again and again, ponder over its every word and pursue
yoga with greater zeal and confidence. Those who have
the slightest inclination towards spirituality will certainly
be influenced by this work. Although it may not have
conformed to the criteria of scholars and critics, it is a
true and simple account of a spiritual journey containing
authentic experiences. This book is not a Tantric treatise,
nor a philosophical work, nor a sectarian text. It will
therefore appeal to everyone. In fact, since the book
narrates the true story of personal sadhana, it has turned
into a spiritual autobiography, which is both interesting
and instructive.

While reading the book, the reader feels that Gurudev is not writing but talking to him affectionately. Gurudev modulates from one tone to another while narrating his own experiences in his uninhibited and intimate style. He reflects a wide range of human emotions. Sometimes he is smiling gently, sometimes laughing heartily; sometimes he is overwhelmed by compassion, other times filled with devotion to his Guru. He feels terrified by frightful visions, and astonished at the marvellous sights of different worlds. He is overcome by sadness and depression; he also floats in the joy and enthusiasm bubbling up from within. His manner of instruction is sometimes that of a story-teller, sometimes that of a philosopher. At times he writes like a sensitive poet, at times like a severe ascetic. He caresses like a loving mother, and he admonishes like a stern father or Guru.

Gurudev's rich and versatile personality is fully revealed in his style. For this reason each reader will find in the book something special that appeals to his own temperament. By composing this work Sri Gurudev has done an immense favour to present as well as future seekers. This will make them his own forever, true heirs in Siddhaloka.

Gurudev, who is Parabrahma, is Brahma because he creates for his Siddha students a new and wondrous world imbued with Chiti; He is Vishnu because he sustains and protects them in their divine life; He is Shiva because he annihilates their world of limited individuality. How can we ever repay the great debt we owe him for this wonderful work, this priceless gift of his grace?

The best way of expressing our gratitude to him is to follow his teachings with implicit faith in him and merge ourselves in pure consciousness wherein the Guru abides. Only then can we truly please him. May we become fully worthy of his boundless grace—this is the sincere prayer of Pratibha, his own divine effulgence, at the sacred lotus feet of Sri Gurudev.

February 10, 1970                              AMMA
Shree Gurudev Ashram
Ganeshpuri

Baba Muktananda

Bhagawan Sri Nityananda

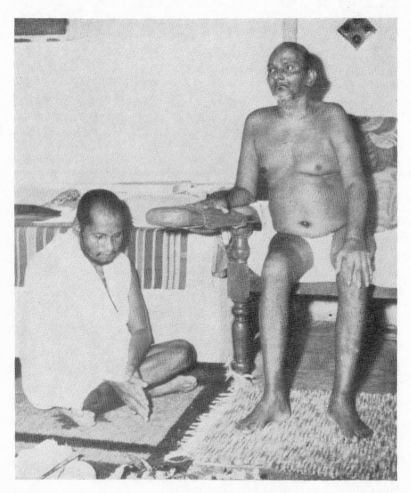

At the Feet of Gurudev Nityananda

# INVOCATION

I invoke the lotus feet of the supreme Guru, Sri Nityananda, the most auspicious one, whose look of grace dispels all misfortunes and bestows the highest good.

I remember the Guru who is the Supreme Being, untainted, utterly pure, the Absolute, whose presence easily grants the transcendental state.

May Sri Nityananda, the goal of meditation of Siddhas, the spring of Vedanta, the divine Witness who is realised through knowledge and detachment, promote our true welfare.

May the highest Guru, Sri Nityananda, by whose favour an aspirant achieves new awareness, who securely establishes his disciples in the state of perfection like his own by transmitting his Shakti into them through Shaktipat, award me full success in the composition of this work.

To obtain his munificence, I bow to Sri Guru Nityananda, the Lord of my heart, who though inhabiting Siddhaloka, pervades everywhere, who is the pure conscious soul, the divine power of grace in his disciples, whose favour is itself the knowledge of the identity of the individual soul and the Absolute.

To invoke his blessings for the completion of this work, I pray to Sri Guru Nityananda, who dwells in the hearts of Siddha students, working dynamically within them in various ways, who is their sole beloved.

For the consummation of my meditation I bow to my beloved Gurudev, my sublime Father, who transcends the distinction of unity and diversity, the torch-bearer on the Siddha path, whose actions are based on equality and on the awareness of the Self of all, who grants the state of perfection easily.

O grace-bestowing Sadguru! I bow at thy lotus feet. Thou art the knowledge of the Siddha path which we receive from thee. O Lord Nityananda of the Blue Form!

Thou revealest thyself within the Blue Pearl when the ignorant notion of "I-mine" is destroyed. Meditation on one's own Self is thy true worship. Repetition of the *So'ham* mantra is thy remembrance. Total surrender is the best offering. The supreme bliss throbbing in meditation constitutes thy pure nature. Thou art the deity of Siddha students, ever dwelling in thy Blue Abode, in *sahasrar*, enveloped by the light of consciousness. May thou, the Self of all, the goal of 'Thou art That,' revelling in Muktananda's heart, ever living in Ganeshpuri, shower the nectar of thy bliss on Siddha students and bestow eternal peace and everlasting joy upon them.

# PRAYER TO SRI GURUDEV

This is my prayer to Gurudev:
May everyone's life be a paradise;
May our trivial notion of "I-mine" vanish
And the knowledge of Chiti arise in our hearts!
Let all beings worship thee with love and equanimity,
And the rhythm of our breath be constantly mingled with
the mantra of *So'ham*.

Bless me that I may adore thee with the awareness of the
Self of all;
May I abandon distinctions of caste, creed and language,
and cleanse my mind.
O Lord Sadguru!
Let me see thee in the high and the low, the suffering
and the needy, the noble and the foolish.
Grant me a heart free from vanity, simple and munificent;
May I spread true knowledge.

Bestow this boon, O Gurudev:
May I ever meditate on thee in my heart.
O Self of all!
May I always love the all-pervasive light.
Sustain my devotion for thee.
Let me pursue knowledge, yoga and meditation
steadfastly;
Let me ever be a worshipper of Siddha Yoga.
Let my mind merge in Chitshakti.

May I always see Rama, Krishna, Shiva and Shakti in thee
And live in Ganeshpuri, the playground of thy Siddha
Yoga.
Raise me above the differences of nation, language, sect
and race.
Grant me the vision of equality.
May Nityananda pulsate in my heart.
May he rule my intellect.

May all attain simplicity, truthfulness, valour, courage,
     discretion and radiance.
May the world be a blissful garden for all, containing the
     celestial wishing-tree and the celestial cow.
Let Siddha students conquer their senses and rejoice in
     Kriya Yoga.
O Guru, O Master!
May I ever see thee in the temples of human hearts and
     feel fulfilled.
May I continue to perform my duties until my last breath
And remember thee uninterruptedly.
May I earn my bread with the sweat of my brow
And ever meditate on thee.

Grant this at least:
May I ever remain united with thee
And see thee at every moment everywhere
Stretching from east to west, north to south.
Thou art Parashiva, pure and invisible.
Thou art Satchidananda.
Thou art in the universe
And the universe is in thee.
Thou art One, undifferentiated, unsurpassed.

Muktananda prays to his Guru:
May the Siddha science bear ample fruit;
May our meditation be dynamic;
May we repose in the Blue Pearl.
May I ever roam joyfully in the world with thee always
     abiding in my heart.
Muktananda prays: O Guru:
Let our lives be the sport of Universal Consciousness!

# DEDICATION

My mother loved me immensely. As I was her only son, I was exceedingly dear to her. In fact, I was the fruit of her life-long worship of supreme Shiva, a boon of His grace to her. But I could not give any happiness to my beloved mother nor make her contented. On the contrary, I left my home at an early age, causing her untold suffering. She languished away in grief for her lost child, remembering him constantly. Mothers do so much for their children and deserve their full gratitude. They nourish them by their own milk and sacrifice their own comforts, feeling happy in their children's happiness. I wonder at everything my mother did for her dear son. She must have entertained great hopes and expectations. How many gods and goddesses must she have propitiated, praying for my happiness? She must have overwhelmed each astrologer who happened to pass by with the questions: "What sort of woman will my son marry? How many children will he have? Will he become famous in the world? Will he go abroad? How many factories will he own? Will he enjoy the love of a brother?" This is how a mother loves her son. If an astrologer makes any bad prediction, she immediately starts appeasing all the deities. She would keep fasts on Thursdays, Fridays, Saturdays, in fact on all days if it came to that. If the child has gone to school, the mother keeps tormenting herself with anxious misgivings: "When will he return from school? Why is he so late today?" Then she keeps looking out for him. She looks at the clock. As the time goes by her anxiety increases: "Why has my dear son not yet returned?" Her ears are eager to catch the welcome sound of her returning child. Thus a mother takes care of her child in countless ways. Yet, the cruel-hearted son leaves her one day. One wonders how many rude shocks he delivers to maternal affection.

I too behaved heartlessly. I had hardly passed fifteen

when one day I forsook parental love. I should not have behaved in this manner, but what could I do? I was destined to commit such a cruel act. It happened. Nay, it should have happened, and it did. Later, after I gained maturity, during the period of my practice of meditation, the time of my spiritual schooling, I began to miss my mother.

So many mothers, including ones from Yeola, Chalisgaon, Kasara, Kokamthan, Vajreshwari and several other places, looked after me, providing food and drink, things for my daily bath, clothes and other necessities. They adapted themselves to my easily inflammable disposition, which involved immense hardship and forbearance. How much love they lavished on me! The fact is that they are my worthy mothers who took such pains over me, fed me with pure, selfless love and devotion and above all, bore my temper. I lacked self-control. I would get enraged at them if they served me food at 11.15 instead of 11 a.m., yelling "Why are you late?" I would also lose my temper if my meal came five minutes too early, shouting, "Why so early?" If the food fell even slightly short of my standard, I would refuse it. If it was cold I would reprimand them. Nor did I spare them if it was too hot. Such was my peculiar, fastidious temper during the period of my sadhana. How deplorable! Even I do not know why I could not tolerate even minor lapses. I felt neither the slightest pity nor forgiveness. Nor did I feel a bit ashamed of it, even in my heart! Those mothers served me with their savings and relentless work, depriving their children for my sake. Yet I extended neither pity nor forgiveness.

O Lord! Why did you make me so particular, so fastidious? I do not know the answer.

All these mothers, including the sweet, affectionate and loving ones from Delhi and Bombay, still consider me a temperamental child and give maternal affection with reverence, devotion and love. If I go on a tour, they accompany me. Why? Because their Baba's food has to be cooked. While touring the country, I take my lunch punctually at 11.30. My mothers have to rise at 3.00 a.m.

to begin to cook my food. They carry it in their cars. To make it harder for them, I absolutely adhere to the timing of my departure. For this reason, they have to get ready in a hurry. Even if I eat on the way the food must be hot, so they use thermos flasks. I must have my tea at 3 p.m. They carry a stove and milk in the car to meet this demand and prepare tea punctually. They have kept my filial feelings alive by undergoing such hardships. They tolerate my peculiar temper, gladly suffering my fastidious ways. They look after me, remaining unperturbed. This would not be possible if my real mother were not acting through them. Many such mothers and their husbands have been good to me in countless ways. Remembering this, I beg them to generously forgive me. I bow to you, mothers, in utter sincerity, seeing my own mother in you all. I pray to Lord Nityananda that I may continue to perceive within you the same Goddess Chiti whom I love so dearly.

One mother in particular has taken care of me as her own son during my tours, enduring all hardships for my sake. She has served me ceaselessly in spite of her poor health. She has never slackened or been negligent. She has not cared for her home or even her college-going son and daughters. She has never worried as to who will look after her household or her worldly responsibilities. She has been cooking and providing for Baba for one month, two and even three months on end, braving scorching heat, freezing cold or tempestuous rains. I dedicate this work to her, Shrimati Sharda Amma, who is particularly dear to me, in memory of my own godly mother, Kusumeshwari.

# PREFACE

I am a follower of Siddha Yoga. I am alive by the grace of a Siddha. It is his benediction which is my life, food, bath, meditation, mantra, prana, highest attainment, salvation and above all, my eternal abode of repose. Lord Nityananda, the supreme Guru, the Master of Siddha yogis, transcending all beyonds, dwelling in Siddhaloka, is the supreme deity of worship for Muktananda and comprises his innermost Self. I live by his kind favour. His divine power of grace abides in my heart, spreading throughout my body.

Let no one think that worldly enjoyments, which lack true joy and flavour, are meant only for the worldly, while yoga and meditation only for renunciants. All people living in the world can easily practise Siddha Yoga while attending to their daily affairs. There are many such practitioners of Siddha Yoga. In ancient times, innumerable householders practised Siddha Yoga and became ideal men and women by harmonising mundane and spiritual pursuits. This path is open to all. The divine Shakti dwells in man as well as woman, about which the *Shiva Samhita* says:

मूलाधारस्थ वन्ह्यात्मतेजो मध्ये व्यवस्थिता ।
जीवशक्तिः कुण्डलाख्या प्राणाकाराथ तेजसी ॥
महाकुण्डलिनी प्रोक्ता परब्रह्मस्वरूपिणी ॥
शब्दब्रह्ममयी देवी एकानेकाक्षराकृतिः ।
शक्ति कुण्डलिनी नाम विसतन्तु निभा शुभा ॥

(The Shakti, Kundalini by name, resembling the pure fibre of a lotus stalk, lies in the midst of golden light in the *muladhar*. She is luminous and is known as the 'coiled one' dwelling within in the form of prana and the individual soul. The great Kundalini is said to be the Absolute Brahman in Her nature. The Goddess is Brahman in the form of words; all letters, from *a* to

xxxiii

*ksha* are Her forms.)

The blissful, divine Shakti, Goddess Chiti, expanding as the universe, is the noble Kundalini. She lies coiled up in the *muladhar* and regulates the functions of the different parts of the body. When she is awakened by the Guru's grace, She makes the best of one's worldly circumstances according to one's destiny. She cultivates supreme friendliness among people, inspiring them to look upon each other as divine, thus transmuting this very world into a paradise. She perfects whatever may be imperfect in one's world.

The divine Shakti, entering a person in the form of grace, transforms that person by Her power. As a husband becomes aware of Her pervasiveness, he develops a new relationship with his wife, based on selfless love. The knowledge that his wife is not a mere woman but divine Kundalini, arises within him. If a wife begins to look upon her husband as Chiti, her heart will be filled with intense reverence and tenderness for him; she will always be ready to serve him. Furthermore, as a result of this influence, she will not see him as merely human, but as an embodiment of God. The mother into whom the Guru's power of grace is transmitted finds her whole world overflowing with happiness. As the Shakti saturates her, she begins to understand the real nature of her children, and she acquires the ability to equip them with learning, modesty and artistic skills, and to lead them towards their highest goal.

This is certainly not imaginary, nor is it true only because Muktananda says it. It is also testified to in the *Rudrahrdayopanishad*—रुद्रो नर उमा नारी तस्मै तस्यै नमो नमः। One comes to know that the supreme Shiva, eternal Truth, divine Witness, fundamental Cause of the universe, noblest object of worship, attributeless, formless, unborn, and without beginning, manifests as man—the husband. His Parashakti Kundalini, his beloved queen and consort, who controls the universe, also called Uma, Chiti, Durga, Pratibha, Malti, Radha, Sita or Mira appears as woman —the wife. She becomes the ideal daughter, the chaste and loyal wife, the exemplary mother and the sublime yogini. All are worthy of reverence. This new knowledge, acquired through the Guru's grace, transforms worldly life into heaven. I am describing this inner Shakti in order to enable man to know and utilise Her while living in the world. The divine Kundalini is of the nature of *pranava*. When She is activated, the same world which once appeared arid and insipid now becomes sweet and fertile. That which previously caused discontent now begins to impart fulfilment.

Muktananda sincerely wishes that this Parashakti be aroused in all men and women. May they grow with the unfolding sport of Kundalini Shakti! May they enjoy Her play within them and live happily with abundant selfless love for one another! Let the husband and the wife not consider each other to be mere means of sensual pleasure, but worthy of mutual respect and love. Let every woman of the world directly experience the might of Parashakti and look upon her husband as a ray of the same. May she become truly pious, extending courtesy, friendliness and service as her most sacred duty!

Let everyone remember that the entire universe is pervaded by Goddess Chiti—it originates from Her and is maintained by Her. Chiti is supreme Shiva, the Perfect Being, transcendent, attributeless, the ground of all, the goal of the Vedantic *neti, neti* (not this, not this); the basis of *aham brahmasmi* (I am the Absolute); the conscious soul. Chiti is the Parashakti of the supreme Shiva, in no way different from Him; She is also called Shivashakti. It is Her beauty that is revealed in our animate and inanimate universe. This sensible world is an outward expansion of Her own vibrations. She appears in various ways, favourable or unfavourable, helpful or obstructive— तन्नाना अनुरूपग्राहकभेदात् । (*Pratyabhijnahrdayam*, 3). (She becomes manifold in the variety of mutually related objects and subjects). She becomes the thirty-six elements by Her own will, in supreme freedom, yet She remains absolutely pure. She appears as male and female or Purusha and Prakriti, which is the chief, all-encompassing division in the world. Birds, animals and trees also fall into these two categories. This dual classification holds good for concepts such as nobility and degradation, virtue and sin, deliverance and bondage, bliss and anguish, as well. Even then, the same Chiti inhabiting the temple of the body as consciousness, appears in the perceiver and the perceived. That the world is permeated by Chiti, belongs to Her, is Chiti, is what I wish to convey. If you see with the eye of true knowledge, you will find nothing but Chiti in the world.

Even though one's inner Shakti has not been awakened, he must remember that God Himself assumes human forms and lives in the world— मनुष्यदेहमास्थाय छन्नास्ते परमेश्वरा: (Pratyabhijnahrdayam) When this is so, a follower of Siddha Yoga can easily develop his inner Shakti. This being the truth, is it not regrettable that people should neither know, experience nor worship Chiti within? She is nobly worthy of our worship. Whereas an ordinary man sees diversities in Her all-pervasiveness, one who is blessed by the Guru perceives only perfect love and unity.

O pilgrims of the world! If you want to complete your journey smoothly, become aware of Goddess Kundalini, the worthiest deity; awaken Her through meditation; see Her unfolding on all sides and live your daily life joyfully. Her blissful Light constitutes the Guru's form. Your Chiti Kundalini, aroused by the Guru's grace, will skilfully accomplish all your tasks. You will achieve greatness by Chiti's favour. Your worldly life will become your yoga sadhana, overflowing with joy, strength, nobility and love. Your home will be holy Kashi, your practical affairs sacred daily duties, your friends gods and goddesses, your food a holy offering to the Lord, and all your actions will be worship of God. This yoga of meditation effects your spiritual development without interrupting your normal life, hence it is called Maha Yoga. In this manner, you will eventually attain the final goal—merger in Chiti.

O divine Chitshakti! Thou art the Father, Thou art the Mother, Thou art Shakti, Thou are Shiva. Thou art the Self that pulsates within every heart. Both of Thy aspects, the external universe and the inner soul are full of Thy supreme bliss and beauty. So long as the true

knowledge of Thee does not arise, ignorant people continue to superimpose imaginary dualities on Thee, such
as Shiva - Shakti, bondage - salvation, enjoyment - renunciation, spiritual - worldly.

O great Shakti, worthy of our highest reverence! When
Thou bestowest grace in the form of the Guru and enter
a disciple, true knowledge arises within him, by means
of which he sees Thee also revelling merrily in the
external world. Siddha Yoga, the great worship of
Kundalini, the yoga of meditation, is Thy own creation
and is filled with Thee. By its means, Thou fulfillest
one's meditation and bestowest intense awareness of Thy
true nature.

Just as threads permeate every bit of cloth, or clay
appears as a pot, similarly, Thou art manifested in this
entire animate and inanimate universe. This insight
enables one to see unity in diversity and God in everyday life.

O Parashiva's Parashakti! When an aspirant, while
remembering Thee by chanting *Om Namah Shivaya* or
*So'ham* forgets himself completely, Thou revealest Thyself within him. O Supreme Existence! O Absolute Freedom! All mantras are Thy names, all patterns are Thy
creation. The universe is Thy visible body. O Universal
Consciousness! This entire world of innumerable forms,
colours and shapes, this vast congregation of countless
objects, unfolds Thy glory. I bow to Thee again and
again.

Just as a ray is not different from the sun, a wave from
water, a dust particle from the earth, in the same manner,
O Chiti Goddess who assumest myriad forms, Muktananda
is not distinct from Thee. He belongs to Thee, being one
of Thy innumerable rays. Muktananda has arisen from
Thee. He is entirely Thine. He is liberated by Thee.
He enjoys his freedom in Thee. I consecrate this work,
this hymn of homage, to Thee.

As a general rule, one should not reveal one's spiritual
experiences, which are gifts of divine grace. But, my
dear students of Siddha Yoga lovingly requested me to
write about my own experiences; and so, owing to the

further persistence of my dearest Amma and Yogini Kusumtai Sharma, I began to compose this work at Anand Bhavan, Mahableshwar on Monday, the 12th of May, 1969.

Now this short work has been completed. Its theme and manner do not resemble those works of the ancient Masters. Their works also possess immense significance. This is entirely Chiti's creation, a gift of Her grace; nay, it is Chiti Herself in action. I am only describing this great Shakti Kundalini, the Absolute, by calling Her Chitshakti. The aim of this work is attainment of Chiti; its name, *Chitshakti Vilas*, was not consciously thought out, but sprang within me spontaneously.

SWAMI MUKTANANDA

Mahableshwar,
June 4, 1969

BOOK 1

# THE PATH OF
# THE SIDDHAS

# 1

# THE IMPORTANCE OF GOD-REALISATION

Although God is all-pervasive, eternal and perfect, only a few individuals know Him directly. Even so, He permeates the inner and outer being of all creatures. He is the inner Witness of all and He dwells in the temples of all hearts as the innermost Self. There are misguided people who hold that there is no such Being either in the innermost heart or anywhere else in the world. Atheism has become quite common. There are philosophers who regard Nature as the original cause of creation. According to them the universe has come into existence by the aggregation of atoms and molecules and has no sentient Creator. According to others, God does not dwell in the heart but in some remote corner of the cosmos such as Vaikuntha, Kailas or the fifth or seventh heaven. Then there is the modern notion that if God did exist, the world would not be tormented with so much conflict, strife and suffering. They say that some places are inundated with rain while others are afflicted with droughts; some regions suffer from famines while others cannot manage their food surpluses. Rain does not fall at the right time for the farmer and at times there are such acute shortages of water that one can drink only the tears that fall from the eyes. There is not enough food and some people are forced to survive on the leaves of plants and trees. Some people have no houses to live in and no clothes to cover their bodies. How can such obvious imbalances be explained? If there were a God, surely things would not be so terrible. Arguing like this, their minds filled with increasing doubts and misconceptions, such disbelievers drive faith

1

away from their own hearts, which become sterile and empty.

There are several countries in the world that are affluent and prosperous, with plenty of food, clothing and other material comforts. They owe this to their persistent and determined efforts. Japan, even though it is a small country without much fertile soil, has managed to become self-sufficient in the fields of agriculture and domestic products. The inhabitants of such countries apply the art and science of agriculture with religious zeal. They do not defend lethargy by pointing out that pythons and birds do not work. Isn't it ridiculous to wallow in sloth, neglect rightful work and then complain to God about your constant hunger?

Once I was introduced to a family in which there were seven doctors, each a specialist in a particular field. A small boy in the family fell ill because he was in the habit of eating indiscriminately. He did not heed the doctors' instructions about food although he took the prescribed medicine. As a result, his condition continued to deteriorate. Can we conclude from this that the doctors were incompetent? The hard truth is that man gets the fruits of his actions from God, and the fruits always correspond to the actions.

It is futile to seek God by theories and conjectures. He has revealed Himself fully but in subtle form. There are so many wonderful places in India and so many abodes of Siddhas. If we have not been able to see them all, is it right to hold that they do not exist? Similarly, the divine power exists in our own being, working ceaselessly. It is only perverse rationalism that denies its existence. It is the Supreme Being who makes this world habitable by pervading its different planes, inner as well as outer, according to the needs of either. Although He is inactive He is the ground of all our inner and outer activities.

If this world were actually without God, who would enjoy living in it? Who would strive to make his worldly life clean and pure? If life is sweet and joyful, it is because of God. His glories are infinite. Whatever sweetness and joy we experience belong to His infinite nature. We are able to enjoy our small pleasures in mundane objects and pursuits only because the bliss of that supremely blissful Being is reflected in this world. The savour of food, the sweetness of water, the melodies of musical compositions, the tender smile of blooming buds and the joyous squeals of small children are all images of divine bliss. If the many-hued beauty of flowers did not reflect God's radiance, why should we be so captivated by them? Why should we love them so? If fruits like mangoes, pineapples, oranges and pomegranates lacked His loveliness, juice and flavour, we would not enjoy them so much. They derive their sweetness, their juicy savour from the presence of God in them. How satisfying plain and pure water is! What treasures of love do we not bestow on the sun's glorious rays of variegated colours! At their soft caress, lotuses open their petals, plants sway with joy and birds pour out their ecstatic strains. Creepers twining around trees and sunbeams surrender themselves to each other in loving worship, locked in a silent embrace. Gentle breezes vibrate with divine music. How sweet and cool and pleasant their touch! Observe all these phenomena carefully and intelligently. God's manifest love flows bountifully in all these. But man, on account of his alienation from God, does not perceive the true nature of this universe, which is alive with consciousness. And in his ignorant condition he finds fault with the ways of God!

This universe is a true image of the Supreme Reality. The Vedantic statement, "All this, indeed, is the Absolute," is entirely true. God pervades everywhere. All countries, holy centres and all names belong to Him. The differences of high and low are only man-made. All places on this globe are, in fact, His abodes. All rivers, lakes and ponds are sacred, as they are His. The many shapes and forms of this world embody the sound of God's name. Infinite are the names, infinite the glory, infinite the play of the Infinite. Limitless is His Being! However much you may read, there is always so much more to read. No matter how many holy places you visit,

there are always many more. However far your vision
may reach, more lies beyond. Such is the all-pervasive,
the infinitely vast, the supremely glorious divine
substance!

Just as man reproduces man, that which springs from
the Divine must also be divine. One seed produces
another identical seed, and the ones yet to come will also
be replicas of the original. Similarly, what is born of
the Supreme must have Its nature. The universe originates from God, who is Himself without origin. The
souls of all human beings come from the supreme God,
each being as complete as its Creator, always fully maintaining His perfection. When such is the truth of divine
law, why should we experience imperfection, disintegra-
tion and unbearable anguish? The reason is forgetfulness of our true nature. Such Self-forgetfulness, though
illusory, is extremely powerful. It has been called *maya*,
ignorance, nescience, illusion and impurity. This very
ignorance reduces the supreme Lord to a mere human
being, the Universal Soul to an individual soul, the free
to the bound. It creates the false notion of 'I' and 'mine'
and condemns a man to all the agonies and conflicts of
worldly existence. Our life span is short, full of stress
and hardship and the body perishable. The attainment
of God or Self-realisation is the one and only means of
deliverance from its clutches. Therefore, it is absolutely
necessary for us to find Him. But it is said that the way
to God is extremely difficult.

## The Need Of Meditation For Happiness

There are many different phenomena inside the human
body. If a man were to see the inner splendour in
meditation even once, he would derive immense benefit
from it. How wonderful the treasures within this body!
So many *chakras* just in the head! Pools of nectarean
juices! Numberless sheaves of sensory nerves! Rever-
berating music concerts! Varied intoxicating perfumes!
Countless rays of different suns! Sacred dwellings of
gods! In spite of such wealth, deluded, unfortunate man

prefers to dwell in the insipid external world. 'Like a dog at his bone' is a perfect description of man seeking satisfaction in outer life. Just as a dog while sucking a dry bone, enjoys nothing but his own blood trickling from his jaws, so also man while looking for sweet happiness in the external world, ends up weary and joyless.

The universe within is superior to that without. How wonderful the seat of clairaudience in the auditory tubes! How significant the centre of deep sleep in the throat which easily dissolves the fatigue of the waking hours! No matter how much a man may acquire during the waking state, he becomes tired. He may ride a horse, an elephant or an easeful palanquin, but he has earned only lassitude at day's end. He may acquire wealth, gold or a kingdom, but finally he becomes weary. He feels tired of dramatic performances, the ravishing beauties of the world, even treasures of pearls and gems. He may obtain titles and honours or become the unquestioned master and ruler of the whole world, but he is greeted by apathy when his waking state ends. It is sleep during the day or night which removes fatigue. My dear ones! When you go to sleep, you have to put away all your adornments, because even your most precious jewels are of no use to you then. If you just happen to remember them, your sleep will be disturbed. You are able to sleep only by forgetting your wealth; otherwise, you have to resort to sleeping pills. After deep sleep, you wake up feeling active and cheerful; but if you cannot sleep, you become restless and tormented, almost to the point of insanity. This proves that sleep is a precious treasure. Its centre lies in the throat, which is also the seat of the *vishuddha chakra* and its deity. If you are not acquainted with this centre of joyful sleep, how can you ever realise the full value of your body ?

In your heart there is a lotus whose different petals stand for different qualities such as desire, anger, infatuation, greed, love, modesty, knowledge, detachment, joy, omniscience and so on. Sages have spent their whole lives trying to behold the scintillating divine light which lies within the thumb-sized *akasha* of the heart. How glorious the Goddess Kundalini who transforms a man as She expands! O soul of man! What joy could beckon you in the external world while such an infinite treasure of marvels lies within? If you neither meditate, perform good deeds nor take good care of your invaluable body, how will you ever find happiness?

O unaware man, become aware. Meditate. Meditate, not just for liberation, religious discipline, high yogic states or praise, but for the fulfilment of your sensuous desires as well. You are in search of beauty in the world. Since you fail to find it, you feel weary. You seek joy in cinemas, theatres and in touring your country and abroad, yet you remain without it. At last, ironically enough, you lose your own beauty and become ugly. You search for happiness but find sorrow and listlessness. Tell me now: is it all worth it?

Be honest with yourself. You seek savour in various foods. You look for it in tea, coffee, soft drinks and sweet puddings. You visit hotels and clubs to find it, but you end up with boredom and emptiness. Your face becomes shrivelled and your wealth expended. You acquire diseases instead of joy and regret that the best part of your life is over. In the process of cooking and eating various delicacies, you lose your own sweetness. The little joy you had before also vanishes. And you never find the true, pure, joyous and invaluable inner nectar.

Your quest for perfumes also meets a similar fate. To enjoy sweet smells, you use fragrant flowers and new varieties of scents, including Parisian ones. But finally old age comes and you yourself begin to emit a foul odour. O soul of man! Meditate and perceive the divine aromas whose centre is situated between the eyebrows. O my brothers! If that centre is opened, bad smells will be transmuted into pleasing scents and you will enjoy supreme bliss.

Then you exert yourself so much for agreeable sounds. You expect to hear courteous words from everyone. For mere praise, you try to please, even fawn on all sorts of people. You peruse the newspapers hoping to find a flattering write-up about yourself. You even secretly commission a writer to compose a book extolling your imaginary virtues. If it does not sell, you distribute it free. How eager you are for words of praise! "What did my husband say about me?" "What did my wife remark?" "What did Baba or someone else say?" "What remarks were made about me in that public meeting?" Although praise pleases you, it cannot impart true happiness, brighten up your face or reinvigorate your body. You hear good music and learn classical compositions to gratify your ear, but your inner bud of love remains unopened. You never care to hear the uplifting word, about which the saints say: सोऽहम् शब्दानि ठाईं पहुडत झालें (I found rest in the word *So'ham.*) In this manner, the word escapes you completely. O soul of man! Whither are you going? You have heard everything except the Guru's word which enables you to taste immortal ambrosia and see the world as aglow with a new light— the light of consciousness.

Next, you go completely mad hankering after the pleasure of touch. You seek it in soft cushions and garments, in beds of flowers and velvet clothes, but you do not succeed. What have you not done for tactile sensations, thinking happiness, peace and joy lie therein? You look for it even where it does not exist. Engaged in this frantic search, you select a woman and try to gratify it through her, only to become disillusioned later on. Her touch, too, does not afford pleasure any longer. You seek it in your beautifully adorned wife, but are only greeted with passionate heat. You touch your wife for highest bliss but ultimately feel bitterly frustrated. Alas! You never experience true joy. You make every possible effort to soothe your sense of touch until it atrophies. You exhaust an entire lifetime seeking it, only to feel frustrated in the end.

O unfortunate fellow! You are not making the right sort of effort. If your inner Shakti is awakened, the blissful Parashakti will spread Her dynamic influence throughout your body. Ah! You will be immersed in an ocean of pure tactile delight.

You will be able to meditate after your inner Shakti is aroused by divine grace. Muktananda says: O man! meditate for the sensuous enjoyments you have been pursuing in the world. You will find all the pleasurable sensuous stimuli, since they lie within. Your world will be filled with utter joy and your life will become a paradise. Meditate on your inner Being. Meditate on the Shakti to whom you owe your individual existence. Love the inner Shakti and respect your inner Self.

Meditate, regardless of your religious affiliation, because no worthwhile creed could possibly prohibit meditation on the Self. O man and woman! Whatever your race, community or country, meditate on the inner Parashakti. O simple-hearted people! You may belong to any party, but your practice of meditation will not interfere with your party obligations. Do not allow your church, party, country, religion or degrees to come in the way of your meditation on the inner Being. Whatever your status, whether you be a leader, high-ranking official, a Swami or the head of a monastery or ashram, meditate. Even if you are a *mahamandaleshwar* or an archbishop, meditate. Do not let your position be a hurdle in meditation. Of what use is such petty status if it interferes with meditation? Meditate, whether you are a boy or a girl, a man or a woman, a celibate or a householder, a hermit or a *sannyasi*. Seek your own Self. You will certainly find It. Meditate on your own soul, wherever you are living—in your own home, a forest, a city or a village. Meditate, whether you are a patient or a doctor, a culprit or a lawyer, hopelessly poor or fabulously rich. Meditate, whether you are accomplished or not, virtuous or sinful. You will attain inner peace through it. Meditation will fulfil you by satisfying your five sensuous appetites, your aesthetic urges of art, poetry and dance and your quest for *jivanmukti*.

When the latent treasure of inner Shakti is released in meditation, you will soon ascend to higher meditative stages. You will see splendid sights and glorious forms. You will apprehend internal divine lights. It is only by virtue of these lights that your fleshly body becomes beautiful and you feel love for each other. As the magnificent radiance sparkles in meditation, your craving for beautiful and loving forms will be satiated. Husband and wife will perceive such magical lustre in each other that even the handsomeness of Adonis and the beauty of Venus will be surpassed. Meditate on Her, by virtue of whom you surrender to each other in conjugal love. The divine power of grace abides in both of you, taking your forms. In this manner you will find one of your cherished objects, namely, beauty. You will begin to see the whole world as radiant.

Along with beholding visions you will hear inner sounds. Sweet, divine music will ring in your ears. This possesses countless virtues. As you listen to it, you will have such sleep as is enjoyed only by heavenly beings. These melodious strains will compel you to dance in ecstasy and eradicate your indifference, distress and ramblings of mind. Your world will vibrate with cheer and joy. O worldly travellers! As you enjoy the divine melodies, radio music, news of different places and conversation will lose their interest. You will then be saved from spending your money on radios and televisions. Not only this, the inner music will release celestial ambrosia and you will relish its sweetness. This nectar, trickling from the palate, is the tastiest of all tastes. Its each drop is worth more than millions. Worldly people in particular should value it. This elixir will expel all your diseases and permeate you with gladness. Then you will equally enjoy all foods, whether plain or sumptuous, properly cooked or not. Your anguish will vanish, desires diminish and the notion of 'I' and 'mine' will disappear. You yourself will exude ambrosial sweetness. You will rejoice in your spouse and children. रसो वै स: । रसं ह्येवायं लब्ध्वानन्दी भवति । (It is elixir. Having obtained it, a person becomes full of bliss). As you taste this nectar and become absorbed in it, you will be transported with inner delight. This is the food of gods, of love, of yoga and of your worldly seeking. Your life, which is dry, cheerless and trivial, will become sweet and meaningful.

O my brothers! You will also inhale divine scents.

Sight, sound and taste—these three are always accompanied by their brother, smell. As your inner aroma is released, not only your home, but your whole world will become tranquil; your body will shed its heaviness and sloth and become lithe and vibrant. Then you will experience perfection in spite of any possible deficiencies in your worldly life. Your heart will throb with selfless love for your relatives, friends, children, teachers and your Guru. Then you will sing the song of love and equanimity while living in the world.

Touch is the fifth object of your pursuit. When your inner Kundalini Shakti is stirred, She will release Her impulses of love throughout your body and its 72,000 nerves. She will thrill your every blood corpuscle with Her ecstatic joy. Only then will your craving for touch be truly gratified. You will recover the lost lustre of your eyes. Your withered face will glow with love again and your lips will become rosy. You will experience delight in every cell on fully experiencing the divine touch. The husband will look upon his wife as a goddess and the wife upon her husband as a god. Your sons, daughters, parents-in-law and neighbours will all appear divine to you. Your home will be transformed into a temple. Divinity will not remain confined only to places of worship, as you yourself will become holy. Then you will behold celestial forms, taste unearthly juices, smell heavenly perfumes, hear ethereal melodies and enjoy exquisite sensations of touch. Your world will quiver with beauty, joy and love!

You will become aware of the omnipresence of the Lord and dance in the ecstasy of pure love at all hours. You will see God in forests and in the mind, Him within you, yourself within Him, and feel that you belong exclusively to Him. You will repeat the truth that God is the husband, He is the wife, He is the power of reason and He is the final goal. You will realise that He pervades everywhere; that this entire world is His and He is maintaining it. O dear men of the world! Thus your own house will become sacred, your household work your worship and your daily life your religion. The husband

and the wife will consider each other divine. Muktananda exhorts you to meditate for this objective. Meditation will satisfy your worldly desires as well as provide
an inner shelter of repose in your life. Meditation is your
best friend, most reliable guide, the celestial wishing-
cow and the celestial tree which will grant all your
wishes. Therefore, practise meditation daily in some
measure.

## Spiritual Pursuit In Worldly Life

Life without God is painful and agonizing. If a man
could combine his daily life with the practice of meditation, this very world of his, afflicted with the threefold
misery, would be transmuted into a paradise. Just as
a pudding containing the most expensive ingredients,
such as almonds, pistachio and cardamom, cannot taste
sweet without sugar, similarly, existence remains joyless
without contemplation of God. Man can make his
worldly conditions most congenial by meditation. Without meditation on the Supreme, life continues to be full
of hardship and suffering. Sri Jnaneshwar Maharaj, the
greatest saint of Maharashtra, says:

अवघाचि संसार सुखाचा करीन ।
आनंदें भरीन तिन्ही लोक ॥

(We shall fill our worldly life with happiness, transmitting the experience that the three worlds are overflowing
with joy and nothing but joy). Worldly existence could,
in fact, be a means of happiness, provided that it were
filled with the full awareness of God. Lacking in
remembrance, knowledge and contemplation of Him, life
becomes limp and lustreless.

My dearest ones! Do not give up your worldly life,
your near and dear ones. Do not waste yourself away
rushing around in search of God in the four directions,
nor lose your own soul while seeking inner peace and
comfort. Live in your own homes with your spouse and
children, making full use of your artistic talents, running your business or factories. In whatever position

your destiny has placed you, be you a millionnaire or a labourer, a king or a beggar, God belongs to you all. He belongs as much to the rich as to medicants; as much to the women living in families as to the milkmaids of Vraja; as much to worldly people as to the ancient sages, seers, yogis and yoginis. If you call Him with love, dwelling on Him with devotion, He will reveal Himself within you. He will grant a vision of the divine light of His love. He will flood your *sahasrar* with nectarean peace. Then you will know that you are an embodiment of bliss. Not only that: you will be utterly transformed. You will realise, "I am Shiva! Yes, I am! I am Rama, I am Krishna! Yes, I am!" You will sing this song with love. Your privations and the torments of countless life-times will come to an end. You will cease to lament: "I am miserable, I am sinful, I am destitute."

Do not consider your body a mere lump of flesh made of the seven components. It is a noble instrument, provided that it is not employed for sensual indulgence. In it are situated all holy places, gods, mantras and the source of all extraordinary powers in the world.

I heard this true story from my Gurudev, Bhagawan Nityananda. Once, a couple had taken a firm vow to go around the whole world, have dips in all the holy waters and worship all the deities. But they could not carry out their resolve. As days went by and their anxiety about this increased, they approached a highly evolved saint, conversant with the scriptures, and put their problem to him. The great man of learning consoled them saying, "Do not be afraid. A short distance from here there lives a couple established in God-consciousness. They have sanctified their worldly life and awakened their inner Shakti by the yoga of meditation. They have completely purified the centres of all the mantras and deities situated in the six *chakras*. Thus they have risen to the supreme, divine status by practising Maha Yoga, Kundalini Yoga. They are holy. The exalted Chiti is playing in them. Although they appear human, the fluids of their bodies are permeated by that divine Chiti. In them dwell all gods and all sacred places. They are entirely absorbed in Parashiva. Go to them. Go round them thrice. Make your offering and remember them with a heart full of love. Thus shall your vow be fulfilled."

This is absolutely true. O man! God dwells within you, with all holy waters, mantras, seed-letters and all gods. He is present as fully in you as in Kailas and Vaikuntha. Why are you exhausting yourself, looking for Him in different places instead of in your own heart? You should live your normal life, but accord Him the chief place among your creeds and daily activities. Whatever your sect or cult or doctrine may be, do not make yourself a foolish, weak and trivial creature. Do not head towards decline and disaster by regarding this body as Godless. Do not commit spiritual suicide by belittling yourself through defective understanding. Remember the Lord's statement (*Gita*, VI-5) : आत्मैव ह्यात्मनो बन्धुरात्मैव रिपुरात्मनः । (One is one's own friend or one's own enemy). Whether you are in hell or in heaven depends entirely on you. Begin at once to seek your true well-being. Just as for material progress you may study at different institutions, go abroad, and after years of diligent pursuit, become an engineer, a lawyer, a doctor or a professor, in the same manner, while working in your profession, seek out the Guru to attain spiritual peace, to transform your home into a temple of yoga, and above all, to find Shiva.

## Sri Guru's Greatness

God-realisation is possible only through a Guru, a spiritual Master, who is a direct descendant of the supreme Lord and who is illumined with divine knowledge. One should endeavour wholeheartedly to secure his sublime grace. So long as one lacks his blessing, the inner Shakti remains unawakened, the inner light unmanifest, the inner eye of divine knowledge unopened and the Spirit chained to the body. In a state of bondage, one cannot be absorbed in the divine experience of the Absolute. Just as a king may, in a dream, believe himself to be a beggar, the Spirit in the condition of ignorance believes Itself to be limited, considers Itself the doer and and the enjoyer, thinks Itself to be a petty, ordinary creature and thus continually experiences suffering in Its destitute plight. Just as an owl cannot see during the day and a crow at night, similarly, without the Guru's grace, a man is unable to see the world as a true heaven, but sees it only as full of grief and sorrow. Therefore, we desperately need a guide, a Sadguru—one who has fully realised the Truth and possesses the spiritual power to enable us to achieve the divine state of Parashiva.

Just as life itself is not possible without prana, without the Guru there can be no attainment of true knowledge, development of inner power, destruction of ignorance nor opening of the third eye. We need the Guru more than a friend, a son, a brother or even a wife. We need him more than wealth, machines and factories, art and music, much more than health and even more than life itself. He brings about the rebirth of man, imparts knowledge to him, sets him on his spiritual journey and develops the love of God in his heart. By his grace alone our inner Shakti is unfolded.

The number of so-called gurus has multiplied in the world, with everybody readily claiming the title. Wherever one goes one encounters hordes of them. Even ordinary people, not to mention true seekers, are now fed up with their conflicting opinions. Whoever appears on the scene attempts to form his own cult. He has never been a disciple of anyone, but tries to impose his own gurudom on one and all. All these new cults and sects, spreading like wild-fire, are in fact nothing more than a means of livelihood, a form of profitable business involving no effort. It should not be so.

If someone performs miracles, he is readily accepted as a Guru. If he gives a little sermon or a mantra, or if he dabbles in Tantric rituals, he is easily accepted. Thus extending devotion to any pretender, one deprives himself of inner certitude. Eventually he loses faith and comes to regard Guruhood as a sham. Then he rejects even a genuine Master. By projecting his image of the Guru on an imposter and receiving nothing in return, he becomes hostile to a true Master and does him gross injustice. Without the Guru, a seeker winds up in despair, having served different teachers, tried different paths and languished under severe austerities in the seclusion of caves, forests or the Himalayas. Then he blames his past actions, his *prarabdha*. Unable to realise God, he is plagued by anxious misgivings: "When shall I find Him? Who shall guide me?"

It is not easy to meet a Master and then it is extremely difficult to understand him. The Guru is a great and wonderful deity. Do not miss your opportunity with a realised one by considering him ordinary. You can understand his greatness only when you are fully blessed by him.

The true Guru is one who awakens the disciple's inner Shakti through Shaktipat and makes the divine energy active within him. He bestows grace on a disciple by kindling a sacred flame in his heart. Thus he enables his disciple to dwell constantly in spiritual bliss. He has realised the mantra and is able to charge it with living, conscious force. He is adept in Shaktipat, possessing great spiritual power. Whether he be a householder or a renunciate, he has the ability to transmit this power. God's power of grace dwells in him in its fullest glory. He unravels the mysteries of yoga and teaches one to work selflessly. He imparts the ecstasy of divine love and the joy of knowledge and above all, brings liberation while one is still in the body. His true nature is enveloped in divine mystery. Such a supreme Master is none other than Shiva Himself, a descendant in the ancient line of Guruhood that began with Shiva, the primal Guru. He is Rama, Shakti, Ganapati, one's divine father and mother.

Such a Guru is above the distinction of sex. Parashiva is the Guru and Parashakti Chiti is the Guru as well. Hence there is no essential difference between male and female from the viewpoint of Truth. Both are pervaded by the one power, one Self, and both experience identical fulfilment. The man or woman whose Chitshakti is activated rises above the distinction of sex. In the external world, such a one may appear masculine or feminine, but in his or her inner being reside both Parashiva and Shakti. As the great Kundalini, Mother of Yoga, is aroused by the Guru's grace, all the inner impurities of the flesh are destroyed and one's consciousness of being male or female is consumed in the fire of yoga. Afterwards, Chitshakti enters all seven bodily components and imbues them with Her own energy. As water mixed with sugar becomes syrup, similarly, the apparently fleshly body becomes pure when fully permeated by Kundalini Chitshakti. How can anyone in this state be considered a man or a woman?

The Guru's life is a constant unfolding of divine play. By his blessing, any man becomes divine, continuously immersed in inner joy. Great is his glory, beyond the comprehension of the obtuse intellects of ordinary mortals. He is worthy of everyone's reverence.

The Guru understands the ways of the world very well. He is fully conscious of the laws of destiny. He is fully familiar with the ways of God. On the one hand, he is adept in spiritual matters and on the other, he is exceedingly clever in his worldly dealings. Those aspirants who live under the protection of such a Master pass through acute crises with ease and meet the most unfavourable circumstances fearlessly.

Leaning on my worshipful Guru for support, his devotees lived without apprehension. He transmitted heavenly joy to his devotees, even to those who did not renounce their homes. He was so great a saint that he enabled a devotee to experience yogic states and a yogi the joy of devotion. He imparted true knowledge by his look of compassion, without imposing any strenuous discipline. He revealed the presence of God in the world. His teaching to men and women was: "Look upon each other as God." He was always poised in the state beyond mind, as though his mind had been transfigured into pure consciousness.

Bhagawan Nityananda was a most divine Guru, who did not display his inner secrets. He possessed unique spiritual power. To people, he appeared as a divinely intoxicated yogi. Although he was omniscient, he affected ignorance. He did not attach much importance to miraculous powers; he maintained that, compared to God's miracle of self-manifestation, all others fade into utter insignificance. The entire universe rests in Shiva. Can there be a greater miracle than this? Even so, wondrous godly powers secretly resided in him. The major *siddhis* exist as a matter of course in Siddhas. Even though such a Master does not display them, they become active in his service of their own accord, dancing attendance on him as it were. Even the earth considers herself fortunate when such Masters walk on her surface.

Bhagawan Nityananda was, and still is, famous throughout the country as an extraordinary saint. He is, in fact, an inhabitant of the glorious Siddhaloka; a completely realised being. He embodied in his person a perfect synthesis of knowledge, yoga, devotion and selfless action. He will be remembered, praised and envisioned as long as the sun and moon exist. He was worthy of the greatest esteem in the world, being nobly exalted and a full embodiment of true Guruhood. Receptive aspirants obtained Shaktipat as they remembered him or sang his praises. Even today, power flows from his shrine and photographs. In truth, he pervades both the inner and outer planes of the universe; a saint who merges his being in the Self of all becomes omnipresent.

The Guru is true. The Guru is perfect. He is simple, straightforward and loving. He is the genuine well-wisher of his disciples. He does not rob them of their money, but of their ignorance. He does not take away their wealth and property, but their anxieties and sins. He is jealous of egocentricity, inimical to bondage and wrathful against a differentiating mentality. His glory lies in leading his disciples to God-realisation without imposing severe austerities. He fills their homes with the peace of solitude and the quiet of a cave, spiritualising their worldly life. He brings the purity of the Himalayas into their everyday lives and reveals the spiritual grandeur of Kailas in their meditation. Such a preceptor does not recommend renunciation of material goods and wealth to an unjust degree nor abandonment of worldly things, which are, after all, created by God, but only makes his disciples renounce their limited individuality. The Guru ennobles one's normal life with his parents, friends and relatives by blessing him with divine favour. With the Guru's grace, one can easily perceive the Self shining in his heart through meditation, even while he lives, works and performs action in society. His entire life becomes worship of God. Thus the inner being does not become sterile and empty. Existence is seen as a divine gift.

The Guru elevates his disciples, shows them their true nature and enables them to realise their Shivahood by merging them into Shiva. His wonderful power is so potent that it can completely transform a human being. He grants a new life, free from sorrow and senility. He makes one attain perfection in the midst of worldly life.

Can we ever adequately repay, honour and adore the venerable Guru who enters us as Chitshakti? O Beloved Gurudev! You care not whether our bodies are pure or impure, diseased or healthy. You never look down on us despite our unclean, defiled, mutable, physical forms. On the contrary, out of compassion, you enter us and cleanse us of all of our sins and impurities. You infuse your activating energy into each nerve, each corpuscle of blood. How great is your mercy! How noble your compassion! How beneficial your influence! What friend can equal the love of the Guru who transmits Shakti and who, with the inner yogic movements, washes away all impurities like phlegm, bile and wind disorders from all parts of the body, all its nooks and crannies and polluted nerves? Working like a menial servant, he turns the body into pure gold, consuming all the inner filth in the flames of yoga. What lover, what mother or what deity can compare with such a one? Can we ever render appropriate service to him? Who can adequately sing the praises of the Guru who embraces us as his own, entering us in his true form, regardless of the status of our family, race, merits or demerits, actions or omissions?

This is why beloved Nityananda alone is Muktananda's

all in all, his divine father, deity, bliss, meditation and
*samadhi.* "I worship the Guru, the dear Sadguru"—can
singing this refrain ever repay you for your infinite
kindness? No, never! Dear Gurudev! You are the most
exalted being. It is only for your worship that Shree
Gurudev Ashram has been established. You are the
*prana* inhaled by me, while I am the *apana* which flows
out. *So* stands for Nityananda and *aham* for Muktananda.
Nityananda is *So'ham* and *So'ham* is Nityananda. This
is my daily worship.

Om Namah Shivaya is your mantra of initiation. My
dear Gurudev! It enshrines your memory in a perfect
way. You yourself are Shiva:

यो गुरुः स शिवः प्रोक्तो यः शिवः स गुरुः स्मृतः ।
उभयोरन्तरं नास्ति गुरोरपि शिवस्य च ॥

(Guru is called Shiva and Shiva is referred to as Guru.
There is no difference between the two—Guru and Shiva).
*So'ham* is the mantra received from you for meditation.
It stabilised my mind's flow in your direction, and con-
summated the sacrifice of my spiritual seeking, thus
making me tranquil and fulfilled. I was transformed into
*So'ham.* You not only gave this benevolent gift, but,
entering me through *So'ham*, destroyed all my sins,
cleansed my impurities, and raised me to Shivahood.
Above all, you accepted me as your own. My adorable
Gurudev! How shall I honour you? How shall I wor-
ship you? One thing is certain: I will always chant:
*Jaya Gurudev! Jaya Gurudev!*

If one recognises such a Siddha as the Guru, is it not
a sign of the greatest fortune to be initiated by him?
Whatever word he imparts constitutes a mantra, endowed
with conscious force. The sublime Guru in whom Chiti
is manifested, enters his disciple by his mantra, thought,
touch or look. It is not surprising, then, that his disciple
should achieve the highest state of perfection by living
with him in his ashram, forging a personal link with him,
worshipping his feet and drinking the water sanctified
by their touch, receiving his *prasad*, serving and adoring
him, absorbing the vibrations of Chiti which flow from

his love-intoxicated state, contacting Her particles that pervade his clothes and receiving Her light-rays which emanate from his incoming and outflowing breath along with the music of *So'ham*. My venerable Gurudev was a Siddha of such great potency. Divine rays of Chiti constantly flowed from him. He could awaken anyone with a mere glance. Whoever was blessed by my Gurudev flourished. Even those who were abused by him achieved noble fame. All the activities of such saints arise from Chiti. The food left over by them is saturated with Her. Even their bathrooms are full of Her highly beneficial beams.

I shall tell you something curiously interesting. My bathroom is well-kept and beautiful. I do not allow anybody else to take a bath in it; I do not even allow anybody to clean it, except Venkappa, who has been my dear disciple for several years. Such a beautiful and pure bathroom is essential for yogis who give Shaktipat. We used to drink the water used by our Gurudev for bathing, considering it sacred, because it was permeated by Chiti beams. That is why I do not allow anyone to enter my bathroom. One day a beloved student of Siddha Yoga, who is an officer with an airline, begged for permission to wash my bathroom. I said, "All right. Go ahead." While cleaning it, he sat down and remained in that position for four hours! The Chiti rays pervading the bathroom pierced him. As a result, he received Shaktipat and was absorbed in *samadhi* for four hours. When I found later that he had not yet returned, I went inside and saw him sitting ecstatically in the lotus posture.

Each activity of my Gurudev was saturated with Chiti beams. Anyone who was penetrated by them had a lofty experience. All the actions of such a Siddha are motivated by Chitshakti. If his finger touches anyone, Shakti flows from him into the latter. Whoever is touched by his body receives Shakti. Even if one wears his old clothes, one is blessed by Shakti. Once while I was composing this work, a powerful impulse of Shakti besieged my body. A college student, a newcomer, was standing near me. I asked him to massage my head for it was feeling heavy. As he was doing so, Chitshakti entered his body, even though he was not in a meditative posture. He received intense Shaktipat. He began to execute *mahamudra* and other postures spontaneously. He experienced high stages of yoga.

It is said in the *Hatha Yoga Pradipika*:

दुर्लभो विषयत्यागो दुर्लभं तत्त्वदर्शनम् ।
दुर्लभा सहजावस्था सद्गुरो: करुणां विना ॥

(Without the compassion of the Sadguru, it is difficult to give up worldly objects, to realise the Truth and to attain the state of natural *samadhi*).

Many paths have been laid down for the attainment of peace in human life, some of which are external, others internal. Various ways to Self-realisation have been described in spiritual works such as the *Vedas*, the treatises of the six schools of Indian philosophy, the *Ramayana* and the *Srimad Bhagavatam*. All these means bear fruit, but only after the exertion of great self-effort, done in full faith for a long time.

But the state of equilibrium is obtained only by intense love of God and by the Guru's grace. No matter what path we follow or form of worship we adopt, we cannot easily reach this state; nay, it is unattainable by any other method:

नानामार्गैस्तु दुष्प्राप्यं कैवल्यं परमं पदम् ।
सिद्धिमार्गेण लभते नान्यथा पद्मसंभव ॥

(*Yogashikhopanishad*)

(O Brahma, it is very difficult to achieve the state of beatitude through various paths. It can be achieved only through the Siddha path and no other way).

The Guru, our supreme father, brings us to that state through initiation. He destroys our sins and enables us to realise our oneness with God:

दीयते शिवसायुज्यं क्षीयते पाशबन्धनम् ।
अतो दीक्षेति कथिता बुधै: सच्छास्त्रवेदिभि: ॥

(The wise men who know the true scriptures say, 'that is *diksha* in which the noose of bondage is destroyed and

union with Shiva is bestowed'). During initiation, it is
the Guru's Shakti which enters the disciple. As the tree
is only its seed in a different form, so the Guru is an
embodied form of Shakti, which causes various yogic
movements in the recipient. When an aspirant repeats
the mantra received from the Guru, sitting quietly in a
meditative posture, absorbed in the sacred remembrance
of his beloved Guru, the Guru himself becomes active
in him through the mantra. These movements are not
without significance or positive results. It is the Guru
who works within, and through his Shakti effects unusual physical movements, postures, *mudras*, various
kinds of *pranayama*, dancing and mantra-chants. An
onlooker may find it all strange and even frightening.
The aspirant, however, is unafraid, experiencing through
these movements a kind of intoxication, ecstasy, lightness of body and physical well-being. Some of these
movements fall under Raja Yoga, some Hatha Yoga,
others Mantra Yoga and yet others Bhakti Yoga. Under
the influence of the Guru's Shakti, a seeker performs
these yogas spontaneously as needed. When all the four
yogas become active together, the result is Siddha Yoga
or Maha Yoga. It is also known as Siddhamarga or
Siddhakripa.

As days go by, the greater the devotion a disciple has
for his Guru, the closer his contact is and the more
intense his absorption in him becomes, the higher will
be the spontaneous movements and marvellous occur-
rences such as effortless postures, clairaudience and
clairvoyance, during meditation. But sometimes, owing
to an impure heart, the disciple begins to attribute attachment, aversion and other weaknesses to the Guru. As a
result, his practice of yoga becomes less intense. Then
he wonders why the movements are not occurring in
him as before. I assure him that they will, most certainly.
But first he must reform himself.

My Gurudev would at times use abusive language and
even hit! There was of course, always a reason behind
it. Sometimes when my adorable Guru became furious,
I would say to myself, "Look, you must not forget that

all the actions and deeds of God are divine. Whatever form they may take, they are always beneficial and blissful." The state which Lord Krishna granted to the milkmaids, being pleased by their exclusive love for Him, or to Uddhava and Arjuna through spiritual instruction, was in no way different from the state He conferred on the demons Kamsa and Chanur by killing them! He awarded the same grace to Putana, who fed poison to Him, as to His mother Devaki, except that He treated the former with wrath and the latter with love. In fact, ultimately both enjoyed the same state.

The divine sport is full of bliss. All the workings and actions of the all-pervasive One are identical in nature. Similarly, all the acts of the Gurudev are motivated by Chitshakti, being only different scenes in Her drama. All of them are salutary, accelerating progress. It is a pity if a seeker courts a setback in his sadhana by a critical attitude towards the motives underlying the Guru's actions. While living in the company of the Guru, great saints or Siddhas, one must never ascribe faults to them. Siddhas behave in strange, puzzling ways, beyond the comprehension of ordinary mortals. They learn from the ignorant, but teach the learned; they fight the valiant but flee from the jackal; they demand when they are not getting anything, but give away what they do get. Everyone asks for something from such an emperor of saints, who, possessing nothing, gives one all that he wants. The most precious things of the world are mere trash to them. Siddhas are, in fact, far beyond our ordinary standards of life.

## Chiti Kundalini, The Divine Mother

The tradition of Guruhood is sublime. The Chitshakti of the Absolute revels freely within the Guru, who, intoxicated by Her joy, remains absorbed in blissful love. It is said of the Gurus that their spiritual power, light and strength have continuously protected us like an unshakable mountain from time immemorial. Such a Guru transmits his Shakti into a disciple, pierces his *chakras*, and stabilises him in *sahasrar*. As the Shakti passes into the disciple from the Guru, She burns away all impurities in the fire of yoga, rending the veil of ignorance from his eyes. Eventually, the disciple himself becomes the Guru.

The energy that is transmitted is the highest Chitshakti, the nature of which is fully explained in the *Pratyabhi-jnahrdayam* as: चिति: स्वतन्त्रा विश्वसिद्धिहेतु: । (Chiti creates the universe of Her own free will). She is indistinguishable from supreme Shiva. She is the ground of the creation, preservation and destruction of the universe.

This Chitishakti, the active aspect of Parashiva, is self-effulgent and transcends space, time and form. She extends grace and restrains excess, dwelling in complete freedom. She motivates all activities, brings all disciplines to fruition and grants worldly fulfilment as well as salvation. Chiti grants easy means to liberation, provides support to all auxiliary powers and illuminates transcendent reality. Both action and non-action are Her manifestations. The glory of this Shakti of Parashiva is manifold. She is the wisdom of the enlightened, the fruit of action of the active, the love or divine intoxication of the devotee and the dynamic Kundalini of the yogis. In fact, She is the beauty of the entire world. She is, indeed, the magnificent lofty power of the Supreme Being which, when realised, fills the heart with wonder. The functioning of the entire universe, inner as well as outer, is carried on by Her.

O Divine Mother Chiti! You are the throbbing energy of Parashiva, His beloved consort and His dynamic expression. You are the Cause of the universe, forming the five elements. You are the sun, stars and planets. O Goddess Kundalini, You are all the heavens and nether regions. You are the three worlds and the four directions. Of Your own divine will, You assume the eighty-four *lakh* life-forms of creatures of the four categories – those born of sweat, seed, egg and womb. You project these countless images on Your own screen. Your ways are so inscrutable that philosophers reach the limit of their intellects trying to comprehend this universe. Innumerable are the manifestations of Your divine light. You bring forth in Your own Being such a vast creation, diverse as well as single, and yet remain supremely detached, constantly engrossed in divine bliss. You are attainable through the *Vedas,* Vedanta, different scriptures and mantras.

O Mother Kundalini! You are the power of bliss received from Nityananda. You are yoga as well as its eight aspects. You are the inner essence of the state of *samadhi,* called *nirvikalpa.* You are the never-failing support of the human body. O Mother Chiti Kundalini! You are the pure-souled Guru of the great Gurus. Seated on the Guru's throne, in the two-petalled lotus between the eyebrows, You serve as the Guru, taking care of Your disciples' necessities.

O Supreme Deity of aspirants! O Yogini Kundalini! O Guru! Giver of love! Dynamic Force! You are the benediction obtained from Nityananda. You are the two-syllabled *So'ham,* his boon to me. I owe my existence to You. Dearest Mother, You are the power behind my initiation. With the supreme Blue Pearl as your vehicle, You appear to my devotees in my form in their visions, fortifying their faith.

O beloved power of yoga! I make an offering of my love for my Guru to You. You are the paramount force, granting fruits of actions and possessing boundless might. Appearing in myriad forms, You are the Sita of Rama, the Radha of Krishna, the Laxmi of Narayana, the Bhavani of Shiva, the Yogashakti of yogis, the activated Shakti of aspirants and the power of grace of the Guru operating through Shaktipat. You are, indeed, the Guru himself.

This venerable Mother Shakti dwells within the Guru, performing his function. Therefore, the Guru is neither male nor female, but only the power of blissful love, revelling in its own being. He is the enlightening force of the fully unfolded Kundalini. He is in Chiti and She is in him, both being absolutely identical.

The Guru is an actual embodiment of the Absolute. Truly speaking, he is himself the Supreme Being. The one who infuses such divine power into his disciples is not just a teacher, but their vital force, their very inner Self. He is not only their prana, but also their true wealth. He is the goal of their spiritual pursuit—the *Gurutattva*, the essence of Guruhood. He is utterly unworldly, supremely intoxicated and blissful. There is no exaggeration in the rhapsodic descriptions of the Guru's potency sung in the *Guru Gita* and in the 13th chapter of the *Bhavarth Deepika* (*Jnaneshwari*) of Jnaneshwar. Nectar is as nothing to the one who drinks the sacred water cleansing the Guru's feet. According to the *Guru Gita* (80), worship of the Guru is the highest worship:

गुरुरेव जगत्सर्वं ब्रह्माविष्णुशिवात्मकम् ।
गुरोः परतरं नास्ति तस्मात्संपूजयेद् गुरुम् ॥

(The Guru is, indeed, the whole universe. He comprises Brahma, Vishnu and Shiva in his being. There is nothing higher than the Guru. Worship the Guru devotedly).

You will realise the validity of this assertion only after directly experiencing the Guru who is one with Chiti. All sacred waters and all heavenly beings are contained in him. In fact, he is the all-encompassing Supreme Reality, manifested as the universe. He himself enters the disciple as grace, bestowing his divine power on him. This is what is called Shaktipat *diksha*, Gurukripa, or the true Kriya Yoga.

## Sadhana

As soon as the grace of such a Siddha is received, the spiritual process is initiated. Some experience it immediately, while others do so over a period of time. If the process is subtle, it may not be perceived at first; but even so, the aspirant must continue his practice with full faith, love, reverence and respect. He should remember that Nature may change her ways, the sun may shed its heat and the moon its coolness, water may stop flowing, day may suddenly turn into night and night into day, but the grace of a Siddha Guru, once bestowed, will never go to waste. This power of grace continually assists the disciple even in his future lives. Just as man can never escape the results of his past deeds wherever he may go, the Guru's grace, once received by the disciple, continues to work wherever he may be. You should, therefore, keep up your practice with perseverance, enthusiasm and devotion.

It is better to choose one spot for meditation. If convenient, it also preferable to set aside clothes especially for meditation. In the place where one meditates, rays of Chiti keep accumulating. If one meditates in the same place every day, one will be able to meditate better as time passes. I meditated for a long time in a certain room. Now others also sit there; all have good meditation and spontaneous initiation also takes place there. Therefore it is always preferable to meditate each day in the same spot. But if such an arrangement is not possible, one may meditate anywhere. The beloved Gurudev will shower his blessings on you without fail.

The human body may appear to be a mere lump of flesh, but it is not so. It is a noble creation, containing 72,000 nerves which, along with the six *chakras* and the nine openings, form a sort of house. Of the 72,000 nerves, one hundred are important, and of these, ten have greater importance. Of these ten, three are major, but the *sushumna*, the central nerve, bears the highest significance. The various activities of life are only possible because of the *sushumna*. It extends in an unbroken line from the *sahasrar*, the seat of supreme Shiva, down to the *muladhar* where Kundalini lies coiled up.

The *sushumna* is the repository of supreme Shakti Kundalini, which when activated by the Guru's grace, permeates the whole body, moving through the 72,000 nerves with the support of the five forms of prana. Pervading the seven components and every blood corpuscle, it makes the body pure, well-formed, clean, beautiful, radiant and sparkling.

Prana is vital to the body. When it leaves, the body completely loses its value. It makes possible the existence of the universe and of man. In fact, we owe everything to it—happiness, energy, powers, health, movements through different worlds, bearing of children, strength and virility, disease and anxiety, delusion and lunacy, beauty, rebirth and liberation. I would even proclaim that prana is Brahman, Shiva, Shakti and Kundalini. प्राक्संविद्प्राणे परिणता । (Universal Consciousness turns into prana). It is said: सर्वं प्राणे प्रतिष्ठितम् । (Everything is established in prana). All the senses of perception and the organs of action are able to function only because of prana. Just as the spokes radiating from the hub of a wheel are supported by the wheel, similarly, the body, senses, mind and intellect are dependent on prana. The prana resolves into different aspects, performing different functions. This prana, endowed with Chiti, takes the five forms of *prana, apana, samana, vyana* and *udana*, in order to organise the functions of the body into a co-ordinated system. Although prana, or the Shakti behind it, is one, in order to maintain life and accomplish its different tasks it pervades the individual body in these five different forms: *Prana* operates in the region of the heart. It ensures a regular, constant functioning of the heart and by its dynamism, keeps an individual alive. *Apana* is that force which presses downwards and expels, evacuating waste products through the anus and the sex organ. *Samana* functions with equal force throughout the body, distributing nourishment to the entire organism. *Vyana* is that which is pervasive, the force which flows to every one of the 72,000 nerves through its various branches. That which moves upwards is *udana*. It is a great friend to a seeker, since, by its force he can conserve his semen, becoming an *urdhvareta* by drawing the seminal fluid upwards, the particles of which are transformed into prana as they come into contact with it. As a result, he is unaffected even by a heavenly nymph. It is this ascending seminal fluid which is the basic source of the power of Shaktipat. It confers energy, strength, radiance and valour. With the help of *udana*, the individual soul migrates to the world of the worthy if it has been virtuous and to that of the sinful if it has sinned, returning to the human world from there. After purification by Kriya Yoga, this same force gives the experience of the bliss of *samadhi*. *Udana* dwells within the *sushumna*.

The divine power of grace performs countless functions. Sometimes it works in wonderful ways with all its powerful, ecstatic and blissful vibrations, through a seeker who is full of unswerving devotion for the Guru. As a result he dances, sings, weeps, laughs, shouts and moves his body in extraordinary ways. Hopping like a frog, gyrating, swaying, rolling on the ground, slapping his own face, making vigorous circular motions of the head, performing different postures and *mudras*, trembling, sweating, doing *jalandhar*, *uddiyana*, and *mula bandhas*, drawing the tongue inwards or pressing it up against the palate in the *khechari mudra*, rotating eyeballs upwards, uttering all sorts of sounds, roaring and making other animal sounds, chanting *Om* or other mantras loudly—all these movements take place spontaneously during meditation. Different kinds of *pranayama* such as *bhasrika, bhramari, shitali, sitkari* and *ujjayi,* are performed involuntarily. *Kumbhaka* begins automatically. As meditation becomes intense, respiration is suspended for longer periods. At times one may even contract a minor ailment, which disappears shortly after. Thus a latent disease is brought to the surface and expelled from the system. All this work is effected by the fully conscious, all-knowing power of the Guru's grace.

The divine power of grace at first may cause a reaction of inertia, sleep and languor as it enters an aspirant. Many seekers glide into a profound slumber. This is a sure sign that all is going well. Sometimes a seeker becomes intoxicated, remaining in the sleep-like state of *tandra*, with his head feeling somewhat heavy. In this state he may see many visions of Siddhas, lights, different worlds such as heaven, hell, Pitruloka or Siddhaloka. Above all, he envisions his own Gurudev.

Waves of divine joy, never before experienced, soar within him. Currents of bliss flow through all his nerves. He begins to dance in ecstasy. All creation, including the most trivial objects, appears to be exceedingly beautiful and exquisite. It seems as if he were re-born in a new world or as though celestial loveliness, charm and delight had descended into the mortal world. He is overwhelmed with inner happiness, realising how joyous and sweet life is. His heart overflows with tender-ness and he feels compassion for all living beings.

The impulses of Shakti are sometimes strong and at other times mild. At times She intensifies meditation for days together, while at other times, She reduces its intensity. O beloved aspirants! Do not worry. Take refuge in the Guru without fear. Rely on him. Let him be your only strength, one hope and faith. Perfection will come to you easily. Keep meditating regularly every day and always observe discipline. Continue to mentally repeat the mantra received from the Guru.

Truly speaking, the divine name is the mantra obtained from the Guru. Repetition of the name activates the inner Shakti with full vigour. All the letters of the Sanskrit alphabet from *a* to *ksha* are permeated by Chiti Kundalini:

अकारादिक्षकारान्ता मातृकावर्णरूपिणी ।
यया सर्वमिदं व्यातं त्रैलोक्यं सचराचरम् ॥

(By whom all these three worlds of movable and im-movable things are pervaded, is of the form of letters in the alphabet, from *a* to *ksha*). The name itself is God. It is enough to repeat it constantly, with full reverence and faith, considering it to be God Himself. Its repetition promotes enthusiasm for sadhana and love for the Guru. It imparts divine wisdom and love. It is indeed, the veritable wishing-jewel, wishing-cow and wishing-tree. Never forget that the mantra, the Guru, the Shakti and you are one and the same. It is said that the mantra protects the one who repeats it – मन्त्रा: मननत्राणरूपा: । Never stop repeating and identifying yourself with the mantra, which bears a conscious force. It is a boon of the Siddha Guru. It embodies your Guru. A mantra charged with the potency of Parashiva, the highest Guru, is not merely an inert pattern of sounds. The supremely glorious, universal, divine power is hidden within it. In such a mantra, Parashiva and the Guru are united. Therefore, it is endowed with consciousness: मन्त्राः सर्वज्ञबलशालिनः । (Mantra possesses the power of omniscience). Keep singing it with love. Keep dwelling on it with tender feeling. Very soon Shakti will work in you with the speed of lightning. Mingle the Guru's secret mantra with your respiration. It will not take you long to be awakened. The movements will occur by themselves. Your spiritual practice will become automatic. Visions will present themselves to you without your asking. Sant Tukaram says that just by repeating the divine name, one will be able to comprehend the incomprehensible. Under its influence, one can see the invisible easily. It has infinite advantages –

न कळे तें कळों येईल उगलें । नामें या विठ्ठलें एकाचिया ॥
न दिसे तें दिसों येईल उगलें । नामें या विठ्ठलें एकाचिया ॥
अलभ्य तो लाभ होईल अपार । नाम निरंतर म्हणतां वाचे ॥

Repeat the name in solitude with a pure mind. When you harbour bad thoughts or your mind is filled with undesirable impressions, you experience corresponding undesirable states. You are familiar with the experience of being seized by lust when you entertain lascivious thoughts. How long will it take you then, to permeate your inner being with the mantra by its constant repetition? The Guru has entered you with the mantra. He will spread his influence throughout your body and make you like himself. How great is his kindness! I remind you once again to repeat the mantra constantly. This way, you will spontaneously glide into the meditative state.

The Gurushakti, seated in the heart, intensifies meditation and stabilises it. She will certainly bring you some extraordinary inner experience, such as a vision of light or a divine sound to support your meditation. You will be able to meditate more deeply afterwards. Do not be frightened of the world 'meditation.' You are already practising it in various ways in your everyday lives although you may not be conscious of it. It is through concentration that you are able to master many artistic

skills. Is it possible, without one-pointed attention, for a
doctor to diagnose a disease, a judge to decide his verdict,
a technician to make a delicate instrument like radar,
a professor to give a lecture, a housewife to prepare food,
a chauffeur to drive a car, a vocalist to render intricate
passages of music, or a mathematician to solve problems?
To achieve success in all these fields, it is necessary to
focus the mind to some degree. But, in all these activities,
your mind is centred on worldly matters, not on God.
Just as you have learned to absorb your mind in mundane
affairs, in the same manner, to immerse it in love of
God is meditation. This is not very difficult, but neither
is it so very easy. The real meaning of meditation is:
ध्यानं निर्विषयं मनः । That is, to free the mind from thinking,
reflection, memory and even knowledge; in short, to free
it from mentation. This is higher meditation, a state with
which highly evolved saints are familiar. It indicates a
high state when in meditation the mind sheds its activity
and remains merged in the soul.

Meditation is the unfailing method of conquering the
restlessness of the mind. It is the wishing-tree which
grants the desired fruit. It is a kind of magnet which
draws the divine power. Never be flippant about it.

Meditation is the heart of yoga, the basis of all spiritual
pursuit, the Guru's key to knowledge, the very flow of
love and the noble sacrifice which confers all the wealth
of the Guru's grace. It is, in fact, only a different form
of the Guru.

How, for how long, and on whom should one meditate?
These are necessary and important questions. The *Gita*
says (XIII-24): ध्यानेनात्मनि पश्यन्ति केचिदात्मानम् । (Through meditation some perceive the Self in their own selves). The
*Srimad Bhagavatam* says: ध्याने ध्याने तद्रूपता । (As one
continues meditation, he becomes the object of meditation). As a caterpillar is metamorphosed into a butterfly
through intense concentration on the latter's form, a
seeker becomes God through meditation on God.

One should not question the validity of meditation or
debate with oneself whether to meditate on the Form
or on the Formless. Both of these bring the same results.

Saints such as Tukaram, Tulsidas, Namdeva, Mirabai and Janabai worshipped the Form, yet they realised the Formless as well. The Form (also called the Personal Aspect of God) is not imaginary, but real. The splendour of God is immeasurable. He created this habitable world out of the pure Void, from the infinite treasure of His own Shakti. In truth, He became the universe, Himself manifesting as all its various objects. How can it be difficult for the One who has myriad forms and names to appear in a human form? Therefore, neither *sadhus*, *sannyasis* nor seekers should become involved in such controversies. ⁀Worship that aspect of God which is in harmony with your own inclination.⁀

The *saguna* is He. The *nirguna* is also He. Choose for meditation that which stills your mind, frees it from agitation and merges it in the pure Self. Do not squander your precious time on futile arguments about the object of meditation. ⁀You may meditate on any aspect of the Divine.⁀ All gods are worthy objects of meditation, all being one in essence⁀ By means of meditation, attain the inner state of supreme peace in which you overcome all sorrow, experience perfection, conquer the nightmare of frustration and rid yourself of the concepts of birth and death. Arguing is a disease. When in his life, man has suffered from so many diseases and repented of his folly, why does he not avoid the disease of arguing about meditation? Become thought-free. Just as, on waking from deep sleep, you experience the thought-free state for a few moments, similarly, let your mind become tranquil, free from anxiety and realise its identity with the Self. This alone indicates progress in meditation.

Here is another hint: consider whatever you see with your eyes to be a form of the Divine. Such an attitude promotes meditation. This is the true vision that delivers one from birth and death. Yamaraja, the god of death, says to his messengers:

सकलमिदमहं च वासुदेवः परमपुमान् परमेश्वरः स एकः ।
इति मतिरचला भवत्यनन्ते हृदयगते व्रज तान् विहाय दूरात् ॥

(*Vishnu Purana*, 3-7-32)

(O messengers! Do not go near those who firmly possess
the attitude that this visible world and themselves are one
in essence with Vasudeva, the Supreme Person, the
highest Lord, who is seated in the heart). What a high
state of meditation! What a lofty feeling! Those who
meditate on God who is in all directions, in front and
behind, above and below, secure liberation instan-
taneously.

This is how the milkmaids meditated. They saw only
Krishna in whatever they beheld. To them the Yamuna
River, groves and forests, the four directions, their husbands, children, cows and their own selves were only His
diverse forms. Krishna pervaded their bodies and their
minds. He was, in fact, everywhere, all around. They
could find nothing which could be distinguished from
Krishna. Such meditation is consummated without the
necessity of having to retire to a cave or a mountain. This
kind of meditation comes as a result of knowledge,
because knowledge of God is important. ⁸ The whole
universe is the perfect form of God.⁹ This is absolutely
true.

### The Significance Of A Siddha's Abode

Many people came to Nityananda and practised sadhana.
Everyone desired to become a Nityananda, possessing his
supernatural powers and his honour. Each claimed, "I
am the most important person here." "Yes, I alone am
dearest to Nityananda." "No one else has been blessed by
him as much as I." Thus, discordant and painful notes
were flung around among devotees, fostering jealousy,
arrogance, ill-will, hypocrisy and affectation. Consequently, their meditative joy decreased proportionately. "What
did he say?" "What happened there?" "What does he
know?" "Who can ever equal me?" "Even Nityananda
respects my word, not to speak of others." "The Swami
must respect our decision." "What do you think of yourself?"—such paltry, deluded notions spread. Regarding
themselves as Nityanandas, so-called devotees became
conceited and hypocritical. Many great obstacles arose.

When people should have become sinless and pure, over-coming all their defects, the opposite happened.

A meditating aspirant should remember that just as love for the Guru purifies the heart more and more, increasing its radiance, likewise, jealousy, arrogance and sensuality contaminate it in an ever-increasing measure. It is certain that unless a man makes an effort to increase his goodness and meditate more deeply, obtaining heavenly peace and joy, he will suffer inner discord, lose merit, fall into sensuality and add to his store of sins, finally plunging into hell.

A Siddha's ashram is a centre pervaded by charged particles of Chiti. All the trees, creepers, fruits and flowers, birds and animals in the Guru's abode are per-meated, within and without, by rays of Shakti. The Shakti of the unseen, motionless, unchangeable, Supreme Guru, whose nature is Satchidananda, passes through Shaktipat to His descendants down to the present day. This Chitshakti, though without beginning, is ever-new. She has been described in the *Shivasutras* by Lord Shiva as: इच्छा शक्तिरुमा कुमारी । (She is will power, the ever-young Uma). God's own sacred will power is not different from Him. She is the celestial maiden who leads seekers through various spiritual stages. This glorious Chitshakti permeates Siddha students as the divine power of the Guru's grace. Such an ashram is protected by all the Perfected Ones of Siddhaloka who also fulfil all its needs. It receives power from the Supreme Being, Parashiva, the Lord of Siddhas and Siddha yogis and yoginis descending from Him. It is a centre of the blazing flames of yoga! This fire, on the one hand, affords mastery of yoga, con-suming all sins, and on the other hand, it deprives one of radiance, lessening the merit of one who spends his days harbouring lusts instead of practising sadhana. Besides, the thought, "This place has lost all its charm. I now must search for another," indicates fickleness of mind. Even if such an inconstant fellow were to go to another ashram, he would only feel frustrated there as well.

An ashram must not be treated as a den of licence. It

is not meant for boys and girls to indulge in idle gossip
or pleasure. It is neither a tennis club nor a bar serving
whisky and brandy to profligates. Such misconduct courts
ill-repute, suspicions and criticism, destroying yogic
attainments. On the other hand, loyalty towards the
ashram, good conduct, noble deeds and regulated life, bring
the significant experience of the bliss of Kundalini, Chiti's
inner miracle, within easy reach. Only recently a girl
attained a high state of meditation, though she first came
less than a month ago. She meditates deeply, performing
several *mudras*. One day she suddenly got up from
meditation and came running to me, holding her right
middle finger in her left hand. She was still in a meditative state. She said, "Babaji, a serpent has bitten me
here. That's why I've rushed to you." What a lofty
experience! How many stages she has crossed in a short
duration! In Siddha Yoga it is a sure sign, predicting
supreme liberation, to be bitten by a serpent on the right
middle finger. If a practitioner of Siddha Yoga is bitten
by a snake even in a dream, he will certainly achieve
salvation. If such an experience is had during meditation, so much the better.

O students of Siddha Yoga, carefully preserve the
Shakti that spreads throughout your body by the inspiration of a Siddha. Make friends only with the divine
Shakti, the power of Guru's grace, active within you.
Enjoy the company of your own spiritual processes.
Rejoice in your various inner experiences, remembering
them lovingly. Do not taint your heart by misconduct or
ill-will. Remember that you will have to follow a strict
discipline to preserve the Shakti. If a pregnant woman
is not sufficiently careful and vigilant about her child,
keeping away from irregular diet, indulgence and cor-
ruption, she will either miscarry, suffer from some other
complication, or else her baby will not be strong and
healthy. If a wealthy or virtuous person does not take
care of his wealth or virtue, he loses it soon. In the
same manner, without self-control, a seeker loses Shakti.
Never treat each other with anger, evil intention or
snobbery. When a Siddha student progresses on the path,

he becomes worthy of great honour. Honouring him
means honouring Parashakti. Each aspirant should
realise that the highest power of his own Gurudev is
working in all others, because it is one Chiti which
dwells in the Guru as well as the disciples. This attitude
will fortify meditation.

Various streams of Shakti continually arise and subside
in the human mind. One is constantly being reshaped by
one's conduct. This is what is meant by the saying
"actions make the man." Whatever ray of Chitshakti on
which your mind focusses with pure feeling in meditation,
should be consolidated and developed until you reach
perfection. You must not stop half-way.

Siddha students in particular, should gather more
Shakti. This Shakti promotes both spiritual and worldly
well-being. I quote the following verse describing the
reward of Siddha Yoga:

यत्रास्ति मोक्षो न च तत्र भोगो यत्रास्ति भोगो न च तत्र मोक्षः ।
श्रीसुंदरीसेवनतत्पराणां भोगश्च मोक्षश्च करस्थावैव ॥

(Where salvation is, worldly enjoyments are not. Where
sensuous pleasure is, deliverance is not. But spiritual
emancipation and worldly delights are in hand of those
who worship the supremely lovely Kundalini. This should
not surprise anyone.

The Goddess, the primal Shakti, is the source of this
world, consisting of the animate and the inanimate. Lord
Krishna says the same in the *Gita* (XIII-29):

प्रकृत्यैव च कर्माणि क्रियमाणानि सर्वशः ।
यः पश्यति तथात्मानमकर्तारं स पश्यति ॥

¶(He sees, who sees that all actions are performed by
Nature alone and that the Self is actionless)¶ Great seers
have addressed this transcendent blissful Mother, Goddess
Chiti, as follows: त्वमेव सर्वजननी मूलप्रकृतिरीश्वरी । (O Supreme
Goddess! Thou alone art the Mother of all. Thou art the
primordial *prakriti*).

The *Spandashastra* says: इति वा यस्य संविच्तिः क्रीडात्वेनाखिल
जगत् । (He knows the true reality who perceives the

entire universe as a sport of the Parashakti of Parashiva, the Universal Consciousness). She expands as the cosmos. It is the same Shakti which is transmitted through Shaktipat by Siddha Yogis.

Seekers should, therefore, live thoughtfully and remain alert in the ashram of a Siddha. Be vigilant and discreet whether you are in the Guru's company or not. Never find fault with others. They who look for defects in others aggravate their own, diminishing their yogic power. Your conduct should be pure. Purity of conduct does not imply caste-system, untouchability, distinction of high and low or personal adornment. It is a reflection of inner nobility. The purer you are, the greater your progress.

## Meditation On The Guru

Get up before sunrise, take a bath and sit peacefully in meditation. Preferably face the east, but you may face any direction considering it as belonging to Krishna. Compose yourself and sit in a proper posture. Remember the divine power of grace. Remember the mantra. Synchronise it with the incoming and outgoing breaths. Let the mantra fill the mind. If the mind begins to wander, persuade it back to the object of meditation.

Shall I tell you another noble method? Listen. An aphorism of the seer Patanjali reads: वीतरागविषयं वा चित्तम् । (Let the mind be focussed on one who has risen above passion and attachment). In Siddha Yoga, one-pointed meditation on one's chosen form holds a high place. The sublime Guru has awakened the inner Shakti, imparted the mantra and taught one how to sit in a meditative posture. Devote your mind to meditation on your beloved Guru. This is the very essence of Siddha Yoga or Kundalini Maha Yoga, the very secret of the yoga of meditation, the Guru's key to spiritual realisation.

Man develops according to that on which his mind dwells. Whatever he holds in his heart with love impresses him with its own character. It is very easy to meditate on the Siddha Guru. The reason is that we are fully acquainted with him, from head to foot, as it were. We have been with our beloved Guru again and again and have travelled around with him. We have heard him speak on various topics: the different spiritual disciplines and their underlying principles; ecstatic yogic movements; high philosophical matters; various modes of sadhana, some of which may be quite peculiar; and the lives and characters of many saints. It is a matter of common experience that all these things which are stored up in our mental world come before us when remembered or even if not remembered.

Once a young man came to me and said, "Babaji, I am very much upset. Kindly restore my peace. I fell in love with a girl. We liked each other and decided to get married. But some obstacle came in our way and our marriage did not take place. Meanwhile, the girl chose another and married him. That is what has made me so sad. I cannot bear my torment any longer."

I said, "Look, why should you be so aggrieved? It is very simple. You should choose some other girl and marry her."

He said, "That would be fine. But that girl has come to possess me so much that, in spite of my best efforts to get rid of her image, I am not succeeding."

I asked, "Why do you remember her at all?"

He replied, "I don't remember her. Her memory springs up in my mind by itself. Her image starts hovering before my eyes of its own accord."

What a revelation! He had not worshipped the girl for any lengthy period according to scriptural injunctions. He had not tried to concentrate on her, employing the seed-mantra of each part of her body. Nor had he obtained a mantra of her name from a Siddha. Yet her image haunted his mind! Such is the consequence of being together. When we seat someone in our hearts with love, we cannot get rid of him, even if we try our utmost. Even the command "Get out of my mind!" has no effect. When this is the result of meditation done with love, why then, do you not meditate on your Gurudev in such a loving manner? If he can enter your heart just once, he will indelibly imprint his image therein. Then he will not move out, even when you try to drive him away.

Worldly people are always repeating this strain: "Babaji, I try to sit in meditation but worldly affairs come rushing to my mind immediately. The same ruddy office! The same old factory! The same blessed children! What should I do? I am very concerned about it. I am not able to meditate at all."

I answer, "Look, you certainly do meditate. Aren't you meditating when you feel your office or factory throbbing within? Besides, you are also having visions of your children. Aren't you content with these fruits of your meditations? Whatever you lovingly pursue in daily life, whatever objects you embrace with feeling, whatever things your mind dwells upon constantly, are all bearing fruit. Sometimes you visualise your office, sometimes your factory and sometimes your children. Don't you regard this as meditation? Look, brother! I am in the same boat. I meditate on Sadguru Nityananda. I loved different elements of my sadhana. I hugged and kissed the feet of my beloved Gurudev. As a result, those impressions and feelings arise in my heart again and again. Even when I am not thinking of him, the chant *Gurudev, Gurudev*, goes on inside my heart. He gushes up in my entire body. I see only him in my dreams. I perceive him, only him."

When the object of our constant thinking begins to vibrate in our heart, it is called meditation. And, as those vibrations continue, there comes a time when the object is not remembered at all. This is a higher state of meditation. Therefore, the scriptures enjoin us to fix the mind constantly on the Guru, who is divinity in manifest form. Occupy the mind constantly with higher contemplation. Meditation on the Guru bears the highest fruit, not even conceivable to us. As the mind is transmuted into pure consciousness, you will realise the One whose nature is bliss.

Dear fellow beings! Consider why our great saints, established in the Truth, urge everyone to meditate. Why do they ask us to spend so much time on it? Their words are true and authentic, aimed at the well-being of every creature, the lasting benefit of all. Their purpose is to impart a spiritual character to worldly life. They reveal God in the world and the world in God. The mind is the instrument for finding happiness in the world. That is why the sages say: "Meditate. Meditate on God. Realise that the nature of the mind is pure consciousness."

## The Mind   *western psych needs to incorporate some of this*

We are furnished with various means for discovering God in our lives. The mind is the most important of all. We may be able to recover everything else, but once the mind is lost it is extremely difficult to regain.

Once a big industrialist who owned several cloth mills and factories, including one sugar factory, was brought to my Gurudev. There were two servants, two nurses and one doctor to take care of him, as he had become a mental case. He had been held in high honour and esteem, but because his mind was no longer functioning properly, the Lord of the mind having deserted him, as it were, he was no better than the living dead. His mind had lost its power and agility on account of constant worry and anxiety. He was suffering from insomnia. His power of reason had been damaged and he had sunk into idiocy. He had lost only one thing, his mind, but it appeared as though he had ceased to exist. Previously, with the assistance of his mind alone, by its grace and friendliness, he had been able to carry on a big business in his own country and abroad. But now that he was no longer in possession of his mind, he had fallen from his previous high status into this pathetic plight.

Once impaired, it is almost impossible to restore it to its original state. For this reason, Indian culture lays so much emphasis on worship and meditation—to make the mind strong, firm, pure, and powerful and enable it to apprehend truth over a prolonged period with its powers unimpaired.   *Do they have less mental break-downs*

Once a foreign aristocrat came to me and stayed at the ashram for some days. One day he complained, "Swamiji, I have no peace of mind. I am very much disturbed. I am not able to sleep well. Life has lost its sweetness. Even though I possess enormous wealth and esteem in my country, I have no peace, no contentment. I suffer from constant anxiety. I cannot understand this. Please show me some way out. I came here with the information that meditation is highly valued in India. On my way, I met a holy mother in Delhi. I was delighted with her satsang. She sent me to you. Please give me a method by which my mind may become steady, quiet and alert."

The different forms of worship, such as chanting mantras, reciting hymns and contemplation of God, are really worship of the mind, intended to strengthen and purify it.

The mind has a great value. All powers are contained in it. Do not treat it as something trivial. One aphorism from the *Pratyabhijnahrdayam* reads: चेत्यसंकोचिनी चित्तम् । (Mind is Chiti Herself, the light of consciousness in a contracted form). The commentary on it states: न चित्तं नाम अन्यत् किंचित्; अपि तु सैव भगवती तत् । (There is no other thing like the mind, for it is that Goddess Herself). The mind is Goddess Chiti or Kundalini Herself. The universe has come into being by Her agency. It is through the mind that the individual carries out his daily activities in his limited universe. The mind is one pulse of Chitshakti. God, who is the light of consciousness, is the infinite treasury of power. As the myriad kinds of rays of the sun are one with the sun, similarly, the divine Shakti, with its countless different functions, is indistinguishable from the Godhead. Although Shakti performs countless functions and appears in innumerable forms, She retains Her immutable character. Chiti becomes the mind to enable the individual soul to reap the fruits of its actions.

Do not minimize the value of the mind. To indulge in undisciplined, futile and impure thoughts, to remain occupied with sinful ideas day and night, to make the mind impure and to become argumentative—such practices lead to the direst hell. One whose mind is disturbed continually suffers, neglects his duty, behaves unworthily and strays from the path of salvation. An impure mind is hell itself. God dwells within you as the

mind and awards the fruits of your actions. Which of
your secret deeds can remain hidden from Him? Therefore, meditate. Let the mind dwell on the Guru with
sublime feeling.

The mind yields fruits corresponding to your thoughts.
With the help of the mind alone, a man becomes peaceful,
wise, intelligent or deluded. By its power he becomes
a poet, an artist, a musician or a yogi. According to the
scriptures, the mind obstructs and the mind also liberates.
The mind is the Guru who activates Shakti. When at
rest, it is the *nirvikalpa* state.

Take care of your mind. It should be your delightful
friend. A pure mind is worthy of the sublime love of
the Guru. Therefore, meditate with a calm mind. God,
dwelling in the mind, will soon be pleased and grant you
a vision of His Universal Form in meditation. By the
grace of such a mind, you will easily realise the Self.

What a precious treasure your mind is! Why should
you ever weep, grieve, or feel inferior and empty, when
such wondrous Chitshakti is within you? Worship the
Chitshakti which is forever dwelling in your mind. Live
in constant remembrance of the Self, which vibrates in
every fluctuation of the mind.

God, who is the very consciousness of all beings, will
also ensure that you enjoy worldly fulfilment. I will give
you a recent example. A young boy from a good and pious
*brahmin* family frequently comes to the Ashram with his
parents. The boy began to meditate spontaneously and
as a result, his inner Shakti was awakened. He was
continuously engaged in the loving repetition of his mantra
and he began to have various experiences. Though very
young, he was blessed with prophetic knowledge by the
mantra-deity as a result of the mantra vibrations within
him. One day, just prior to his annual examination, the
mantra-deity appeared to him in meditation and said,
"You are going to receive an injury in a motor accident
and it will incapacitate you for your examination." When
he reported this to his parents, they laughed at him,
adding, "Since you don't want to study, you are indulging
in fantasy." But, exactly three days later, the predicted

misfortune came to pass. His right arm was injured in a motor accident and as a result, he missed the examination.

A week later, another surprising event occurred. He and his brothers went to the family farm, intending to enjoy shooting with his airgun. In the morning, as he passed into the *tandra* state, the mantra-deity appeared again and forewarned: "Your gun is thirsty for human blood." However, he disregarded the warning and that evening he went with his brothers to practise shooting. Later, on their return home, he was bending over, with his gun placed upright between his knees, trying to unlock the door to his room. The gun slipped. One of the other boys, who stood nearby, tried to catch it, but happened to press the trigger. The gun went off and a bullet was lodged in our young man's chest. He sustained a wound near his right lung, about two and a half inches long. But, miraculously, he did not become at all perturbed. While he was being taken to the doctor, he remained calm and composed. On the way, the mantra-deity appeared again and communicated some secrets to him. He wrote them in a note in spite of his wound. Later, he passed the note on to me.

The doctor was required to perform an operation which could have proved fatal had the boy not been under the protection of Parashiva. Then, after the operation, with the onset of chest pain, he slipped into the *tandra* state, in which he envisioned a saint passing his hand over his chest. His pain vanished at once. From this, you can easily imagine how beneficial meditation may also be in your daily life. Therefore, meditate.

Meditation is, beyond doubt, conducive not only to spiritual enlightenment, but also to material welfare in the world. As meditation clears the mind, a student can pass any examination with a high grade. I have personally known many boys and girls who have progressed by leaps and bounds, becoming more inspired, vibrant, pure and noble through meditation. Meditation calms the mind and makes it stable. As the mind becomes steady, the breath is retained for short periods. This

The benefits of meditation.

strengthens muscles, tones up blood circulation and helps
in the assimilation of food. Furthermore meditation
increases one's alertness. One who meditates regularly
overcomes various common diseases. As a result of inner
peace, one's life becomes inspired.

## The Method Of My Meditation

It is not necessary to elaborate on the various
techniques of meditation. As I have said before, the best
and quickest method of stabilising the mind is contained
in the following aphorism of Patanjali: वीतरागविषयं वा
चित्तम् । (Let the mind be focussed on one who has risen
above passion and attachment.) Meditation on one's Guru
is a noble, nay, the noblest and loftiest form of meditation. For years I had practised many different disciplines,
including *pranayama*, concentration, and repetition of
mantra, but, at long last, I devoted myself entirely to
meditation on my beloved Gurudev.

Meditation on the Guru is the basis of all methods of
meditation. When I read in the *Guru Gita* (76):

> ध्यानमूलं गुरोर्मूर्तिः पूजामूलं गुरोः पदम् ।
> मन्त्रमूलं गुरोर्वाक्यं मोक्षमूलं गुरोः कृपा ॥

(The root of meditation is the Guru's form
The root of worship is the Guru's feet
The root of mantra is the Guru's word
The root of liberation is the Guru's grace),
I obtained my supreme mantra. I accepted it with great
love and reverence. This form of meditation is, indeed,
superior to all sacrifices and all forms of worship. In the
following mantra-like verse, Sant Tukaram says:

> गुरुचरणी ठेविता भाव । आपे आप भेटे देव ॥
> म्हणुनी गुरुसी भजावे । स्वध्यानासी आणावे ॥
> देव गुरुपासी आहे । वारंवार सांगूं काये ॥
> तुका म्हणे गुरुभजनीं । देव भेटे जनीं वनीं ॥

(God can easily be attained without any travail of
sadhana, by maintaining deep faith in the Guru's feet;

therefore, worship the Guru and let your thoughts dwell on him. God is quite close to the Guru. How many times should I tell you: Tukaram says that by constant remembrance of the Guru, one can meet God anywhere— in an uninhabited forest or in the midst of multitudes). I adopted this passage as my ideal, embraced the truth contained in it and enjoyed its reward. I firmly resolved to meditate on Sri Guru Nityananda. Sitting in a remote and quiet corner of the hall, in a position where I could behold Gurudev, I began to stare at him for prolonged periods.

What a beautiful, dark-complexioned form he had! What a sublime body! Harmonious limbs, veins overflowing with joy of life, dark skin glowing with crystalline sheen, teeth like tiny pearls, long tapering fingers, abdomen fully strengthened by spontaneous retention of breath, wearing only a pure white loin-cloth, the fingers of the right hand in *chinmudra* and those of the left wide open in *abhaya mudra*, his divine, full-throated sound of 'hunh,' neck swaying rejoicingly, body moving in ecstasy, cells quivering with supreme bliss, rays of celestial glory emanating from all parts, bubbling laughter illuminating all directions—all these were forever imprinted on my heart. I would gaze and gaze at his divinely beautiful form and always discovered a new fascination, a new magic in it.

Gurudev reclined on a wooden cot which was covered by a woollen blanket. Countless tins of sweets and biscuits were lying everywhere, in front and behind. Two cots, one bearing fruits for *prasad* and the other bundles of cloth, were placed on either side of him. I would continue to stare at the auspicious form of my Gurudev, a king among yogis, seated gloriously in the midst of all these gifts. Gurudev swayed his lotus feet up and down, back and forth. His wide celestial eyes, at times remaining only half open, were always filled with ecstasy. A smile would play on his lips, signifying inner quietude. His mind was always free from entanglements, personal or social distinctions, dualities—of possession and renunciation, thine and mine, dual and non-dual, virtue and vice—in short, it was always still. He was securely established in the thought-free state. Sometimes I saw him with my eyes wide open and sometimes with them closed. I tried to visualise inwardly what I beheld outside. Thus gazing and meditating on him alone, I discarded all previous methods of meditation. As I contemplated him, I became immersed in a divine feeling of oneness with him.

I meditated on his various expressions—his *chinmudra*, reassuring *abhaya mudra*, ecstatic movements of hands bestowing benediction, oscillating neck, full-throated musical sound of *Om* arising from utter blessedness, and a mantra-like sound of 'Aah! Aah!' granting inner initiation. A length of time passed in this manner. I saw his form in meditation, sometimes clearly, sometimes not. As my meditation became deeper, my inner joy, steadfastness, strength and radiance increased proportionately. In the course of time, I began to experience *Gurubhava* in meditation. I have proclaimed again and again that meditation on the Guru is the most beneficial. One can never over-estimate its significance.

I observed all his daily activities with close attention— walking towards the hot springs for bath well before 3 a.m., bathing, worshipping his own Soul, laughing, humming, talking and listening to himself, being aware of his own inner bliss and enjoying his own rapturous play. I fully practised all these attitudes of Bhagawan Nityananda. At times, this so intoxicated me that I completely identified myself with him, exclaiming inwardly: "I am Nityananda." In this state, I experienced a secret glory. My inner being scaled previously unknown divine heights. Sometimes I was wholly enveloped in the rapture of spiritual joy, filled with the thought: "I have become perfect. Yes, I have." Sometimes I practised the transcendent attitude of detachment of Sri Guru Nityananda, who remained for long periods in a state in which mentation was suspended. Then his countenance became solemn, teeth clenched, lips pressed upon each other, eyes half-closed and prana flowing evenly. My eyes also became half-closed, teeth clenched, lips pressed together, breathing slowed down and my mind became utterly quiet. Subsequently, my head moved gently forwards and backwards like that of Bhagawan Nityananda, as if my inner state and its outer expression were united with his in sheer ecstasy. Thus, I faithfully practised meditation on the Guru according to the mantra: ध्यानमूलं गुरोर्मूर्तिः। (The root of meditation is the Guru's form).

During these days I was not myself, but often identified with Nityananda. If someone approached me or my acquaintances began to talk among themselves, I flew into a rage, sometimes abusing them in Nityananda's manner. I was fully conscious of a double identity, Muktananda alternating with Nityananda. I would get up from meditation when my identification with Nityananda had ceased and take a brief stroll around my dwelling. At that time it was Muktananda walking around, not Nityananda, and I only carried memories of the previous identification. Sometimes while I practised *Gurubhava* I became furious, only to regret it later. When I recollected that I had scolded or abused someone and even rushed to strike another, I felt distress and remorse over my lack of self-control.

One day I gathered courage and approached Gurudev, addressing him as 'Appa' which means 'Baba' in our language (Kannada). While I spoke, Baba continued to make his characteristic 'hunh' sound. I said, "Sometimes during meditation, I lose my temper and even abuse people. I feel so ashamed of it later."

He replied, "That's not you . . . not you at all . . . only a fleeting condition. Aha! . . . that's certainly not you."

I found it hard to understand. For eight long days, I mentally debated the meaning of the words: "That's not you at all. That's certainly not you at all. That's certainly not you." But I did not succeed. Then the question arose: What should I do? I prayed inwardly to Bhagawan Nityananda for an answer.

Gurudev was my only deity, constituting the sole object of my *saguna* adoration, *saguna* worship and *saguna* meditation. I worshipped him, seeing Sita-Ram, Radha-

Krishna, Girija-Shankar and the Guru Dattatreya in him. I was not at all concerned with any other god. I did not repeat the name of Rama, worship Krishna, nor meditate on Shiva, but this did not worry me. I believed with all my heart that the Guru encompasses all gods. Worship of the Guru includes that of all deities, meditation on the Guru that on all gods and repetition of the Guru's name that of all the seventy million sacred mantras. I had been blessed with the darshan of sixty great saints, including Sri Siddharudh Swami, Zipruanna, Hari Giri Baba, Madiwala Swami, Athani Shivayogi, Narsingh Swami of Pandharpur and Sri Bapu Mai. They all had proclaimed, "There is no path higher than meditation on the Guru, obeying and serving him." I had met many other *sadhus* and *sannyasis*, including Vaishnavites of a high order, and naked *avadhoots* who had lived in the Himalayas for many years. Each one of them had declared at the end of his discourse that meditation on the Guru, service to him and obedience to his command are the noblest virtues. It was asserted again and again that the best method lies in merging oneself in the Guru. Furthermore, I had come across several Shaivite saints, who exalted Shiva and identified themselves with Him in meditation, and whose mode of initiation was Shaktipat. They, too, stressed the same truth: "Approach the Guru. Adore him. Live with him." I had also read the writings of various other saints. Eknath Maharaj writes: "Meditate on the Guru." Sri Jnaneshwar says: "The Guru is the mantra; the Guru is the Tantra; in fact, the Guru is all in all." Sri Gorakhnath, Sri Nanakdeva and Sri Kabir have all celebrated the Guru's glory.

Thus I was totally convinced that meditation on the Guru is the highest. I engaged myself constantly in the *saguna* worship of the Guru. I meditated on Nityananda, sang his praises and practised the Guru-mantra received from him. I drank water from the hot springs sanctified by his dip. When visitors put questions to him, I carefully listened to his answers and reflected on them. At noon, nobody was allowed into Bhagawan Nityananda's kitchen. No one could obtain the *prasad* of his left-

overs, even if he begged for it. Therefore, I sought out
the corner where Kariyanna Shetty and Monappa, Bhagawan's cooks, dumped the kitchen refuse after washing
the utensils. I would steal quietly to that side and joyfully eat a few grains of the food as *prasad*. I picked up
the dust particles from where Bhagawan Nityananda sat
and smeared my body with them. Thus my *saguna* worship, adoration and meditation on Nityananda grew more
intense each day. I never harboured critical thoughts of
my Guru, found fault with his ways or argued about
him. I never lent my ear to any disparagement of him,
no matter who it came from. At times I also had the
opportunity of massaging his sacred limbs or pressing his
lotus feet. In this manner, my devotion for him increased steadily, my faith in him strengthened and my
reverence deepened.

My beloved Gurudev knew all my thoughts. At times,
he would make me aware of this in a subtle manner.
Bhagawan Nityananda sometimes spoke to me of his own
accord, being aware of what passed in my mind. One
day at 4.30 p.m., when the atmosphere was tranquil, I
was sitting in the old hall with many others. Bhagawan
said: "Meditation on the Guru saves one from death . . .
highly mysterious process . . . complete yoga . . . full
knowledge. Yes, all knowledge . . . inherent in it. Great
worship of the Guru . . . sublime meditation on him . . .
themes of *Jnana Sindhu* . . . lofty work." Saying this, he
fell silent again. I pondered his statement deeply. For
me, it had the force of a mantra. I always regarded
Bhagawan's statements as gospel truth. Musing thus on
his words, I went towards the springs and found a
devotee from Bombay, Krishna Shetty, sitting with a copy
of *Jnana Sindhu* in the Kannada language. He said,
"Swami, I have a book called *Jnana Sindhu*. As I read
it, I become quite confused. Let us offer it to Baba
Nityananda." I said, "All right." Both of us went inside.
He placed the book before Babaji. Making his characteristic 'hunh' sound, Bhagawan Nityananda said to me.
"Take this." I took it, considering it his *prasad*. In fact,
I looked upon everything I received from Gurudev as

*prasad.* If I received a fruit from him, I did not regard
it as a mere fruit, but ate it with utmost devotion as a
symbol of unfolding Shakti. Then I would meditate for
a short while. Likewise, I took the book and touched it
to my forehead. I had already read it twice. This work
was composed by a distinguished Siddha called Sri
Chidananda, who was an *avadhoot* through and through.
He had directly realised Goddess Baglamukhi. His abode
was situated on the mountain known after the name of
the Goddess as Baglamukhi Mountain on the bank of the
Tungabhadra, beyond Hampi. Though it was no longer
something new, I accepted it as a new *prasad* from
Gurudev. I sat down in a corner of the hall and opened
it at the chapter dealing with the lofty worship of the
primordial Guru. I read that chapter three times with
rapt attention. It was impregnated with profound
meaning. The book contains a dialogue between Parashiva and Kartikeya. In its description of the mode of
meditation on the Guru, it says one should meditate on
the Guru after installing him in one's inner being and
identifying oneself with him.

My dear ones, devoted to the Guru! Listen now with
full attention. The chapter begins as follows: Parashiva
spoke: "O Kartikeya! You are the most devoted of the
devotees of the Guru. Meditation on the Guru is
supremely elevating—the mysterious mode of the Perfected Ones. It bestows not only worldly enjoyments and
spiritual liberation, but in the end also transmutes the
meditating aspirant into the highest Guru, immersed in
transcendental bliss, being pure effulgence in essence. O
Kartikeya! Despite his physical form, the Guru is without beginning or end. His nature is truly beyond thought.
The Guru Principle is the primordial Principle, composed
of supreme bliss. Though itself motionless, it forms the
primeval source of all movement. All thoughts subside
and transmigatory motion ceases in it. It is the ground
of the animate and the inanimate universe. This Truth
is the goal of *Om*, and is the abode of Siddhas, beyond
the reach of the *saguna-nirguna* controversy. It is
accessible only to a Guru, and there is no return from

it. It is the deity of all gods, support of all, the ultimate
destination of all, and their innermost Self. Such is the
true nature of the Guru. From time to time he incarnates
in human form and lives within as the Guru Principle.
He elevates his disciples to his own plane by bestowing
grace and also controlling its activity. Meditation on the
form of such a Guru bears noble fruit. O Kartikeya,
established in yoga! The transcendental glory, without
form or attribute, the substratum of all existence, is in
fact the Supreme Guru Himself. All directions, spaces,
mountains, forests, rivers, oceans and vast earthly regions
consisting of the five elements are His different forms.
The supremely blissful Guru stretches from east to west,
north to south, above and below, from paradise to inferno
and over Kailas and Vaikuntha. He is the highest destination of the liberated. He assumes all forms, but
remains different from them. In fact, He belongs to none,
and none belong to Him.

"The Guru is the final goal of *So'ham*, manifesting
himself as *So'ham*. He embraces the animate as well as
the inanimate. He appears as the primordial cosmic egg,
and the cosmos as well. He descends in the human form
of a spiritual Master to impart his power to his beloved
devotees, subjects, children, nay, his own Self. He is the
founder of the Siddha path. His manners and ways are
inscrutable. He is neither male nor female but pure
Guru. His body has been purified in the flames of
Kundalini Yoga, with its seven components permeated by
Chiti. The primal *Om*, becoming *So'ham*, plays in his
prana. Worldly existence, which appears tangled to
others, is only a play of Chiti to Him.

"Meditate on such a Guru, installing him in all parts
of your body. O, thou devoted to the Guru! This is the
highest worship. Become tranquil, overcome thought
fluctuations and free the mind from all internal and
external supports. In short, eradicate mentation. Sit
down feeling that the Guru is confronting you. Kneel to
him who comprises all gods, mantras, saints, sages and
seers. Prostrate yourself to him in each direction. Address
him, saying, 'O Gurudev! You comprise all! You appear

as the universe.  I prostrate myself again and again to each of your innumerable forms!'  Thus, bowing to him inwardly, meditate on the Guru, realising that the Guru Principle envelops you from each direction, above and below, front and behind.  Afterwards, install him in your body.  Remember that just as threads permeate cloth and cloth is present in every thread, likewise, the Guru is in you and you are in him.  See the Guru and yourself as one.  As a pitcher is not different from clay, even so your Guru is not different from you.  With this knowledge, sit in a meditative posture, touch your head with your hand and feel that it is the Guru's head.  Then touch your forehead, eyes, ears, nose, tongue, throat and shoulders in turn, regarding them all as his features.  Likewise, while touching your chest, heart, abdomen, back, waist, thighs, knees, calves and feet, feel that they are all his and his alone.  Finally, touch your toes, considering them his.  Along with this movement from head downwards, continue to chant *Guru Om* mentally.  O Kartikeya, full of the love of the Guru!  Then, start from the toes, and in the same manner touch all the parts, such as feet, calves, knees, thighs, back, abdomen, and so on, continuously reciting *Guru Om*.  Thus installing the Guru throughout the body, finally, touch the head, uttering *Guru Om*.  Then begin to meditate, feeling that you yourself are the Guru, the mantra, nay, everything; the Guru is in you and you are in the Guru.  Meditate daily in this manner, without the slightest doubt that the Guru is in you and you are in the Guru.  While meditating and repeating *Guru Om*, let go of the consciousness of self."

Then the Supreme Lord adds, "O Swami Kartikeya, while bathing, feel the Guru dwelling in your entire body. While taking food, know that the Guru who resides in your heart receives it.  Offer it to him and then eat. While bathing think that the Guru is bathing, while eating, that the Guru is eating.  Surrender all other actions to the Guru who promotes your true welfare. Consider him to be the giver, enjoyer, sacrificer and all sacrifices.  Thus being completely possessed by the Guru, continually repeat *Guru Om, Guru Om, Guru Om* each day. This is what is meant by his supreme worship."

Parashiva spoke again: "O Kartikeya! A disciple soon becomes the living image of his Guru by this Guru worship. One becomes like him of whom one sings, on whom one meditates and whom one worships. Meditation on the Guru, worship of him, repetition of his mantra and the awareness of his presence in each cell—together these make an instantaneous impact on the disciple's heart. Therefore, meditate in solitude on the supreme Guru, deeply identifying yourself with him. This is the secret mode of Siddhas, the master key of Sadgurus, the blessed divine couch of the Guru's devotees for inner repose and the ladder to the City of Liberation. This truth will not interest those who lack devotion for the Guru. O Swami Kartikeya! Only those blessed by the Guru can fathom its mystery. Without God's grace, Guru worship will not hold any charm, but will escape all comprehension."

Thus, having described the Guru's glory, the manner of his worship and meditation, Lord Shiva left for Kailas. Then, Sri Kartikeya became absorbed in meditation on the Guru.

This is the theme of *Jnana Sindhu*. I, too, was practising sadhana in this manner. As I read about Guru worship in this book, presented by my revered Gurudev, I realised it was more than a hint for me. Believing it to be my Guru's command, I did not return to my dwelling, but remained at the Ashram, close to Guru Nityananda. As night fell, the day's routine ended and the atmosphere became quiet. Gurudev retired into his room. I went into the big hall and sat in a meditative posture facing east. Musing on the instruction of Lord Shiva to Kartikeya in *Jnana Sindhu*, I began to meditate. I took the all-pervading consciousness to be Nityananda, firmly regarding the five elements, rivers, oceans, caves and mountains as his different forms. Considering the sky to be his head, the earth his feet, the directions his ears, the sun and moon his eyes, I began to meditate on the all-pervasive Nityananda. My mind became increasingly more absorbed in this contemplation. Thus I meditated considering the entire outer universe to be his embodiment. Whatever awareness was left, I turned it to contemplate Nityananda within. First, I touched my head with my hand, thinking of my beloved Gurudev. "Nityananda is in my head; he is in my forehead. My beloved Nityananda is in both my ears. Nityananda is in the light of my eyes, he is in my throat. Nityananda is in my arms. He is in my hands. Baba Nityananda is in my fingers. He is the soul dwelling in my heart. Sri Nityananda is in my abdomen. He is in my back. Sri Guru Nityananda is in my thighs. He is in my knees. Nityananda is in my legs. He is in my feet."

Thus I installed him in my body. While touching all these parts, I continually repeated *Guru Om, Guru Om* and felt him in each. What a joy! There was lightness in my heart and its anguish vanished. Fresh, cooling impulses flowed through my being. I plunged into ecstasy. Thoughts of the ecstatic saints release rapture in the heart. I once heard it sung:

सफ़ा से मिला तो सफ़ा हो गया मैं ।
खुदी मिट गई, खुद खुदा हो गया मैं ॥

(When I realised the Pure, I became pure;
   My ego was obliterated, I myself became God).

Thus installing the Guru in my body with a deep feeling of love, I was fully immersed in adoring him. What a joyous couch to recline on, free from anxiety! What delicious delicacies, containing all six savours, satiated me! What a heavenly kingdom I dwelt in! Sitting in the boat of love, gliding on the ocean of the Guru's bliss, playing among the waves of delight, I rejoiced in the cool breezes enfolding me.

In the meantime, the clock struck midnight. I had been meditating for three hours! But so far I had only practised the first half of the new technique. I now started upwards from the lower extremities. I touched my feet, saying, "O Gurudev! Dwell here. Nityananda is in my feet. He is in my knees. Nityananda permeates my thighs. My Guru Nityananda is in my back. Sadguru Nityananda is in my abdomen. Baba Nityananda is in my navel. He is in my ribs. In the centre of the heart

lotus resides Lord Nityananda in his transcendental bliss.
Nityananda is in my rosary of *rudraksha* beads. He is
in my arms. Guru Nityananda is in my throat. He is in
my mouth. Nityananda is in my tongue. He is in my nose.
Nityananda is in my eyes. He is in my forehead. Sadguru
Nityananda is the efflulgence of *sahasrar* in *brahma-randhra*."

As I plunged deeper into meditation on Guru Nityananda, from toe to crown, the prana became calm and
steady within my heart. I felt acute pain in the *mula-dhar*, as though it had been struck with divine lightning.
As the prana moved forcefully throughout my body and
the various nerves thrilled, I became completely absorbed
in meditation. I heard Nityananda Baba call me at
3 a.m., saying: "Get up." I arose in rapture. The intoxication melted gradually. Babaji took a bath in the hot
springs and I did the same after him. Then I was besieged
by meditation once again. My *Gurubhava* became more
intense. Rays of peace spread within.

As the morning broke, Bhagawan Nityananda came out
and sat on his couch. All the visitors used to receive his
darshan from a distance. My turn often came last. After
the darshan I remained standing there. Babaji said,
"That's it. That's the right form of meditation." Lifting one hand in *chinmudra* he added, "That's genuine
meditation. . . . Yes. . . . O Yes . . . it is . . . includes
knowledge . . . worship . . . ecstasy, yes, ecstasy . . .
O Yes . . . subtle, perfect meditation." Then he started
humming. I realised that I had been fully initiated in
meditation.

I accepted meditation on the Guru as the kind of
meditation I should practise. I got up each day at
3 a.m. when the atmosphere is entirely free from noise.
This period is eminently suitable for worship and
meditation. After a bath, I bowed to all the directions,
feeling that one Spirit pervades them all. Then I
meditated on my beloved Gurudev. During a silent
period of the night I meditated again. I was able to
meditate deeply during both periods. Sometimes, unable
to take a bath, I washed my hands, feet, face and tongue.

Thus cleansed, I sat in meditation. Afterwards, I took a walk. All around my meditation room I put up photographs of Gurudev and other Siddhas. I sat in their midst for meditation. To me his picture was not something lifeless. Just as I conducted myself with awe, restraint and purity in his actual presence, likewise, in my meditation room where his picture hung, I never sat with my legs outstretched towards it. Inside the room I moved about with scrupulous care. The reason is that the meditation room is filled with rays of Chiti, particularly during the period of meditation. Moreover, the Guru dwells fully where his picture is worshipped. While meditating in this room, I also invoked all the Siddhas in the following manner: May all those Siddhas who have realised the highest state by the Guru's grace, through the worship of his sacred feet, including all past, present and future ones, protect me and bestow Shakti on me in all its fullness.

During this period, I generally kept away from people, as each one carries his particular aura, which may or may not be congenial. The subtle power of the divine name permeated the atmosphere around Kakabhushandi's ashram in the Himalayas for miles and miles. As soon as anyone, however dull, slow or stupid, entered this hermitage, he began chanting the name of Rama spontaneously. Similarly, Sri Nityananda had instilled the atmosphere with his stillness, silence, detachment and freedom from thought. So powerful was his presence that restless people from Bombay, of whatever class or disposition, shed their agitation and became quiet as they entered his orbit after a dip in the hot springs. Bhagawan Nityananda's personality dominated the atmosphere. Under the influence of his perfect detachment, silence and quiescence, each one sat in peace, fully observing the discipline. In his presence, each one meditated spontaneously. My own regular meditations increased my enthusiasm, bringing new experiences. I seemed to be advancing towards my spiritual goal with enormous speed.

# 2

# MY SPIRITUAL EXPERIENCES

Thus, I was worshipping and meditating on the Guru. One evening I went for the darshan of Bhagawan Nityananda. After the darshan, he always asked me, "Are you leaving now?" But that day he did not put his usual question, so I stayed on. I spent the night immersed in the sublime joy of meditation on the Guru.

## Initiation

The morning of the fifteenth of August, 1947, dawned. What an auspicious day! How nectarean! What merit and exceptional fortune it held in its womb! It was the most remarkable day of my life—the most significant day, not only of this lifetime, but of many lifetimes! The holiest of the holy, O yes, the most auspicious of all auspicious days, broke.

The sun rose slightly above the horizon. The atmosphere was tranquil. I was standing in the eastern corner of the hall absorbed in contemplation of the Guru. In the opposite corner stood Monappa, Gurudev's cook. Inside the meditation room, Gurudev made his characteristic 'hunh' sound to indicate that he was about to come out from his meditation. Soon he appeared, revealing a form which I had never seen before. He was wearing beautiful wooden sandals. He moved forward and backward, smiling to himself, and walked around chanting certain mysterious mantras. Then he would stand in front of me, smiling and humming. He was wearing a white shawl, a loin-cloth and the sandals on his feet. He faced me again and again, uttering a loud 'hunh.' One hour passed in that way.

Then Gurudev came close to me and his body touched

mine. This surprise completely benumbed me. I was standing facing west, while Gurudev faced east, his body adjacent to mine. I opened my eyes to look at him. Lo! His eyes, wide open in *shambhavi mudra*, were gazing straight into mine. I was dazed. I could not close my eyes; I had lost all power of volition. The divine rays emanating from Gurudev's eyes virtually paralysed mine. We remained in this stance for a short while. Then I heard the heavenly strain of his 'hunh.' When I had somewhat regained consciousness, I found he had stepped back about two feet.

He was saying, "Take these sandals, wear them. Would you like to wear these sandals of mine?"

Though amazed, I replied reverently and firmly, "Gurudev, these sandals are not meant for me to wear, but to worship. Sire, if you kindly agree, I shall spread my cloth. Please be so gracious as to place your feet on it and leave your sandals."

My revered Gurudev accepted my request. Making his sound of 'hunh,' he lifted his left foot along with the sandal and placed it on my cloth. Then, bringing the left foot down and lifting the right one, he put in the other sandal as well. He stood facing me directly. He looked into my eyes again. Watching carefully, I saw a ray of light entering me from his pupils. It felt hot, like burning fever. Its light was dazzling, like that of a high-powered bulb. As that ray emanating from Bhagawan Nityananda's pupils penetrated mine, I was thrilled with amazement, joy and fear. I was beholding its colour, and chanting *Guru Om*. It was a full unbroken beam of divine radiance. Its colour kept changing from molten gold to saffron to a shade deeper than the blue of a shining star. I stood utterly transfixed. Then as Gurudev moved slightly, chanting his 'hunh,' I stirred, partially recovering my wits. I bowed to the sandals in my cloth. I prostrated myself at his feet. I rose with my heart pulsating with bliss.

I said in a soft, tender tone, "Gurudev! What divine luck! I have obtained the highest boon today. Kindly dwell in your fullness in these sandals and allow me to

worship them, though I do not know the proper manner."
As I uttered these words, he went towards the western
wing of the hall. He returned with some flowers, two
bananas, a few incense sticks and a pinch of *kum-kum*.
He placed them all on the sandals. Meanwhile, I was
chanting *Guru Om, Guru Om*.

He sat down and said in his aphoristic fashion, "All
mantras . . . one. Each . . . from *Om*. *Om Namah Shivaya
Om* . . . should think, *Shivo'ham*, I am Shiva . . . Shiva-
Shiva . . . *Shivo'ham* . . . should be internal repetition.
Internal . . . superior to external."

Making his 'hunh' sound, he went inside. This sound
sometimes indicated different instructions. If he turned
his head while uttering this sound, it was a hint for me
to leave. But he had not yet made that gesture, so I
remained standing. Bhagawan came out, holding a blue
shawl which he put around me. What marvellous
fortune! Since early morning I had been receiving
precious gifts, one after another. Then he rushed towards
the kitchen where Monappa was cooking *bhajiyas* of
unripe bananas and putting them in a plate. Taking two
handfuls of them, he came over and put them in the
same cloth which held the sandals and other gifts. Finally
uttering his blissful 'hunh,' he made the sign for me to
depart.

What a significant day! How sacred and auspicious! As
I came out I began to congratulate myself: "Aha! What
an hour! How fruitful! What meritorious deeds I must
have done to deserve all this!"

I was beside myself with amazement. I had never
expected such an event to occur. It was unlikely for one
such as I to receive the Guru's sandals, because at that
time Bhagawan Nityananda had many ardent devotees
who had been devoted to him for years. Some were
quite old; some were business magnates. Each claimed
to be an advanced and experienced seeker, being closest
to Bhagawan, while I was an ordinary and unfamiliar
visitor, rather new to the place. I had not performed any
special kind of sadhana nor had I achieved any worthwhile stage. I owned neither a mansion nor a business

concern. I was in every way a poor man. Therefore all that had happened showed that I was exceptionally fortunate.

My Gurudev was a perfect *avadhoot*. He used to travel barefoot throughout the country. But on that day, he had worn sandals on his lotus feet—those sacred lotus feet which are worshipped by gods as well as men, which grant yogic knowledge and destroy all sins. He had then walked around, finally stopping in front of me. He had bestowed his sandals on me straight from his feet. Thus my anguish had been overcome, my sins annihilated, the cycle of birth and death ended and the veil of ignorance torn away. What a glorious event! Nityananda *Avadhoot* did not bestow his grace in such a direct manner, usually granting it through a seemingly purposeless *mudra* or movement. That he himself should confer his sandals on me was inconceivable. He who never wore sandals, had worn them and put them in the empty cloth of my mendicancy, not with his hands, but straight from his sacred feet. Not only this. He never looked directly into anyone's face. Even if he sometimes directed his glance towards a certain face, he would shift it in a moment. That day he had gazed into my eyes with his eyes wide open in Parashiva's *shambhavi mudra*, as if he had never seen me before. He had entered me with his divine ray of Chiti that grants all powers. Beholding that ray, I had experienced different states—tremors in the body, tears flowing from the eyes, stupefaction, detachment and supreme joy. Thus he had blessed me with sublime initiation. Then he had called me towards him. This poor *sadhu*, who had been staying at a great distance, had received his first opportunity of going near the Lord. It was unusual for a helpless stranger to sit so close to Bhagawan in the presence of all others. In fact Parashiva, my adored deity, had rewarded me generously in keeping with His epithet—*ashutosh*—which means the One who is easily pleased, for my inadequate Monday fasts and repetition of His name. That which a poet says about the munificence of Lord Shiva applied to Bhagawan Nityananda fully:

धन्य धन्य भोलेनाथ !
आप बाँट दिया सब जग एक पल में ।
तेरे सम दाता नहीं और कहीं जग में ॥

(O simple-hearted Lord! You gave the whole world away
in a moment. There is none else in the entire universe
as bountiful as you).

Sri Gurudev had seated me near him. By imparting
the electrified mantra *Om Namah Shivaya*, indicating the
true meaning of *Om*, and uttering *Shivo'ham*, he had
made me fully aware of my identity with Shiva. He had
explained a mode of external worship that consists of the
repetition of the highly beneficial Shiva mantra, composed
of five Sanskrit letters. By uttering *Shivo'ham*, which
means "I am Shiva"—who dwells in the inner heart—he
had conveyed the immortal message of the immortal
Lord. By declaring "All is *Om*," he had bestowed the
knowledge that all is one Self.

If a miser starts giving away his hoarded wealth, one
receives so much that one becomes satiated. That is what
had happened in my case. As Gurudev had uttered the
words "*Shivo'ham*. . . . Inculcate this attitude," he had
destroyed, by the stroke of the supremely radiant mantra
of Parashiva, all the innumerable sounds arising in the
*akasha* of the heart from time immemorial—sounds
which cause transmigration through innumerable forms
of existence. He had also exterminated the countless
impure attitudes characterised by desire, frustration and
delusion, springing from the notion 'I and mine.' He had
transmitted into my inner heart the great mantra of the
form of Shiva, illuminated by consciousness, ever-rising
and ideally luminous, embodying the truth 'I am perfect,'
and the transcendent word of Shakti. In the flames of
his grace he had consumed all my sins and karmic impressions, accumulated through myriad incarnations.

Then he had put a blue shawl around me. Just as
armour protects a warrior from enemy strokes, bullets,
knives or swords, likewise, the shawl afforded me protection against the assault of suffering, the taint of sin, the
thievery of delusion, the vile dacoity of all attachment

and aversion and the wild onslaughts of pain and disease. Furthermore, serving as the priest, he had offered flowers, fruits, *kum-kum* and incense sticks to the sandals. How amazingly good my fortune! I had received sandals for worship consecrated by the naked informal priest, Bhagawan Nityananda. My luck was indeed exceptional. Moreover, what followed reflected his grace in even greater measure. He himself had gone in, to the accompaniment of his 'hunh' music and had come back with both hands full of sizzling *bhajiyas* and placed them on the sandals. He had worshipped the sandals with the same hand that he used to lift in *abhaya mudra*, and his divine, conscious lotus hands had also offered the *prasad*. At this instant my mind was flooded with ancient memories. I was able to recollect similar acts of worship performed in past lives.

As I came out of the hall, I began to touch my head with the holy sandals again and again, relish the *bhajiyas* one by one and inhale the fragrance of the flowers. The softness and beauty of the precious shawl gladdened my heart. My mind became as swift and sprightly as it had earlier become one-pointed, silent and motionless. My new exuberance was, of course, untainted by insipidity, sadness, inertia or anxiety. I was overflowing with joyous ecstasy, zest and enthusiasm. My thoughts rushed again and again to Sri Gurudev's sandals, expanding with delighted high spirits. I hummed the following verse of *Gurupaduka-ashtakam*:

ज्याच्या कृपेचा मज लाभ झाला जन्मांतरींचा भवताप गेला ।
श्रीदत्त ऐसा उपदेश केला विसरूं कसा मी गुरुपादुकांला ॥

(Such was the teaching of Sri Dattatreya; by his grace I was benefited; the worldly fever of many births was destroyed. I cannot forget those Sri Guru-sandals).

Congratulating myself on my splendid fortune and praising Parashiva, my former deity for His generous grace, I moved slowly towards my dwelling. *Gurubhava* and devotion to the Guru began to arise again on the way. Following my recent mode of Guru worship, I said to myself once again, "The Guru is within, the Guru is without," and plunged into joy. The intensity of my feelings fortified *Gurubhava*. I was carrying the Guru sandals on my head. As I crossed the Gandhi Square close to a small culvert with a tree adjacent to it, from where the boundary-line of the present Shree Gurudev Ashram begins, *Gurubhava* was transformed into *Brahma-bhava*. For a short while, I experienced the One in many, abandoning the tendency that differentiates the inner from the outer and shows many in One. While I was repeating *Guru Om, Guru Om* with the thought: "The Guru is within, the Guru is without," the Vedantic doctrine of the Absolute, in which I had been instructed by different teachers, flashed spontaneously within me.

God Varuna also showered kindness on me. Tiny drops of gentle rain began to descend softly. A cool breeze flowed peacefully. I was blinking my eyes. Within me, countless sheaves of bright rays began to sparkle and myriads of tiny sparks twinkled. I gazed at them and admired their wondrous beauty with my eyes closed. I could perceive infinitesimal dots shimmering and rushing throughout my body with astonishing velocity. I was overwhelmed with joy and wonder. I opened my eyes and looked outside. Lo! There too legions of the minutest blue particles were scintillating in rows upon rows. I soared into rapturous regions. I was beholding a marvellous new scene, not on a screen, but actually unfolding all around me. I was walking gently, hardly conscious of whether I was following the path or the path was following me. I stopped near the Gavdevi temple. (At that time, Gurudev was renovating the Gavdevi temple and building three small rooms near it). My face turned of its own accord towards Ganeshpuri. I remembered my beloved Gurudev and inwardly bowed to him again. I moved on along the edge of the road. Varuna's grace was still descending in a gentle drizzle. Delicate drops of rain combined with tremulous rays of blue light. What a glorious sight! I was walking slowly, remembering in my heart the Guru who is the Self of all and carrying his sacred sandals. Even today I can vividly recollect that experience of oneness. I am still seeing those minute blue dots.

I reached the Vajreshwari temple which is sacred to the supreme Shakti, the Mother of Yoga, there known as the Goddess Vajra. The temple of Goddess Vajreshwari grants high powers. It is a unique sacred place. According to legends, many Siddha yogis, sages and seers stayed and performed worship there in times past. Even Lord Rama is said to have visited this place. It is surrounded by lovely hills. Several hot springs possessing healing powers are also situated close by. A small river flowing nearby adds to the beauty of its environment. Behind Her temple there is another small temple consecrated to Dattatreya. I always stayed there. I used to have my lunch with Baba Saheb, the head of the temple. Every day he served me one meal punctually and respectfully. I worshipped the Guru's sandals in the Datta temple and also meditated there at night. For a time my daily routine included a regular visit to Ganeshpuri for the darshan of Gurudev, preceded by a bath. My faith, devotion and reverence for my beloved Guru increased progressively. I spent a long period of time at the temple blessed by the grace of the Goddess Vajra, the Mother of consciousness. I drank Her water and ate Her food.

Several days passed. One morning I remained standing after the darshan of Sri Gurudev. He uttered 'hunh,' gave me a fruit and asked me to go. But I still remained standing. Gurudev spoke again: "Go . . . to your hut . . . at Yeola . . . Yes . . . Yeola . . . Pursue knowledge . . . meditation there . . . Go."

I went away feeling aggrieved and anxious, but entirely willing to obey the Guru's mandate. I attached greater importance to obedience to the Guru than ever before. Obedience to the Guru's command is the highest austerity; it is the most effective mantra repetition; it is true sadhana; it is, in fact, one's supreme duty. For a disciple there is nothing more rewarding than obedience to the Guru. Service to the Guru is the highest worship. It is, indeed, adoration of the entire universe. Such was my belief. Being aware that obedience to the Guru's command is a disciple's noble duty, I left for Yeola the following day.

I reached Yeola. The next day I returned to my hut at Suki for sadhana. My hut faced north, situated between two mango trees, one to the east and the other to the west. All these seemed to be awaiting me. I installed Gurudev's sandals inside. After eating the fruit given by him, I sat down to meditate.

## My Confused Condition

I do not know why, but the next morning I passed into a strange state. I had had bad dreams the previous night and I was still feeling uneasy. I was seized by restlessness. My entire body began to ache. It felt as if every cell were being pierced with a needle. I could not understand what could have happened so suddenly. Where had my earlier ecstasy and joy vanished? My mind was moving to the other extreme. My pride and arrogance were humbled. I was once again rendered poor and destitute as before. My mind was filled with remorse. Where had that rapture disappeared? Alas! What had happened? How did my new world of unfolded bliss dissolve? I had been in such a wonderful state. What had vitiated it? Swami Muktananda fell into that sense of unreality which overpowers one who regards the ruins of his capital, once so beautiful and dear, now razed by fate.

I came out of the hut to sit under my dear mango tree, which was always unperturbed. "What has gone wrong? How has this come about?" Such anxiety was gnawing at me. I was losing my composure. The anxiety deepened into dejection. My old companion, Babu Rao Pahalwan, used to come and stay with me for the night. I asked him to return to his house at Yeola and he left. I was tormented by the anxious questions: "Where is the ecstasy? Where has the new kingdom of joy, found at Ganeshpuri, evaporated?" My previous inner joy gave way to anxiety and all sorts of doubts and misgivings. Every part of my body was aching. My head was so heated up that anger, fear and worry took complete possession of me.

It was 11.30 a.m. My landlord brought a plate of food for me. Those days I was only taking millet *chapatis* with one vegetable curry and some milk. I sat down to eat. I did not like the food at all, but I forced myself to eat half a chapati and gulped some water. Then I stood up. I went and sat down in the swing hanging from one of the mango trees, old companions of my earlier sadhana days. I still lacked enthusiasm.

My glance returned terrified from wherever it fell. I was far away from Gurudev. Whom could I ask about my present condition? I got up from the swing, climbed my dear mango tree and sat peacefully in it for a while. But soon the same anguish returned. My mind became more unsteady. I do not have the heart to confess what impure feelings dominated it. This is true. I was occupied with unclean, hostile and sinful thoughts until 3 o'clock. The landlord came again with a hot drink. I took it and then began to pace up and down near my hut, east to west and back again. All this time people from neighbouring villages were coming to visit me. I did not treat them well. If anyone put a question, I did not give a proper answer. I was constantly shifting my seat. I sat in my favourite places, for example under the mango tree, but acute discontent chased me away.

Gurudev had once narrated a story. I recollected it then because it aptly described my own condition. There was a certain idle, utterly poor and good-for-nothing fellow. Wherever he went he was accompanied by sloth and destitution. If he visited any liberal, noble-souled and wealthy person the latter also became poor and miserly. One day, in sheer desperation, he set out for Mount Kailas. He espied another man going ahead of him. The luckless fellow quickened his pace and caught up with the other. He asked, "O brother! Where are you going? Let us walk together." The other was a still more hopeless image of destitution. He said, "O lazy sire, I cannot walk with you. I am a messenger of your own fate. I must precede you to prepare for your welcome by

want, poverty, insensitivity, mental agitation and
stupidity. Now do you understand why I am in a hurry?"
Gurudev had commented that such a luckless fellow
would be warmly greeted by utter misery, even on Kailas.

Some of the new visitors to our present ashram also
fall into a similar plight. Those unfortunate fellows may
be anywhere, even at an ashram with a Siddha, or in a
satsang group; they will always look hopeless, lacking in
lustre, peace and joy, exuding sadness and apathy. They
are constantly obsessed by their Bombay mode of life,
dreaming of movies, pleasure-hunting at clubs, comfort
and ease. "When shall we get back to Bombay?" Such
anxiety continues to weigh on their hearts.

Muktananda was in the same condition as that poor
specimen. Even the mango trees under which I used to
sit so joyfully, perturbed me acutely that day. My dear
visitors from Yeola, so fond of satsang, appeared heartless
to me. At 6 o'clock, Babu arrived accompanied by a dear
old woman who delighted me every afternoon by singing
verses. As soon as she arrived, I said, "Now sing my
favourite verse." Immediately she began to sing:

शेवटिली पाळी तेव्हां मनुष्यजन्म । चुकलीया वर्म फेरा पडे ॥
एक जन्मीं ओळखी करा आत्माराम । संसार सुगम भोगूं नका ॥

(We are finally born as human beings. If we miss that
opportunity, the cycle repeats itself. Delve into your soul
now. Don't just indulge in easy living). This is one of
Namdev's songs conveying profound meaning. (He calls
upon us to experience the inner Self right in our present
bodies.) The human form is not easy to acquire. Live
discriminately in it or else you will be born again. The
woman used to sing this passage with deep feeling. But
even such an intoxicating verse did not delight me.

There is another verse composed by Janabai, Namdev's
dear disciple. Janabai was a great yogini and devotee.
She was fully enlightened and possessed high powers.
She was entirely dedicated to her Guru. In her poetry
she calls herself again and again "Nama's Jani" and
"Nama's maid," and this shows that she was a perfect,
devoted slave of her Guru. Being fully pleased with her

loving service, Lord Pandurang, who is attained with
difficulty even by yogis, washed clothes, plied the grind-
ing stone, cleaned the house, sang for her and talked with
her. He became her constant companion. This should
not come as a surprise, for it is not an uncommon miracle
of devotion to the Guru.

That verse also embodies deep feeling. I asked the old
woman to sing it:

नाहीं केली तुझी सेवा । दुःख वाटतसे माझे जिवा ॥
नष्ट पापीण मी हीन । नाहीं केलें तुझें ध्यान ॥
जें जें दुःख झालें मला । तें त्वां सोसिलें विठ्ठला ॥
रात्रंदिवस मजपाशीं । दळूं कांडूं लागलासी ।
क्षमा करावी देवराया । दासी जनी लागे पायां ॥

(O Lord! I have not rendered the slightest service to
Thee. Yet, O Vithal, Thou hast borne all my troubles
and torments inflicted on me. Dwelling with me day and
night, Thou hast even helped me to grind and crush
grain. O Lord! Forgive me. Jani, the maid of Namdev,
entreats Thee most humbly).

This poem had always inspired my heart with purest
emotion. That day, however, it had lost all appeal. I
was without zest, without love. Alas! Alas! What had
happened? What misery!

I asked the singer to leave and went inside the hut.
Unnatural, impure and painful emotions overwhelmed
me. My body moved independent of my will. I was
becoming more and more confused. At sunset, Babu lit
a lamp and an incense stick. He performed *arati* and
sang devotional songs to the accompaniment of the
tamboura.

In a short while my breathing was affected. At times
my abdomen became distended and I exhaled forcefully.
Quite frequently, after exhalation, the breath was held
outside, and after inhalation, inside. This disturbance,
which seemed to threaten an early death, shattered my
composure. I became more terrified. I went outside in
this befuddled condition. It was about 8 p.m. The moon
was shining but I found it dark. Strange noises, coming

from afar, fell on my ears. I was frightened. I called Babu Rao and said, "Babu, you had better go home now. The condition of my heart is not good and my mind is disturbed. I am certain I shall die of heart failure to-night. Go away; otherwise people will harass you. I feel certain I am not going to survive the night; but even if I do, I may go insane. My brain is becoming affected. Do what I say and go away." He left me with a sad heart.

The night advanced. The atmosphere was completely still and silent. The landscape around was bathed in pure moonlight. I was repeatedly visited by a strong inclination to dance, jump about and scream. This desire gathered momentum. Deluding and harmful thoughts flooded my mind. My body became heated up and my head became heavy. Each cell of my body began to groan.

The whole earth was spinning. The sky was twirling and so were the trees. I would rise from one spot only to sit down there again. I could understand neither what was happening to me nor who was responsible for it. Suddenly I felt drawn towards the mango trees. As I looked in their direction, I saw Sri Gurudev sitting between them, facing me. It was now past 9 o'clock. Somebody seemed to have overpowered my eyes, showing me all sorts of sights. Again and again I looked towards the trees and saw Sri Gurudev appearing and disappearing. During those experiences I felt that some Shakti was overpowering me, forcing me to behave in queer ways. I had lost my freedom of will and was behaving more and more crazily. My mind had become thoroughly ruffled. I went round the mango trees thrice. I bowed to my Guru and entered the hut.

As I looked outside, I saw the sugarcane field on fire. The flames were spreading rapidly. This scared me all the more. I heard multitudes of people screaming frightfully, as though universal dissolution had begun. I espied strange creatures in human forms, ranging from six to fifty feet in height; they were neither demons nor demigods. They were dancing naked with their mouths agape. I again heard terrified screams. All this time I was fully conscious, objectively witnessing a state of madness. Soon I remembered I was going to die.

As I sat down, my legs locked themselves in the lotus posture. I looked around. The flames of a vast conflagration were raging in all directions. The entire cosmos was on fire. A burning ocean had burst and swallowed the entire globe. An army of ghosts and other evil spirits encircled me. Meanwhile, my lotus posture became firmer. My eyes were closed and my chin firmly pressed against my throat, so that no breath could escape from the lungs. Then the knot of nerves in the *muladhar* was rent with acute pain. My eyes opened. I wanted to get up and run away, but my legs were still locked. It seemed as though nails had been driven through my feet to maintain the posture. My palms were also closed. I was fully aware that everything I was seeing was unreal; yet I was very frightened. I tried to close my eyes but couldn't. I could still see the earth submerged in the waters of dissolution. The whole world, except for me and my hut, had been destroyed.

Then a moon-like sphere, about four feet in diameter, came floating over the water, entered the hut and stopped in front of me. The radiant white ball struck against my eyes and pierced me. (I want to assure the reader that all these events were not dreamt or imagined, but sights actually seen). The white sphere, having descended from the sky, entered me. As this light penetrated my nerves, my tongue curled up against my palate. My eyes were closed. I saw a dazzling brightness in my head and was terrified. My head moved downwards and was stuck to the ground while I was still in the lotus posture.

## The Red Glow

My eyes opened after some time. An exceedingly sweet, soft red glow appeared, shimmering and moving gently. It emitted countless sparks which spread throughout the universe. While I was beholding it, my legs unlocked themselves and I recovered body-consciousness. I got up from my seat and went outside. I looked to the right and to the left. The atmosphere was calm. I was plunged in amazement, recollecting all that I had envisioned. I went inside. On closing my eyes, I saw the red light as before. I opened my eyes and went out again but saw no trace of the previous sights. The night was far advanced. I tried to sleep but could not. My head was heavy. I remained in this condition until 4 a.m. and then took a bath. Afterwards I sat in the lotus posture and began to meditate on the Guru as before. In a moment, my mind was completely indrawn. My body, locked in the posture, began to sway. The *muladhar* was again pierced with pain. I became absorbed in the rapturous inner echoes of the sacred strains of *Guru Om*, beholding a light shining in the *akasha* of the heart that gladdened my mind. I meditated continuously for an hour and a half and then a new process began.

Sometimes I cried like a camel and at others roared like a tiger. I must have roared convincingly, because people outside actually thought that a tiger had entered the sugarcane field. This lasted briefly. I got up after meditation with my body aching terribly and stiff as wood.

When I had fully regained my normal state, I came out of the hut and sat in the swing. It was very peaceful. The sun rose in the east. Birds chirruped in the mango trees. The landlord came, burnt incense and carried it around. The gentle fragrant vapours filled the atmosphere around the hut. He said to me, "Babaji, I am wondering what happened today. When I came here, I found you in meditation. It appeared as if a tiger had come. Babaji, I'm speaking the truth. I am now coming from the fields outside. I heard a tiger roaring for at least half an hour." He uttered these words in a tone of surprise.

It was time for me to have a hot drink. I usually prepared it myself inside the hut, but today he made it. I drank it in a reflective mood. It was true that in meditation I had roared like a tiger, but I wondered how it could have been audible so far away. If I spoke the truth, I would be taken for a madman; so I kept silent.

I had neither heard nor read anything about such an experience. I had only heard high-flown Vedantic talk and abstruse explanations of scriptural verses.

I sat calmly in the swing. That morning Babu came rather early. He was smiling, pleased to find his Baba quite all right, neither dead nor insane. He bowed and sat down. One Patil, who was very dear to me, swept the area daily. He also arrived and began to clean.

Babu said, "How are you, Baba? You had declared that you would either die or go mad. I prayed to God that neither might happen. I was sure that nothing of the sort would."

I said, "You say nothing happened, but universal death took place last night. The entire cosmos was reduced to ashes. The earth was under deluge. I alone narrowly escaped death. Babu, my condition is not good. I have become a lunatic. I may not appear so from the outside, but inside I am crazy."

Babu brought out the tamboura and began to sing some verses. I strictly enforced the rule that visitors should either sit silently or not come at all. Hence, silence prevailed. I listened with rapt attention to the following verse from *Shruti Ki Ter*:

तू आप अपनी याद कर, फिर आत्म को तू प्राप्त हो ।
ना जन्म ले मर भी नहीं, मत ताप से संतप्त हो ॥
जो आत्म सो परमात्म है, तू आत्म में संतृप्त हो ।
यह मुख्य तेरा काम है, मत देह में आसक्त हो ॥

(Recollect your own Self and then realise It.
Be free from birth and death. Do not let suffering
    agitate you.
The individual soul and God are one. Repose in the
    soul.
This is your main duty. Do not become attached to
    the body).

As I listened, a sublime feeling was aroused. My body began to twist. I entered the hut and slipped into meditation. These days it took no effort to meditate. On the contrary, meditation was forcing itself on me. I was meditating involuntarily in every joint, as it were. All my blood cells were stimulated and prana was flowing through the nerves at an astonishing speed. A red light suddenly appeared, as though it had emerged from me. It measured about two feet from top to bottom. As it shone, its radiance spread. I saw vividly that I was on fire and heard my body crackling loudly, but I did not feel any heat at all. Even though I was absorbed in the vision of this light, I was fully conscious of what was happening. Soon I felt inwardly heated up by the red tongues of fire and my worship of the Guru began.

When I came out of meditation, my ecstasy also diminished. I stepped out of the hut and sat in the swing under the friendly mango tree. I was occupied with the questions: "What was the nature of that light? How did I see it? What precisely did I see?" I always reflected on my inner experiences in this manner. I would re-collect all the movements and visions that came during meditation. Sublime feeling, body aches, varied thoughts, all sorts of desires and confusion—thus my day would pass.

I began to meet people less and less frequently. The reason was that if I entertained a visitor and chatted with him, I could not meditate properly later on. My mind would be disturbed and the flow of meditation obstructed. Then visions would not come. Lights did not appear and I felt disappointed. Besides, my purity was also affected. Any spiritual experiences I might have had were delayed. So I did not encourage visitors. I did not touch anyone nor sit with them. I sat alone.

I had made a new rule for all visitors: "Do not come in the morning. Come only in the evening and leave immediately after darshan." I had it written on a plaque and hung it up. All the inhabitants of Yeola were completely familiar with my insistence on discipline and my temper. They obeyed the new rule with love and respect, for they as well as others from neighbouring villages loved me greatly. I had, in fact, grown up at Yeola and learnt Marathi there. Now I had my second birth at the sadhana *kutir* of Suki, near Yeola. All the devotees from the town came for darshan every evening. They brought

different offerings which were later distributed as *prasad*.
The people of Yeola, young and old, considered me their
beloved Baba. Babu Rao came every morning and left
at night. After everyone's departure, I would burn
incense again, meditate on my dear Gurudev and worship
him ardently.

Various feelings emerged during meditation. Sometimes I saw a burning red light. As I continued to watch
it, my mind became completely focussed. Sometimes I
felt and behaved like a camel and sometimes like a bird.
Sometimes I enjoyed bliss, followed immediately by
agitation, anxiety, impure thoughts and finally Guru
worship. Such was the content of my meditations. And
then I would go outside, sit under the tree and think
about my meditative states.

Innumerable unwanted thoughts again began to rise in
my mind, so I forbade people to either come for darshan
or touch my feet. My reasoning went like this: "My
mind is contaminated. My heart is impure. I am an
ignorant creature, deluded by *maya*. Why should I, if
such is the case, commit the sin of having myself worshipped? Look, I am not fully purified within. Why
do I deceive people in the garb of a holy man?" At times
I said as much, but the people took it lightly. They
believed that I said these things only to hide my attainments. The fact was, I was trying to obey my con-
science, but the people thought I only wanted to conceal
what I had obtained from Nityananda. Each day the
visitors came in larger numbers! But I continued to
meditate in solitude with scrupulous regularity and had
numberless experiences. Sometimes I was happy, sometimes sad. Alternating between smiles and tears, I continued my inward journey.

Our saints, such as Jnaneshwar Maharaj, Sant Tukaram and Janardan Swami, have depicted these experiences
in their poetry, but in veiled language. The words of
these perfected sages and seers constitute true descriptions of God. They have described the Truth after having
reflected deeply on the individual and the Universal Soul
and having directly experienced It through spiritual

disciplines.

For the satisfaction of seekers, I quote one composition by Jnaneshwar in support of the truth of my experiences and the sequence in which they occurred:

आकाशाचा शेंडा कमळ निराळें । त्यासी चार दळें शोभताती ॥
औट हात एक अंगुष्ठ दुसरें । पर्वार्धं मसुरें प्रमाण हें ॥
रक्त श्वेत शाम नीलवर्ण आहे । पीत केशर हे माजीं तेथें ॥
तयाचा मकरंद स्वरूप तें शुद्ध । ब्रह्मादिकां बोध हाची झाला ॥
ज्ञानदेव म्हणे निवृत्तिप्रसादें । निजरूप गोविंदें जनीं पाहतां ॥

The meaning of the stanza is as follows: The lotus of the human form consists of four petals of four kinds, colours and sizes. Each bears a unique significance. The first petal represents the gross body, perceived by the senses. Its colour is red. The second stands for the subtle body, in which we experience dreams; it is white in colour and thumb-size. The third signifies the causal body; it is of the size of a finger tip and black in colour. The fourth denotes the supracausal body; it is as tiny as a sesame seed and its colour is blue. It possesses the greatest significance. It is uncommonly brilliant and forms the essence of the path, being the highest inner vision.

Sri Jnaneshwar, Lord of Yoga, inner Self of all Gurus, emperor of the enlightened, king of divine lovers, worthy of our reverence and daily remembrance, has fully described in the above verse all the different stages of Siddha Yoga, including the final state obtained by the Guru's grace, and all the subtlest visions perceived during the period of sadhana. This passage is the best testimony, embodying, as it does, complete truth. It serves as a guiding light for all seekers on the spiritual path.

Depending on their worth, some seekers perceive this Reality, while others do not. However, the practitioners of Siddha Yoga have a vast variety of experiences about which one neither hears nor reads. Even if one came across such an account, it would be indecipherable without the aid of a realised Master. For this reason, aspirants are unable to comprehend the marvellous spiritual processes of sadhana. They abandon the path out of sheer fright. I have met many seekers who complain: "Babaji, as soon as I sit for meditation, a snake appears and rushes to bite me." "Babaji, when I sit for meditation, a naked woman appears and I feel scared." "Babaji, evil thoughts rush into my mind during sadhana." Sometimes, during the period of sadhana, a seeker feels frightened by the innumerable movements, which are an outcome of the grace of divine Shakti, inspired by the Lord. He becomes confused and gives up his practice. This is mainly due to his ignorance of the path. By discarding his own sadhana through ignorance, he begins to frighten others as well, saying: "This is not a good path. It will affect your brain, causing insanity."

I will give you one such example. Last year, one Swami saw a good Siddha student of mine performing yogic movements. The Swami considered himself to be fully realised and competent to pronounce judgment on all spiritual practices. He approached my student privately and exclaimed: "My God! You are making a grave blunder. This cannot be yoga. Brother, I want to warn you. I have experienced the highest *samadhi* state but nothing of this sort ever happened on the way. You will certainly go mad in a few days or else die." To frighten him all the more, he repeated, "You will either go insane in a few days or die in a couple of months." The student wrote me a letter saying, "Babaji, a Swami is trying to scare me by uttering these warnings and he told me not to mention what he said to anyone."

I let the letter lie for a few months. Then I wrote in reply, "My dear Siddha student, your time limit is over. Four months have elapsed instead of two. Your sadhana is going well. You have passed through different stages. Your experience of inner bliss is commendable. Reap the fruits of your sadhana and remain happy. Remember one thing, however, if you run into that Swami, have his head examined by a doctor and look carefully at the report. Then say to him: 'My dear and wonderful, knowledgeable Swamiji, you had predicted that I would either die within two months or turn into a mental case.

Since neither happened, I conclude that you are a mere
parasite, pretending to be learned when you are ignorant.
I am certain that you must be either crack-brained or
hankering after the undiscerning praise of your admirers.
At least you have a weakness for speechifying.'" On
account of such circumstances, a seeker strays away from
the path.   Therefore, we greatly need an experienced
saint, or at least a work containing his direct spiritual
experiences.

At that stage, however, I had not the least understanding of the various experiences, such as the scenes of
dissolution and the unearthly radiance of the light which
I saw on the first day.  Later I came to know that all
these were the different processes natural to Shaktipat,
which is only another name for the full grace of the
supreme Guru, the benediction of a Siddha, or *shambhavi*
initiation.  The realised ones call it the awakening of
Kundalini.  The experiences I had had under the mango
tree were gifts of the Guru's blessing.  If I had known on
that day that all of them flowed from Bhagawan Nityananda's grace, from his benevolent *prasad*—the sandals,
the shawl and his explanation of the meaning of the
mantras—they would have been welcome, like nectar.

I was progressing in sadhana each day.  As I glided
into meditation, the scintillating sparks I had seen previously were now replaced by a steady red aura of my
own size and shape, which enveloped me within and
without.  I would behold this for a long time.  Countless specks of light shone within it.  While seeing it I
became fully absorbed in meditation.  Sometimes during
meditation my body swayed or performed other movements, while at other times it remained motionless.
Various postures, which I had never practised before,
occurred easily.  At times I hopped like a frog.  Occasionally my body moved violently as if possessed by a
spirit.  In truth, it was the Guru who manipulated me
from within as Chitshakti.

The Guru's power of grace subtly penetrates the
disciple's body and carries out its significant work.  Just
as a tiny spark soon ignites a heap of grass into a blaze,

likewise, Chitshakti entering Siddha students and combining with their prana, performs many functions. Its first task involves the red petal, which measures three and a half arm-lengths, from the top of its head to its toe. The 'red stage' of meditation, during which one beholds the red aura, concerns the physical body, which is described by Vedanta as the field of all activities. The individual soul, by means of this body, experiences happiness and sorrow, performs good and bad deeds and pursues the path of deliverance. Equipped with five organs of perception, five of action, five pranas and four psychic functions, it inhabits the eye and experiences gross stimuli in the gross body. This red body is the experiencer of the waking state. But for this, the existence of the soul would not be known. It is symbolised by 'A,' the first letter of Aum; the individual soul in this body is known as Vishva.

The ignorant man identifies himself with it, since he is absolutely unacquainted with the inner Self, the Witness-consciousness. He who knows a pitcher as 'this pitcher,' remains different from it. Again, he who perceives a car as 'this car' remains different from it even while sitting in it. Similarly, the One who lives within the red aura, being its Witness, knowing it as 'this,' remains different from it. He is the pure Divine Principle, which is the final goal of meditation.

The Kundalini Shakti, aroused by the Guru's grace, accomplishes new tasks each day. She penetrates the system of 72,000 nerves, purifies and strengthens all the circuits which carry blood and prana, then releases vital energy into all, thus transforming the body. By entering the *sushumna* within the spinal cord, piercing the *chakras*, and rapidly changing its state, She renders the body suitable for spiritual sadhana. A Siddha seeker should remember that this Parashakti efficiently reorganises one's worldly life. She takes care of one's children and helps one acquire and maintain all the necessities of life. She imparts the knowledge required for any task one is confronted with. There is not the slightest doubt about this.

Though scripturalists have divided life into two compartments, mundane and spiritual, these are reunited when full knowledge dawns. The external world is an expansion of Parachiti, Her sport and dynamic manifestation, being replete with Her. The universe is not different from Chiti, as She alone continues to assume ever-new forms throughout the infinite stretch of time, without beginning or end. Siddha students must never forget that concepts such as 'matter,' 'void,' 'perishable' and 'objects' hold good only so long as one is not enlightened. In fact, the distinction between spirit and matter has meaning only until the attainment of true knowledge; after that, the seer and the seen are perceived as one supreme consciousness, Parashakti. The witnessing Purusha, who on assuming a physical form, appears to be physical, is in fact the Self of all. He is described in the scriptures as "the Absolute endowed with knowledge and bliss."

Tukaram Maharaj says: Through a direct experience bestowed by inner Shakti in meditation I realised that the supreme Lord Himself is everything. He says in one of his verses:

रक्त श्वेत कृष्ण पीत प्रभा भिन्न । चिन्मय अंजन सुदलें डोळां ॥
तेणें अंजनगुणें दिव्यदृष्टि झाली । कल्पना निवाली द्वैताद्वैत ॥
देशकाळवस्तुभेद मावळला । आत्मा निर्वाळला विश्वाकार ॥
न झाला प्रपंच आहे परब्रह्म । अहंसोहं ब्रह्म आकळलें ॥
तत्त्वमसि विद्या ब्रह्मानंद सांग । तेंचि झाला अंगें तुका आतां ॥

It means: When, by the grace of my Guru, Sri Babaji, I perceived the extremely subtle and luminous conscious Self, which is different from the red, white, black and yellow lights, the lotion of consciousness cleansed my sight, rendering it divine. Subsequently, the imaginary distinctions between dual and non-dual vanished. I completely overcame my sense of difference regarding space, time and substance. In reality, there is neither space, time nor substance. Differences are not real. My own Soul appeared as the universe, and the universe— so-called objective reality—appeared as my own Soul.

## THE FOUR BODIES OF THE INDIVIDUAL SOUL

| BODY: | GROSS | SUBTLE | CAUSAL | SUPRA-CAUSAL |
|---|---|---|---|---|
| SIZE: | 3½ ARM LENGTHS (Full Body Size) | THUMB | FINGER-TIP | LENTIL SEED |
| COLOUR: | RED | WHITE | BLACK | BLUE |
| STATE: | WAKING | DREAM | SLEEP | TURIYA (Transcendent) |
| NAME: | VISHVA | TAIJASA | PRAJNA | TURYA |
| SEAT: | EYES | THROAT | HEART | SAHASRAR |
| SYMBOL: | 'A' | 'U' | 'M' | ☽ CRESCENT |

The outer world never *is*.  The Absolute alone *is*.  I had
the direct realisation: I am That, I am indeed the
Absolute.  I, Tukaram, became That which is attained
through the Vedantic contemplation, 'Thou art That,' also
called the transcendental bliss.

What appears to be a differentiated universe during
sadhana is apprehended as the supreme Lord in the
perfect experience.  Tukaram says: "I am perfect in my
own being."

We too have to gain the same perfect experience by
penetrating deeper through the red aura in meditation.
That will reveal that God is all-pervasive; nay, He
appears as the world.

Sri Shankaracharya says:

सर्वोंऽपि व्यवहारस्तु ब्रह्मणा क्रियते जनै: ।
अज्ञानान्न विजानन्ति मृदेव हि घटादिकम् ॥

*(Aparokshanubhuti*, 65)

(All the activities of men are possible because of the
existence of the Absolute, but they are not aware of It
due to their ignorance.  In fact, a pot or any other
earthen vessel is nothing but earth.)  This is similar to
a spider weaving a web from her own secretion, dwelling
in it and finally merging it in her own being.

Reasoning thus, we find that the whole world is made
of Chiti.  All its material objects contain Her substance.
She Herself appears as all its men and women.  If this
Chiti Shakti Kundalini is awakened in you, it is no
wonder that She will also bring material prosperity.  It is
true that, while living with your consort, pursuing your
normal activities and enjoyments and leading your life
in the world, you will be able to fill it with happiness
and joy only if you receive the blessing of Parashakti.

On the awakening of Shakti, this physical body
performs innumerable movements, which are not meaningless, but purify the nerves and destroy disease.  These
movements are different from those of the other bodies.
Generally, physical movements of numerous kinds continue for a prolonged period.  The vision of the red aura
is attended each day by varied experiences which pro-

gressively increase one-pointedness of mind.

I decided to eat less and so changed my diet. I took a little rice with one or two plain vegetables. At night I took only milk from a beloved cow of mine which stayed with me, and felt satisfied. I advanced in this stage, gradually becoming thinner. I shed a good deal of fat without any medicine. Sometimes I felt some force moving through the nerves of both hands. Sometimes prana coursed through the nerves of my lower back. I wondered what was working so fast and so actively inside my body. Many astonishing movements were taking place. Sometimes I would twist and hiss like a snake. At times my neck moved so violently that it made loud cracking sounds and I became frightened. Was it due to some wind imbalance? During its most violent movements my head would sometimes be thrown backwards below the shoulders, so much so that I could see my back. As the intensity waned I became calmer. But since I did not understand the significance of these experiences, I was always in a state of fear and anxiety. Afterwards I learned that it was a Hatha yogic process effected by Goddess Kundalini, in order to travel up the spinal cord to *sahasrar*. Sometimes after my neck had rotated for a while, my chin would become firmly fixed against the jugular notch below the throat. This is known as *jalandhar bandha* in Hatha yogic texts. As the *jalandhar bandha* took place, my anus was alternately drawn upwards and then released downwards.

All these movements were automatic. It was the beloved Sri Kundalini, the inner Self of Gurudev who pervaded my body, causing all these physical movements. Thus I was getting to know yogic processes through direct experience. Sometimes while I was sitting in the lotus posture, my head would arch downwards and touch the floor in *yogamudra*, remaining in this position for a long period. Sometimes my eyes were focussed on the tip of the nose. While in that position I breathed quickly in and out, like a blacksmith's bellows. Sometimes all the air was expelled and the breath was held outside. I learned that this was a variety of *bhasrika*, which eliminates various stomach ailments and purifies the prana completely.

Even then I did not know that I had been blessed with divine Shaktipat. For two days I saw not only the red aura but also many other different lights. I remained fully conscious during meditation, continually experiencing delight. I meditated for two hours or even more, every morning and evening, without fail. At times I became intoxicated during meditation. Oh, what pure and ecstatic intoxication! But I did not have the strength to bear it and fell asleep as it became more intense.

## Tandraloka—The World Of Higher Consciousness

While sitting in the meditative posture I slipped into the *tandra* state (which I also refer to as Tandraloka), which came spontaneously under the inspiration of Shakti. Though it resembles ordinary sleep, it is quite different from the dream state. For each morning when I awoke from sleep, I found that I had neither enjoyed ecstatic experiences nor visions during the night, whereas in the *tandra* state, I would see prophetic sights that transported me with joy. Sometimes I saw the temples of neighbouring villages with their idols. While seeing lights I would also see naked men, children, cows or hosts of gallant war horses. Tandraloka is endowed with omniscience. Whatever vision is apprehended in this state turns out to be true. For instance, if I saw somebody coming to me in such a vision, he actually came later. My own experiences in this state convinced me that our ancient seers and sages were far-sighted and all-knowing.

Thus I would spend a period of time in a different world. I was immersed again and again in a rapture of delight. After I got up from *tandra*, I would sit in the swing under the mango tree, thinking about the day's experiences and the different worlds that I visited. After meditation I continued to experience great love, joy and gladness the whole day and I overcame all physical weakness.

A noble white cobra lived near my hut. I called him

Baba Nageshwar. Cobras possess intelligence and extend utmost courtesy to holy men. He was old and wise. I saw him, if not daily, at least once or twice a week. He had been there a long time. Other people also saw him occasionally. I had great affection for him. I had heard that some sign of Lord Shiva must be present wherever yoga is practised. A cobra is an obvious sign of Parashiva, the supreme God of yoga. My meditation was especially blissful on the days on which I saw him.

During meditation bad thoughts would arise as well as good ones. Unnecessary feelings of anger, infatuation and cruelty sprang up. I did not know why. All of a sudden I would recollect someone who had been unkind to me ten years before and inwardly I would rage against him. I felt remorse and shame after my wrath had subsided.

The duration of my meditation increased, bringing me new experiences each day. While sitting at Nagad I would see my hut at Suki. The red aura endowed me with divine vision, enabling me to actually see the entire cosmos. Nay, the cosmos itself lay in just a corner of the light that appeared in meditation. My dear aspirants! This should neither surprise you nor raise doubts in your mind. I will take an example from modern technology, which is a matter of your everyday, factual experience. By means of your tiny radio you can hear a programme from Bombay while sitting in a distant city. As you turn the dial just an eighth of an inch, you are tuned in to Delhi and Calcutta lies just a little further on. If you change the waveband, you may hear news from England or America, while the dial remains stationary on the mark representing Delhi. Within the space of only one inch, you are connected to different cities and countries. If, by means of a mechanical aid, you can receive news from all over the world while sitting at home, what could prevent you from receiving news from different places in meditation? What is at all surprising about this? Moreover, we now also have television. It proves the validity of the science of meditation all the more. On a TV screen you can even see the person who is speaking and the place from which he is speaking. Then it should not appear fantastic that one can see the entire universe in the inner light.

In meditation I would also clearly see the entire nervous system and the prana flowing throughout. This flow of prana is usually obstructed by impurities caused by irregular habits of food-taking and pleasure-seeking. By means of the processes of Siddha Yoga, I realised that these obstructions produce disease and age.

## Sensual Excitement

Each day I had new experiences. It now so happened that my body and senses became possessed by carnal craving. What should not have taken place began to occur. I had, in fact, no desire for any sensuous object or enjoyment. I had travelled widely and seen the conditions of all classes of people, from the highest to the lowest, and I knew the final outcome of their modes of living. At Ganeshpuri all kinds of people came to my Gurudev, including wealthy tycoons, men of status, good artists, famous film actors, singers, orators and important officials, as a great saint belongs to all. But each of them complained of some want or another in his life. Despite their wealth and possessions, each lacked one thing miserably—physical health. They would say, "Bhagawan, I have everything, but my heart is giving me trouble. The doctors permit me neither to move about nor eat my fill. Besides, my senses have lost their strength." "Babaji, my stomach aches terribly. I have been to England and America, spending thousands for a cure, but to no avail." "Bhagawan, I have no material want, but I can neither digest my food nor sleep at night. I have already spent two *lakhs* on treatment." Somebody had trouble with his eyes, another with his ears.

Thus all the miserable visitors narrated their woeful tales to Bhagawan Nityananda. Each suffered from some deficiency and wept pitifully. If he possessed wealth, he was poor in health or vice versa. Another was illiterate, poor in learning. A third was ugly, poor in beauty. A fourth was a widow, a fifth a widower and a sixth was childless. Thus, whoever came was afflicted with some privation and would relate his pathetic account. I listened quietly. I considered what lesson I could learn from them. Truly speaking, I was in the same boat: poor in sadhana, Self-knowledge and Self-realisation. I regarded these people carefully. They were without brightness, equanimity and health, frustrated in spite of their riches. Nor did they possess any strength or energy. New diseases were always attacking them. The reasons for all this were the waste of seminal fluid, sensuality and an irregular life.

It is a strange irony that man regards himself as fortunate if he can enjoy sensual gratification. But he is only deluding himself, unaware that instead of enjoying pleasures, he is being enjoyed by them. As a result, he falls a helpless victim to all kinds of sicknesses. Even now people weep to me in the same manner. I keep seeing pitiful cases of new ailments. At that time, after constantly seeing the distressed condition of the many who visited Gurudev, I had only one desire left and that was for sadhana.

Why should I be harassed by sensual craving when I was so vividly aware of its consequences? As I meditated in my hut at Suki, the red aura would appear. I would feel at peace, but not for long. A new occurrence soon filled me with a sense of shame. I should not even talk about it here. If I were to tell anyone about it, he would immediately brand me as indiscreet. If I told it to ordinary worldly people, they would say: "The *sannyasis* of today are quite dissolute and fatten themselves on charity. Doesn't it show that the life of a householder is much superior, since he can pursue his spiritual goal while still enjoying every pleasure?"

I am now going to tell my shameful story. My dear mothers! My dear sisters! You are all different forms of Shakti. Please do not feel offended by my hateful account. Bless me, paying attention to its real purport. My dear readers! My dear seekers! Try to understand the purpose behind this description.

As I sat in meditation, the red aura appeared immediately. I felt intoxicated, swaying, jumping and frolick-
ing around. I worshipped the Guru. While I was
engaged in meditation on the Guru, within and without,
chanting *Guru Om, Guru Om* and plunging into blissful *Gurubhava*, my mind became filled with lustful
thoughts. What shame! How disgusting! I still beheld
the same red aura, though with a slightly different
shading. It was of my size, glowing like the tender red
morning aura in the east. As my mind was invaded by
sensuality, I lost the ecstasy of love and also the Nitya-
nanda-*bhava*. I could not continue with the sublime
Guru worship either. Even the *Guru Om* mantra
vanished and was replaced by a strong sexual desire. I
was amazed. What secret lair did it emerge from? From
where could so much life flow into my male organ, which
was hitherto a mere lump of flesh? An acute lustful
craving tortured me. Alas! Alas! This was worse than
the scenes of dissolution on the first day. My sexual
sense was pulled towards external activity.

Sex, sex and sex! I could think of nothing else. The
only saving grace was that my meditative posture was
not disturbed; my legs remained firmly interlocked. My
whole body felt the stirring of lust. It is difficult to
describe the agony of my organ. I tried to reason it out
with my mind but could not succeed. As I closed my
eyes I saw a ravishing naked maiden within the red aura.
I tried not to see her, but seeing her was all I could do.
I was full of fear and remorse. I opened my eyes and
there she was—stripped of all her clothes. I could
not avoid her whether my eyes were open or closed.
What should I do now? To whom could I talk about such
a disgraceful condition? I was greatly troubled, as this
was being forced on me against my will. How powerful
the craving of the organ! Only Bhagawan Nityananda
or a seeker who has experienced this could understand
what was happening.

My mind would be overcome with acute self-loathing
when I recollected my sexual excitement and I could not
meditate any longer. Feelings of fear, shame and dis-

content afflicted me, affecting even my brain. "If I do not die a natural death, I will have to commit suicide. My present miserable condition must be the result of some grave sin in the past." Brooding in this vein, I was invaded by anxiety which mounted relentlessly.

I went outside and sat in the swing, still occupied with thoughts of disgust: "What is this new weakness in me? What has gone wrong? Alas! What shall I do now?" At noon I meditated again. The same nude female! Sometimes she laughed, sometimes smiled. At times she sat down, at times stood up. I was soon fed up with this sight. The other visions which had calmed and purified my senses, releasing the flow of love in my heart and imparting celestial delight, had vanished, being replaced by their exact opposite. My sexual organ became energised, excited and restless. Other shameful things would follow, so I would get up immediately.

This condition was repeated during the evening meditation. I began to meditate. The red aura . . . mind delighted . . . heart gladdened . . . Guru worship with faith and reverence . . . intensified *Gurubhava* . . . *bhava-samadhi*. Then suddenly the scene changed. The same naked nymph was chasing me! She danced in front of me, a short distance away. She made peculiar gestures with her body and frisked around. When I opened my eyes she was still there. I was losing control of my senses. I was afraid that something regrettable would occur. I decided that I must reduce my physical vigour, so I stopped taking milk. Instead I drank a little water. I was unable to sleep until late at night because of self-loathing. Thinking of Ganeshpuri, I remembered Bhagawan Nityananda. I bowed to him and fell asleep.

I awoke early in the morning. Sometimes I would take a bath at 3 a.m. or simply wash my hands and feet. Then I would smear my body with the sacred ash, charged with mantras. I sat down to meditate. Immediately my meditation became dynamic. The red aura of my own size arose at once. I worshipped the Guru. In a short while, as I went into *bhava-samadhi*, the same sexual desire became active. The naked woman pursued me, finally standing in front of me. She began to torture me excruciatingly with only one apparent objective: she wanted no other sacrifice save my sacred vow of celibacy.

A woman seems to bedevil every man's existence, constantly harassing him with some demand or other. One pesters her man for food, another kicks up a row for clothes. One clamours for jewellery, another will have nothing to do with her husband's relatives. One attempts to keep her man away from friends and saints, another takes the life out of him, breaking his heart with bitter remarks. She complains, "I have fallen on evil days since I married you. My parents treated me with such love and care. I bathed in milk and drank honey. Each day I soared in the empyrean blue. You are a wretched fellow ruining my life. I have been utterly miserable ever since my first thought of you." With such acidic words, she drives her husband out of his wits. Such a one lacks true femininity.

I did not know from where that incredible woman appeared. This blessed siren would turn up even though I did not invite her or extend any courtesy to her. She did not make any overt demand. She only blasted my meditation, exciting my sexual organ. She tried her utmost to blow my vow of chastity to smithereens. What a trial! It was the most distressful phase of my life. I had never been tormented like this before. After a while, my meditation could not continue. I came out and sat on my cot. I brooded on the question: "What shall I do? How can I tide over this crisis?" I became more distress-ed, anxious and deranged as time went by. I used to sit with a sad heart, afraid of women. I lost patience. I was afraid that I might indulge in licentious behaviour. I remembered again and again the past seekers who had fallen from yoga, spirituality and virtue. I cried as I remembered the stories of Ajamila, Surdas and Tulsidas. I remembered one old story about the behaviour of the sage Parashar in his boat. Recollecting numerous such incidents, I felt greatly troubled. I was afraid of the force of sexual passion. I thought I had made my organ lifeless and inert through mastery of the *siddhasana*. But it had sprung to life again. I was utterly astounded.

During the afternoon session of meditation, I again felt excitement in the sexual organ. I asked my landlord, whose wife cooked for me, to have my food cooked not by a woman but by a man. I subsisted on a small quantity of rice and gave up vegetables. Leaving my stomach half empty, I drank some water.

One day I came out of meditation thinking: "How can I escape this torture? Who shall guide me? When my organ, rendered inactive by the *siddhasana*, can become active again, what grace can save me?" While reflecting in this manner, I felt more desolate, concerned and dissatisfied. The evening fell. There was a Siddha called Hari Giri Baba staying at Baijapur, twenty miles away. He was very dear to me. I remembered him intensely. He must save me, otherwise tomorrow could prove fatal. I could not take anyone else into confidence about my secret misery. I wept bitterly; so much so that my head split and my ears deafened. Night came. I did not take any food. Babu turned up in a short while. He muttered something which I did not hear. I said to myself: "O my mind, do not get flustered."

I commenced my nightly session of meditation, keeping to my schedule. I meditated nobly. The red aura arose, which should signify good fortune for a yogi. As I looked at it, I was confronted by tiny refulgent saffron sparks. Then I performed the sublime Guru worship. I was absorbed in *Gurubhava*. While numerous *mudras* took place and different feelings emerged, I began to hear an indistinct sound inwardly. I was overjoyed. But lo! The same female stood in front of me, unclad except for ornaments. The moment I saw her I opened my eyes, but she was still there.

Again my joy disappeared and the meditative posture was upset. I got up slowly and came out. I sat listlessly under the mango tree until midnight. Then I went to bed, but I could not find my usual peaceful sleep. I became quite crazy and confused. Sleepless, I tossed on my bed, right and left, until 3 a.m. I closed my eyes for a while, but finally got up and took a bath. I sat to meditate. I did not feel at all well. I was not physically sick, but I was disturbed and crazed. I bowed to all directions, mentally invoked all deities and began to meditate. At once I plunged into meditation, passing into *tandra*. The red aura began to shine brilliantly within and without. My body executed movements. For a moment my throat was blocked. The *jalandhar* and *mula bandhas* occurred, but soon unlocked. I heard a vague strain within. As my attention focussed on it, I floated in bliss. An egg-shaped white light flashed. This new vision renewed my zest for worship and meditation on the Guru. I attributed this to my invocation of all the gods and goddesses.

But the scene changed rapidly. The red aura turned another shade. What, again! The same damsel. I was taken aback. This time she was richly adorned, captivating me with her beauty. My mind shattered. My sexual organ reacted violently. If I opened my eyes, I saw her without. If I closed them, I saw her within. My loin-cloth was rent and the tip of my organ forcibly pressed up against my navel, digging into my navel pit. Who was driving me so forcefully? I was, however, fully conscious. Then I came out of meditation. I used to wear only a muslin loin-cloth for meditation. I was furious that it had been torn, so much so that I could not think clearly. It was 5 a.m. I got up and put on another loin-cloth. I came out of the hut. I considered going to a place where I was unknown. My mind was utterly confused. I was either going to become insane or act in a deplorable manner. Thinking thus, I sat outside. I was terribly worried about my passionate reaction.

Morning came. I sat calmly in the swing, brooding: "Where shall I go? My present condition is not at all good. It indicates neither success in sadhana nor the grace of God. This must be the evil fruit of some past sin." While occupied with such thoughts, I slipped into the *tandra* state. I went inside and began to meditate again. In a moment, I was absorbed in it. I began to roar like a lion. My tongue stuck out completely. I kept roaring for half an hour. I became more and more frightened. After three quarters of an hour, I came out of meditation. This time I was not clutched by the sexual urge. However, having escaped one enemy, I was gripped by another. It seemed as though I had only jumped from the frying pan into the fire, as the saying goes. My identification with a lion aggravated my self-disgust. I decided to quit that place. I will add here that all these emotional states were in fact the lofty workings of the grace of a Siddha, the ennobling processes of Siddha Yoga. But being ignorant, I felt confusion instead of joy.

In a short while, I saw a *tonga* approaching the orchard. The driver was sitting in front, but I could not see who was sitting in the back. The *tonga* drove right up to the mango tree and someone stepped out. I recognised him. What a blessing! It was Hari Giri Baba, the great Siddha yogi and unique *avadhoot*. He started calling me right from there: "O King! O Emperor! O Swami! Get up." Having uttered these words, he began to laugh heartily. I was beside myself with joy and got up from the swing. He was an omniscient saint, always laughing. He used to wander on river bank, wearing expensive shoes, a number of coats, one over another, and a silk turban. Whenever he felt hungry, he would ask anyone for food, saying: "Give. Give me something to eat," and then ate. At once he would wash his hands and start off again on his jaunt. He was a saint of devilish disposition. He would collect tiny round pebbles from the river, look at one, then at another and mumble: "Yes . . . yes, Coral, you are worth two million." He would talk like this, roaming around by himself. He walked at a flying pace. He would go to the river bank at 2 a.m. and return after dawn. If questioned about it, he would mutter an incomprehensible reply.

Hari Giri Baba came forward. I bowed to him. We loved each other greatly. I said, "Baba! I am in a sorry condition. I am feeling terrible."

He said, "I know what the matter is. I will explain it only if you give me two rupees." I was familiar with his jocular manner. Whenever he came, if asked about anything, he would demand money. I gave him the two rupees. Hari Giri Baba spoke again, "O Emperor! You are in a wonderful state. You are going to see much better times. You will become divine. You are suffering from a beneficial fever. Becoming infected with your fever, many people will overcome disease and sorrow. You will influence a large number of people." Having uttered these words, he walked away. I accompanied him a short distance, but on the way he said, "Go, go away. If one does not go, how can one return? Do not be afraid." Then he moved away. The neighbours began to run after him exclaiming "Hari Giri Baba has come."

I returned and sat in the swing. Once again my mind was in disarray, recollecting the sexual excitement of the morning and also the identification with a lion. I became more and more bewildered, since it is the nature of the mind to become like that on which it dwells intensely. It merges with its object of constant thought, assuming its qualities. I would quote a favourite stanza of mine:

जो मन नारिकि ओर निहारत, तौ मन होतहि ताहिकु रूपा ।
जो मन काहुयूँ क्रोध करै पुनि, तौ मन है तबही तदरूपा ।
जो मन मायहि माय रटै नित, तौ मन बूड़त मायके कूपा ।
सुन्दर जो मन ब्रह्म विचारत, तौ मन होतहि ब्रह्मस्वरूपा ॥

(The mind, always occupied with women, acquires
    their character,
The mind, constantly excited with anger, burns in
    its fire,
The mind, ever dwelling on *maya*, sinks in her
    bottomless pit,
But, Sunder says, the mind, continually resting in
    the Absolute, eventually becomes It).

These words of the poet-saint Sunderdas, who was established in Truth, are entirely true.

My mind was utterly befogged by those two disturbances. I said to myself, "I have been living at Yeola for a long time, commanding great respect. I am a self-respecting person. Why should I dishonour myself by letting them suspect my present predicament? I shall retire into a remote forest where nobody will recognise me." I resolved to leave at once. I got up and embraced the photograph whereby I worshipped my beloved Gurudev, saying, "Forgive me, but what can I do? I am helpless. You are a liberal giver, but I am unfortunate." I bowed to him repeatedly, and then put the frame down. I looked at the hut and said: "My dear hut, I don't know when I shall see you again. I spent a long period happily inside you. I bow to you." I touched the swing tenderly and also knelt to it. I hugged the mango trees, who were my dear friends, and said, "I spent many happy days in your shade. I have no alternative now, since I am utterly wretched. I must leave you." I went inside the hut again. I took off my saffron clothes, tied them up in a bundle and left it to hang on a tree because I did not want to dishonour the garb of a *sannyasi*. Afterwards I wore white clothes for a long time. I left the door of the hut open. I was wearing only a loin-cloth and a shawl over my shoulders. I picked up my water-bowl and secretly set off eastwards. I covered some distance and paused at a point from where I could still see the hut. I bowed again. My mind was full of intense grief and bitter remorse. I began to walk towards the Sahyadri range. I pushed on, walking between hills. I was determined to go far away and I would not have cared had my body collapsed on the way.

I continued my journey. From Daulatabad I reached Nagad via holy Ghrishneshwar. I stood on a Sahyadri peak and looked northwards. From there I could espy a large orchard of oranges and sweet limes. There were also many mango orchards and sugarcane fields of various sizes. Hunger was gnawing at me. I finally ended up in an orchard whose owner turned out to be quite wealthy. He was a practitioner of yoga, having great love for saints and *sadhus*. He was called Dagadu Singh. He approached and inquired after me. Then he took me with him and affectionately had *khichari* cooked for me.

As I looked around, I caught sight of a small hut intended for sadhana, where a certain yogi had practised yoga previously. Dagadu Singh made arrangements for me to stay there. As I sat inside the hut, my legs locked

themelves in the lotus posture and meditation began.
The beloved red aura appeared before me. A voice called
from within, saying: "Open that cupboard over there and
read the book inside." At first I did not pay much
attention to it. But when the voice spoke a second and
then a third time, my meditation was disturbed. I opened
my eyes and saw an old cupboard. I opened it, found the
book and took it out. It opened automatically at the page
that dealt with the process occurring in me. I read it
and felt completely relieved. All my distress evaporated
in a moment. I was no longer confused or worried. I
realised that whatever had happened was a result of my
Gurudev, Bhagawan Nityananda's bountiful grace. It
marked a definite stage of the spiritual journey in Siddha
Yoga. With my doubts at rest, I ate the *khichari*
contentedly. Later I glided into a sound slumber.

I practised meditation at Nagad for some time. Now
I understood that the process which involved sexual
excitement was, in fact, turning the flow of seminal fluid
upwards. One gains the power of Shaktipat only after
becoming an *urdhvareta*. The process was taking place
in order to annihilate the sexual urge once and for all.
As *svadhisthan chakra* is pierced, sexual impulses are
aroused. But this happens in order to make an aspirant
an *urdhvareta*, to expel sexual lust from his system
forever.

When I realised that the sexual excitement was a great
and significant event, I was delighted. How could I
describe it? The previous joy flooded my being again.
The vision of the naked woman had brought me so much
distress because of my own ignorance, my erroneous
notions. She was, as a matter of fact, the great Goddess
Kundalini. I begged forgiveness of the Mother and
recited a hymn to Her. After that, I began to meditate
even more deeply.

The next day, Mother Kundalini stood in the red aura
again. But now I could perceive Her celestial loveliness.
She was the divine power of grace, ravishingly beautiful.
As I saw Her, I congratulated myself on my good fortune
and bowed down to Her. As I knelt down, the divine

Goddess merged in the red aura. From then on the divine Shakti became my Guru. She had looked naked to me because I myself was naked, lacking in true knowledge. My lustful reaction was because of my inability to see Her as the great Shakti Kundalini. I had regarded Her as an ordinary woman of this world. My suffering had resulted from my own ignorance. But now it was all over.

I went to see another saint I knew, Zipruanna, who was a great Siddha. Though he remained naked and roamed through the village of Nasirabad, he was revered as a great soul by everyone, addressed as 'Anna' by old and young alike. He preferred to stay in uninhabited corners, dilapidated houses or huts, far from the rural folk. He had attained a very high state in yoga. He was far-sighted, being able to see into the distant past and future. His body had been so completely purified by the yogic fire that even when he sat on a heap of garbage he remained untainted. I was greatly surprised to see that he had raised even his body to such a high level. Just as the inner Self of a yogi is never sullied by impurities, even so, Zipruanna's physical form could not be con-taminated. The first time I went for his darshan he was relieving himself in a corner. As I approached him, he began to smear his body with his own faeces! I sat near him. His body, amazingly enough, was emitting fragrance instead of foul stench. When I revisited him, I found him sitting on a pile of refuse without being polluted by it. I did not have the courage to go close, so I kept standing at a distance. In a short while he came down from the heap. I washed his feet. His limbs were exuding an aroma resembling that of *ashtagandha* (a fragrant herb). Zipruanna loved me greatly. To this day, I have not ceased marvelling at the extraordinary state of this great saint. Once I asked him, "Anna! Why must you sit on such rubbish?" He replied, "Muktananda, inner impuri-ties are far more revolting than this. Don't you know that the human body is a chest full of waste matter?" This silenced me. Zipruanna was a supreme *avadhoot*, the most precious of saintly jewels.

I went to see him then. He received me lovingly and
sat down with his body pressed against mine. I told him
about my experiences in the Suki hut. He said, "That is
the grace, initiation, benevolence or Shaktipat of a great
saint. Such experiences are possible only because of
sublime benediction. One envisions the great conflagration, ghosts, demons, demigods, cobras, *kinnaras* and the
spectral companions of Parashiva. This is exactly what
you have seen." When I asked him about my sexual
agony, he answered, "The sex organ's erection and its
subsequent digging into the navel happens only in the
case of a rare aspirant. This is due to the extraordinary
divine grace of yoga. Do not underrate the phallus, which
generates all and determines one's sex. Its absence makes
one a pathetic eunuch. This highly worthy generative
organ of man should be restrained and disciplined as
much as possible. If, on touching the navel, it stays in that
position for a while, the entire seminal fluid accumulated
in the testicles starts flowing upwards towards the heart.
Then it gets purified by the gastric fire and moves on
into the brain, strengthening all the sensory nerves and
greatly enhancing a yogi's powers of memory and
intelligence." Then he added, "O Swami! Such a one is
called an *urdhvareta*. In the future, on the strength of
this, you will achieve Guruhood and bestow grace. As a
result of this *vajroli* process which you have undergone,
you will acquire the inner power of Shaktipat. The great
Kundalini Shakti has entirely uprooted your previous
sexual appetite by means of the sexual torture which you
had to endure. In the future, not the sexual urge, but
pure love, will inundate your heart. The rays of your
love will enkindle love in innumerable hearts."
    I then referred to the naked female who appeared in
my meditations, saying, "I always sat down for meditation after putting on Shiva's armour and sealing off
different directions. How, then, could that naked woman
make her appearance?" As I put this question, Baba
Zipruanna brightened up and spoke in a serious tone.
"O Swami! Who can penetrate your inner being, the
radiant city of meditation? That is the refulgent land

of Mother Chitshakti. None except Chiti, the Chiti-endowed deity and the Guru can ever gain admittance there. Your own idea of femininity was responsible for your confusion. What's the difference between a naked and a clad woman? The Mother assumes all forms. When you saw that nymph, you should have looked upon Her as Goddess Chitshakti. Nobody else can enter there. The fruits that you reap correspond to your own attitude. From now on look upon whatever you see, whether good or bad, as different forms of Chiti. When you consider the naked maiden who arises from the inner heart to be the supreme Goddess, Her form becomes divine. Countless are the marvels of Chitshakti. She travels at an enormous speed. You must have seen how rapidly the red particles, subtler than the subtle, move within. You will see the infinite worlds existing in Her. This Chitshakti, who assumes innumerable forms in a moment and reveals many in One, is the supreme *maya*, Mother Yoga Kundalini. O Swami! Whatever happened was for your good. Whatever happens in the future will also be for your good. Always remain aware of the true nature of Kundalini.

"Another thing. The yogi on the Siddha path should always remember that whatever he sees from time to time in the light of the inner heart, whatever emanates from Chiti, whether high or low, noble or ignoble, acceptable or rejectable, worthy or unworthy, beneficial or harmful, is nothing but Chiti in Her fullness. None but Chiti can ever have a place there. The numerous visions and movements occurring there are entirely the Goddess Chiti, regardless of what you may take them to be."

Having listened to such sublime wisdom, I fell at the feet of 'Zipreshwar,' Lord Zipru. What wisdom! How true! What an authentic description of reality! "O my dear Baba!" exclaiming thus, I embraced him. He seated me on his lap. He licked my head, passed his hand over it and said, "Your glory will reach the highest heavens." Those days I used to suffer from acute headaches. From that day on that ailment vanished. Thus Zipruanna resolved all my problems. I had profound reverence and great faith in him. I loved him like my Guru. It was he, in fact, who had sent me to Bhagawan Nityananda, saying, "You are going to reach the highest summit under his guidance. Your future with him is bright."

My dear students of Siddha Yoga! Listen carefully. Once you have been blessed by the Guru's grace, you should discard all fears. Do, however, remember that in Siddha Yoga you must fully carry out the Guru's orders. You should understand this essential truth: the Guru's word alone matters. Fully bear in mind Anna's statement: "How can a full-grown woman enter the tiny cavity of the inner heart?" Can an ordinary woman pierce your armour, forged by mantra and Tantra? You will be able to see everything in the red aura arising from Chiti Kundalini. Can you ever have such a vision without Her wish? Think it over. Remember that the cavity of the heart is minute. None other than Kundalini can penetrate it. Therefore, whatever happens within you, the visions you see and the movements you undergo, accept them all as the divine Shakti's precious gifts and offer them all to Her. Know that whatever happens is for your own progress. The forms Chiti assumes, the movements She motivates, the shapes or colours or states She reveals—bow inwardly to each, considering them Her manifestations. This attitude will fill you with peace at once. If you look upon it otherwise, you will suffer remorse as Muktananda did.

After returning from my visit to Zipruanna, I began to practise sadhana with full faith, in my beloved hut at Nagad. The duration of my meditation increased automatically. I acquired various books since I did not feel satisfied unless I knew more about meditative states. I studied the *Mahayoga Vijnana*, containing experiences which are helpful for a meditator to know. I sent for other similar works such as *Yogavani* and *Shaktipat*, and studied them closely. In fact, Maha Yoga holds a special place in the Shaivite philosophy. Such works as *Shivasutras*, *Pratyabbijnahrdayam*, *Tantraloka* and *Shiva Drishti* are written by experienced sages on the themes of Shaktipat, the grace of a Siddha and the dynamic play

of Mother Kundalini. My stay at Nagad was solitary and
fascinating.

### Spontaneous Yogic Movements

I was making great advances in yogic practice. All
three important factors—divine Shaktipat, the grace of a
great Siddha and a burning desire for God-realisation—
had combined in my case. So far I had lacked only in
the knowledge of the various movements and experiences
which follow Shaktipat. Now that I had gained a full
understanding of this subject by reading the relevant
books, what deficiency could possibly obstruct me? My
sadhana progressed rapidly, like the mighty flood of a big
river. Each day new movements occurred. I awoke at
3 a.m. when the *brahmamuhurta* begins. The moment I
sat for meditation, I was seized by a powerful force. Then
the red aura shone, in which an oval of white light
appeared and vanished, appeared and vanished again; but
the red aura continued to gleam in its fullness. I performed Guru worship in ecstasy. While I worshipped the
Guru, within and without, all thought fluctuations ceased.
The three *bandhas* took place of their own accord. These
three *bandhas*—*mula, uddiyana* and *jalandhar,* have great
advantages. My heel was pressed upon my anus,
contracting it forcefully. The *apana* was sucked upwards.
This is known as *mulabandha*. It equalises *prana* and
*apana*, destroying disease and aging. An aspirant, by
sitting in the lotus posture and mastering prana through
this *mudra*, acquires the power of stabilising himself in
the Void. The frog movement also takes place in this
*mudra*.

Along with this, my breath was expelled and the
abdomen drawn upwards, thus forming a small pit. It
seemed as though the air below the navel were being
drawn upwards. This is called *uddiyana bandha*. In the
Hatha yogic texts this is highly praised, so much so that
it is claimed that death can be conquered through this.
It purifies the prana and the nerves. As the nerves are
purified, the gastric fire begins to blaze. The purification

of the prana puts an end to mental wandering, making the mind stable. In the next movement, called *jalandhar bandha*, my chin was pressed forcefully on the jugular notch. This is highly significant. It blocks the downward flow of the drops of nectar trickling from *sahasrar*. If they were allowed to flow downwards, they would be consumed by the fire of the sun in the navel *chakra*, but in this way they are saved. By means of this *mudra*, the yogi's mind soon attains stillness.

Gradually, my *prana* and *apana* were balanced. I had also mastered the lotus posture. It is said that if a yogi can sit in a posture for three hours at a stretch, he has perfected it. As the three *bandhas* occurred, I hopped like a frog with my legs locked in the lotus posture, from one place to another in the hut. Whatever movement took place was attended with inner joy. In meditation, I effortlessly performed several *mudras* such as *mahamudra, mahabandha, mahavedha, viparitakarni* and *vajroli mudra*. Sometimes I pressed the anus with either heel. Stretching out either leg, I firmly held its toes with both hands and placed my head between my arms. This is called *mahamudra*, which forces the Kundalini into *sushumna* along with the prana. It activates all the nerves, dispelling physical inertia. It helps in the retention of semen. It calms and irradiates the body, intensifies the gastric fire, and brings the senses under control. It arrests aging. By its constant practice, diseases such as tuberculosis, leprosy, piles, hernia, enlarged spleen and dyspepsia are eradicated.

Sometimes I folded one leg, placing the foot on the opposite thigh. My abdomen was filled with air. The *jalandhar bandha* followed and my breath was held. Then the retained air was released slowly. This is *mahabandha mudra* which sends the prana up the *sushumna*, strengthens the body and makes the bones firm. Then the *mahavedha bandha* took place, which is a modification of *mahabandha* with *uddiyana bandha* added to it. After full exhalation, the breath was held outside in external *kumbhaka*. This *bandha* also helps the prana rise into the *sushumna*. It pierces all three knots: Brahma,

Rudra and Vishnu. The Kundalini starts travelling to *sahasrar*. It gives control of prana. Sometimes I would place my hands on the floor, with palms upwards. Putting my forehead between them, I straightened my legs upwards and remained in that position for a while. This is known as *viparitakarni mudra*, or headstand, which has numerous advantages. It increases the gastric fire and removes wrinkling and greying. It prevents the drops of nectar from *sahasrar* from flowing downwards. Sometimes in this very posture, my palms were turned downwards. I supported myself on my hands, remaining with my head hanging downwards between my arms. This is *vajroli mudra* which imparts perfect control over semen, prevents its release or discharge and develops the power to retain it. It prolongs life.

Apart from all this, several kinds of *pranayama* took place. Sometimes, stretching the mouth in the *bhujangini mudra*, I drank in the air. Sometimes the tip of my tongue dug into my palate, followed by retention of breath. This *nabhomudra* eradicates all diseases and enables the tongue to pierce into the nasal pharynx. In the later stages it develops into *khechari mudra*. At times, I would roll my tongue into the shape of a crow's bill and suck air inwards. This is known as *kaki* or *sheetali mudra*, which prolongs life, purifies the blood and eliminates fever and bile disorders. Sometimes profuse secretions flowed from the cranial region and my eyeballs rolled upwards, with my vision focussing on the space between the eyebrows. This *shambhavi mudra* is highly comforting. It steadies the mind, raising a yogi to Shiva's level. As the mind becomes concentrated on the space between the eyebrows, the light of pure consciousness shines.

My identification with a lion had become more intense. I roared so loudly that the cows tethered at a short distance broke free and ran helter-skelter. The dogs barked loudly. The people rushed towards my hut, but were astonished to find only Babaji roaring. I was no longer concerned whether I was granting darshan or not. I myself was having repeated darshans of the great

movements of Kundalini. Each day I sat in meditation
three times—at 3 a.m., at 11 a.m. and from 7 to 9 p.m.
At times, I lay supine like a serpent, zigzagging about.
I hopped like a frog and roared like a lion. While experiencing the extraordinary inner states of Mother Chiti,
my mind was held fascinated.

My joy multiplied. I did not know why, but I wanted
so much to dance. This urge to dance thrilled the whole
of my body, while I beheld the red aura and the thumb-
sized flame within it. The movements involving the
physical body became more forceful. Many Hatha yogic
*mudras* and postures occurred, not each day, but every
second or third day. I gained a new inner eye. I did not
know exactly what it was. With this eye, I saw various
places in the red aura. Afterwards, I also saw the
splendid effulgence of the golden *akasha* followed by the
white radiance of the silvery *akasha* in the red aura. This
red aura extends over three and a half armlengths while
manifesting in an individual, but in its universal manifestation, it spreads from east to west, north to south,
above and below, containing the entire body of the
cosmos. Within the red aura I saw many holy centres of
our India. I reached a new stage in meditation during
which, along with the red aura and the white flame, I
saw vast stretches containing ranges of mountains and
forests. I saw the Himalayas which I had visited and
Himalayan peaks which I had never seen before. Thus
while meditating, I was also having visions. I was fully
conscious of all that was happening and I was also
experiencing bliss.

Though my body became thinner, its strength increased.
It was being purified. Sometimes I had a slight fever or
bad cold which soon cured itself. Sometimes I was
attacked by dysentery but that too soon ceased. Whatever
ailment I contracted at that time was overcome by
meditation.

I was progressing daily in meditation. As I sat I went
into a new *tandra* state. I began to see a yellow light.
At times I also saw a mixed light blending red and white
shades. While I saw that exceedingly beautiful yellow

light in *tandra*, new regions were revealed. This new state resembled *samadhi*, but I remained fully conscious, distinguishing the perceiver from the perceived. After I had remained in that state for a short while, I experienced great joy which dissolved all my fatigue. I started meditating for longer periods. My body was becoming slimmer, so much so that even my calves were shedding their flesh. The seven bodily components were being purified. Though my food intake was still the same, my waste products were reduced. I passed faeces as hard as wood, which were less odorous. The smell of perspiration also decreased. I was feeling lighter and more vibrant. Immersed in the ecstasy of love, I sometimes danced vigorously in the solitude of the orchard.

I had mastered the lotus posture and could sit in it for three hours. Then my tongue began to undergo a new, rather strange process. Sometimes it descended to the heart. At other times, it was held upwards through the nasal pharynx, returning to its normal position only after meditation. Many such supernormal movements occurred. I was having more visions in *tandra*. My perseverance in sadhana, faith in Gurudev and surrender to Chiti grew. An indistinct shape appeared in meditation and said, "Your tongue is opening the heart lotus by its downward movement. Its ascent into the nasal pharynx is the *khechari mudra*. This process will lead you to a high state." As the tongue is held upwards, the passage to *sahasrar* is cleared. This is effected by the awakened Kundalini Shakti in order that She may meet Parashiva residing in the centre of the thousand rays of *sahasrar*. Sometimes I beheld the deities of all the *chakras*, along with their characteristic lights. But none of these experiences depended on my own will. They were the spontaneous gifts of the Guru's grace, motivated solely by Parashakti. Sometimes during meditation, my legs became inert, devoid of prana, but later returned to normal.

One notable characteristic of my sadhana was that I regularly sat in a proper meditative posture for a fixed duration, even if I was unable to meditate or the mind did not become one-pointed. This helped me considerably.

My dear Siddha students should bear in mind that the lotus posture, maintained for three hours, completely purifies all 72,000 nerves and this purification is the most significant one. As the nerves are cleansed, the prana is automatically purified. Then *pranayama* follows in a natural manner. In the sadhana of Shaktipat, *pranayama* takes place spontaneously during meditation, owing to the Guru's grace. As the prana is cleansed, the mind also becomes pure. In this manner one reaches higher states in meditation. Therefore, practise a meditative posture earnestly.

What happiness can there be in life if the nerves are impure and foul-smelling, clogged with unwholesome filth? I will make it clear by an analogy. If each room and each corner of your residence is emitting a noxious smell, mosquitoes and insects are humming around everywhere and the atmosphere is being contaminated by the rotten stench of drains and lavatories, can you enjoy peace and delight? Similarly, if the body is terribly impure and prone to all kinds of ailments, with the mouth exuding bad odour, the nose running owing to a bad cold requiring several handkerchiefs each hour to clear, and the rank smell of unevacuated waste matter issuing from entrails nauseates one's neighbours, what joy, what happiness can one derive in such a body? Can perfumes and scents dispel the internal foul smell? Can layers of lipstick, cream and powder ever impart that brightness to the face which captivates the heart? Remember: शरीरमाद्यं खलु धर्मसाधनम् । (The body is, indeed, the first means to *dharma*).

As time went by, a kind of fire was liberated inside my body, heating all its parts. No matter how I tried to cool my body, it still felt as though it were burning. My body burned so much inside that I could not cool myself even by sitting in a pool of cold water. It had become completely emaciated. A trickle of saliva dribbled from my mouth. I began to take boiled rice water instead of solid food. Then I received a message from Bhagawan Nityananda, who was in Ganeshpuri. The inhabitants of Yeola had been astonished at my sudden and strange departure, as I had neither closed the door of my hut nor taken anyone into confidence about it. They had informed Nityananda Baba, adding that I was at present in the neighbourhood of Chalisgaon. His message said that my sadhana was going well, that my experiences were authentic and that I should continue to practise meditation steadfastly. I was delighted with the message.

My beloved Gurudev sent another message of love through Shri Narayan Sando, one of his most ardent devotees whom I loved greatly. He took out a phial of genuine Khus scent and gave it to me. I asked him, "Why have you brought perfume?"

He answered, "Swami, I took this bottle to Bhagawan Nityananda for his personal use. When I offered it to him, he asked me to go to Nagad and pass it on to you. Please accept it." I took the scent, opened the bottle feeling it was a gift from Bhagawan and applied some. The scent was of a high quality. I applied it on my entire body. Its fragrant fumes filled my nostrils. We talked heartily about Bhagawan Nityananda. I received some news about him. Subsequently my meditation became more intense. The very next day Bhagawan Nityananda appeared in my *tandra*. He handed me the same bottle of scent and said, "Meditation will liberate more heat. This is due to the all-consuming fire of yoga. Use a little of this fragrant lotion each day." Thus on receiving the perfume and also his instruction in meditation, my heart rejoiced.

My meditation each day was followed by lunch, after which I read books concerning yoga while sitting under a mango tree. I came upon the injunction that yogis should wear fragrant flowers, as they alleviate the heat generated by yogic practices. I became aware of the rationality of our culture. In the Indian mode of worship, fragrant garlands are offered to the Lord for the same reason. Thus there is a sound justification behind the offering of costly garlands of fragrant flowers to saints. I also understood why fragrant sandal paste is applied to their feet. Thereafter, I wore a garland of *mogra* each morning before I sat in meditation. After meditation, I sometimes used Heena and sometimes Khus scent.

I was meditating more intensely. I saw a yellow and blue light and slipped into a wonderful *tandra*. The joy of this state is sublime. It is much greater than the pleasure derived from eating, drinking, seeing external beauty or gratifying desire during waking hours. It is also greater than the repose of sleep during which dreams arise. Sometimes I could even witness the sleep state, discovering that its joy is not true joy and that it cannot compare with *tandra*, which it resembles. Then I began to experience the delight of Tandraloka more and more.

Sometimes I saw a beautiful, slender golden tube standing like a pillar extending from the *muladhar* to the throat. That bewitched me. I wondered how that fine tube could become permeated with golden light. Sometimes I discerned a deity in each *chakra*. I also felt slight pain in their centres. Sometimes in meditation I perceived the system of nerves, veins and arteries and the digestive and eliminative tracts. A multicoloured light spread through all the nerves, making them visible. I also perceived the increasing intensity of Shakti throbbing through them.

## The White Flame

Every day, as I sat in my meditative posture, the same red aura appeared, followed by the beautiful egg-shaped white light. These stayed for increasingly longer periods. I was becoming a little more steady each day. I also began to experience a new kind of sleep during meditation. Mother Kundalini Shakti, my beloved Guru, who had previously frightened me with Her naked form, also appeared during these meditations. But now I did not become distracted. I experienced high meditative states. The oval white light, resembling a long *gulabjaman* in shape, stayed for longer periods within the red aura. I looked upon whatever vision I saw as a form of divine Chiti and knelt inwardly to it.

Gradually, my mind in meditation shifted its focus

from the red aura to the white flame, which stood before me in its full glory. From the gross body I penetrated to the subtle. That which I have called the white flame is actually the thumb-shaped subtle body described in Vedanta. In this body the individual soul experiences dreams and enjoys some respite after the toil of its waking hours. It supports the physical body. It is represented by the second letter 'U' of Aum. In this subtle body, the individual soul is known as Taijasa. Its seat lies in the throat. The subtle body can be directly experienced either through a vision of the white flame or in a simple dream. Without direct personal experience, Vedanta is a lame, second-hand philosophy, like the spoon that does not know the taste of the pudding it serves.

As I sat in meditation each day, prana currents would at first begin to speed through the body, followed by the red aura and the white flame. I was becoming more absorbed in meditation on the subtle body, apprehending the subtle form of the outer world within me. At first I slept a little too much during meditation, but this gradually passed. As my mind became concentrated on the subtle, I had more and more prophetic visions. For instance, I would see a fire, which would later break out somewhere, or an impending motor accident. Within a couple of days, I would receive the news of such incidents. This increased my zest for meditation, filling me with wonder at its glories.

While meditating, I had also begun to see numerous other worlds. Again and again I beheld various deities and also the *shivalinga*. In such a state, as I passed into Tandraloka, I beheld strange cobras of different kinds and terrible serpents that somewhat frightened me. Afterwards I carefully pondered the experiences of meditation. I was talking much less for I spent most of my time reading, meditating and resting. If a group of devotees turned up on a particular day, I had some conversation with them. But as a result, my schedule was disturbed and I could not slip into *tandra*. On such a day, my experience of bliss was also much less intense. Whenever I became agitated owing to inner or outer causes, it was not possible for me to meditate and visit Tandraloka. I would feel dejected on this account. For this reason I stopped meeting people and indulging in small talk with them.

Sometimes I was able to perceive the events of the outer world in meditation. As a result, I understood the external world better. I beheld the lotus of the heart in the midst of the white flame. Even a fleeting vision of this supernal radiance held me spellbound. If the light in the heart continued to sparkle with lightning speed, I experienced a state of bliss overflowing with ecstatic love. If I happened to be close to the mango tree at that time, I embraced it lovingly!

One day as I began to meditate, I beheld an amazingly beautiful child in a cradle. The little baby was about one and a half years old and wore a necklace of pearls and a crown of gold. He was celestially adorned. His cradle was made of gold, studded with the rarest jewels. He was swinging in it. There was nobody around him. I saw the enchanting child enveloped by multicoloured light. I still remember him. He turned towards me and laughed ecstatically. He was beckoning me with his big eyes. How joyful this meditation! That day I travelled beyond Tandraloka where I could see nothing for a long time. This is the pure, untainted state. When my meditation ended, I closed my eyes again and tried to visualise the baby, but I could not. I was fully convinced that he was Lord Hari. After seeing Him, my meditation improved even more. For the next two or three days I meditated unusually well. One day I saw a pile of pearl necklaces. On another I saw an uncommonly beautiful milch cow suckling her calf, which had the complexion of the baby in the gold cradle.

Before I would sit for meditation, I was curious about what I might see that day. In the afternoon, my mind would wait impatiently for evening. At night I eagerly awaited morning so that I could meditate. This was because of the captivating sights that I was seeing during meditation. My mind had become addicted to such visions. After meditation, as I recollected the visions again and again, my body was thrilled. In sheer ecstasy, I congratulated myself on my good fortune. Thus most of my days and nights were spent in meditation and recollections of the meditational visions.

## The Black Light

After meditation on the white flame, meditation on the black light began. This light marked the next higher stage in meditation. The black light stands for the causal body. It has been called 'finger-tip size' by Jnaneshwar Maharaj. Its seat lies in the heart. It is represented by the letter 'M' in Aum. It indicates a pure state which transcends the senses. It is the centre of profound, dream-free sleep. On reaching this stage, one overcomes all desires. Here one enjoys only bliss. The individual soul in this body is called Prajna. It is possible to have concrete visions of the gross, subtle, causal and supra-causal bodies. The causal body, apprehended as the black light, forms the third petal of the lotus, of which the first two are red and white. O Siddha students! Find this out through meditation.

My mind was spontaneously focussed, sometimes on the heart and sometimes on the space between the eye-brows. First my attention was fixed on the red-white-black trinity. I saw the white flame within the red aura and the black light within the white. From time to time, while gazing at these three, I also apprehended other bright, multicoloured lights. But at this stage my mind was fixed firmly only on the black light. I felt peace within, accompanied by a pleasant curiosity and expecta-tion of further visions, which occasionally disturbed it.

During this phase, I sometimes perceived frightfully thick folds of darkness such as I had never seen before in the external world. On account of this darkness, I became frightened even of meditation. Yet I had to remain in the darkness for long periods. Then suddenly the scene would shift and the familiar lights—red, white and black would return. I rejoiced in their radiance again and again. At this time, I also suffered from agonizing pain in the space between the eyebrows. The *chakra* situated in this region kept aching for several days. Together with this my eyes would revolve rapidly, causing terrible pain. My eyeballs rolled upwards and the pupils whirled like wheels. Thus I began to have a new experience. When my eyes spun, I felt the prana moving gently only between the throat and the space between the eyebrows. I smelled different fragrances during meditation. I do not know whether they were of this world or not. At times, even the people around me could detect these fragrances. My hut was also permeated by them. Every now and then my eyes stopped spinning. Sometimes they moved upwards, perceiving the region within the cranium, where I saw a dazzling bright sun. I also beheld some stars there. Then my meditation ceased. I would compose myself and come out of the hut to sit under the mango tree, reflecting and musing on my new visions.

One day, while my mind was concentrated on the black within the white within the red, I discerned a city enveloped in impenetrable masses of darkness. I do not know how deep I penetrated into the city, but I covered a considerable distance. As I approached the end, the scene in the black light changed suddenly. While gazing at the red-white-black trinity, I found myself sitting under a tree in a dense forest. A black cobra crawled rapidly towards me and bit me. Its poison spread through my body and I was about to die. Just then a devotee from Yeola came by. He was the one who usually arranged for my bath and sometimes cooked my food. He now prayed to Parashiva for me. After the prayer I recovered from my critically-poisoned condition.

All this resembled a scene in a drama and I remember it still. Later I came upon a book dealing with sadhana. I learned from it that a snake-bite during meditation is a lofty vision, a sign of supreme fearlessness on the path of Siddha Yoga. This signifies that the aspirant will ascend to still higher planes in course of time.

Now I was sometimes meditating on the white flame, sometimes on the black light. Within the latter, I could see mountainous regions like Sri Shailam with their large caves, the abodes of seers. Sometimes I discerned different kinds of lights in the caves of the Girnar hills. Wherever my eyes fell I beheld an enchanting light, combining red, blue and yellow shades. I could see everything there by the glow of this divine radiance. Three or four days after the snakebite, I visited Nagaloka, the world of cobras. Cobras and more cobras all around! They gleamed with a blue lustre. I beheld a huge cobra whose brightness was dazzling. There were flower gardens for them on all sides. Thus innumerable sights and places appeared in blissful visions.

I would remain quiet after meditation. As days went by, my mind became more and more tranquil. I could behold the three lights even with my eyes open during normal waking hours. This happened particularly when I was full of *Gurubhava*. I was more deeply immersed in joy. If I took a stroll in any part of the orchard, I was greeted by the same lights. Wherever my eyes fell, those lights sparkled. I was amazed at this condition. How magical was that snake-bite! Perhaps the god of cobras had blessed me with his grace for my higher spiritual progress.

Then my eardrums were afflicted with an acute but temporary pain. My pupils continued to revolve. The upper eyelid was stuck above and the lower below, and I would not blink for two hours at a stretch. As a result, my eyes appeared to be so swollen that the people who saw them whispered to one another that I looked angry! I did not know why I looked at each one with gaping eyes. When I returned to the normal state, they would remark that I looked quite gentle then. My spontaneous comment was that I was only myself, neither angry nor gentle.

I began to visit the moon world in meditation. That there is a world on the moon is entirely true. All its inhabitants are of the same age. There in a garden I saw many male and female figures walking up and down the flower-strewn paths. All of them were youthful and free from disease. I did not see any aged inhabitants. I gazed at the garden while sitting on its edge. The heat of the sun did not reach there. A soft and sweet glow was spread all over. From a look at the towns, I concluded that neither rain nor hot sun visited that region. All the buildings were made of gold and silver.

Not only were strange movements taking place in my nerves and body, but I was having countless visions. I was making a keen and sincere effort in my sadhana.

## Visions of Hell and God Yama

Several days passed in such an intoxicated condition. Once again I was meditating on the black light. One day I visited an extremely filthy world. Siddha students should read this passage carefully. That day as soon as I sat in meditation, my whole body began to shake violently, as though possessed by some deity or evil spirit. In that meditative condition I noticed that I was travelling to a distant region. I did not know where or how I was being transported. Although my physical body was still sitting in a meditative posture, I reached a region that was disgustingly squalid, being filled with excrement. I found myself right in the midst of garbage. I am fully aware of what I am saying. Muktananda advises Siddha students to read this with attention. Wherever I looked, I found excreta. I wondered for how many ages those wastes had been accumulating there. Just as I see hills all around while standing on any point in Mahableshwar, even so, there I espied excrement in all directions. As I moved some distance, my feet began to sink into the mire. A revolting stench was issuing from all around, making me nauseous and affecting my head. The pathways were rough and crude. The little water that was there was also polluted by excreta. There were not many men and women around. The few who were there were naked. Some of them were sitting on heaps of filth, dejected and ugly. All this horribly repulsed me. I struggled hard to move further. I could see light but no sun. In that region I lost all my radiance. With great difficulty I stumbled upon the exit, but that too was slushy. Then I saw a hill of dry faeces on which men and women were sitting. All this took me greatly aback.

After this I entered another world that contained gardens, orchards and forests, full of flowers and fruits and various kinds of cattle and horses. Soon I saw several black masculine figures about twenty feet tall, with sabre teeth, holding shining daggers in their hands, each about six feet long. They also held long goads. Some of them wore silken garments, some animal skins and some plain clothes. The eyes of all of them looked red and swollen with anger. I was surprised not to find any feminine face there. Then I saw black bulls about twenty feet long. After that I came upon an enchanting lake around which fascinating birds were warbling. A beautiful river was flowing nearby. There was a brilliant light all around—whether of our sun or some other star, I did not know. I beheld a black-complexioned god in the midst of that radiance, sitting on a black bull, which was overspread with a silken sheet and adorned with garlands. The bull's horns were inlaid with gold and its anklets were of solid gold. The god wore a red silk *dhoti*, a sacred thread over his shoulder and a crown beset with jewels. He was about ten feet away from me. As I saw him, I smiled and so did he, lifting his hands to grant fearlessness. I was overwhelmed with gladness as I had seen Yama, the god of death. After some time, two messengers of Yama led me out, taking me through the hellish mire again.

Meditation ceased then. I came out of the hut. When I thought of that hell, my heart became dry. I tried to drink water but began to vomit. My mind was filled with loathsome feeling. I could not eat for three days. I feel disgusted even now when I recollect those hellish sights.

While gliding into meditation, I was seized again and again by intense impulses of Shakti. My tongue curled upwards, eyeballs rolled in the same direction and I apprehended divine light manifesting without. I was progressing steadily. At times I was so deeply plunged in meditation, that the fear of death gripped my heart. "I am going to die, yes, I am going to die." This fearful thought would disturb my meditation. Sometimes in the *akasha* of the heart I beheld the divine thumb-shaped light which gladdened me. The sequence of experiences in meditation during this phase was as follows: first, I slipped into Tandraloka; then I saw all external objects bathed in a multi-hued light; finally, my meditation was interrupted by the fear of death.

## Bindu-bheda: Piercing of the Bindu

It now seemed that the pupils of both my eyes coincided within. This is known as *bindu-bheda* in the scriptures. Then a blue radiance arose in the eyes. This is a prelude to the *shambhavi mudra*. The appearance of the blue light signifies the beginning of the highest fortune. Many aspirants become scared during this process lest they should lose their eyesight. My pupils rotated violently upwards and downwards and sideways. It seemed as though my eyeballs would fall out. Even an onlooker became afraid. But complete reliance on the Mother, the attitude that the inner divine Shakti is the real agent of action, not we, eradicated all fear. As the eyeballs revolve, the optical *chakras* are pierced, which pleases their deity. The aspirant should never forget that each of his senses is presided over by a deity. So long as the *chakras* are not purified, the senses work in an ordinary manner. But when purified, they become invested with divine powers. After the visual *chakras* are cleansed, the god of the eyes grants clairvoyant divine vision.

During meditation I felt not only more bliss and energy but also pain in the eyes, ears and the space between the eyebrows. While suffering pain, my mind became centred first on the red aura, then on the white flame and finally on the black light. As soon as I sat for meditation, some physical movements occurred, prana flowed forcefully through the nerves and the *khechari mudra* took place. It was only then that my mind became firmly one-pointed. This released joy within. Furthermore, I also understood the significance of whatever was happening. My insight into these phenomena has not altered even slightly. Such understanding is greatly significant. Sometimes I felt that this power of comprehension was also new, as I did not forget even the minutest details of my experiences. I remained alert and tried to understand this power of intuitive intelligence.

By this time the sexual urge had been completely overcome. Instead a new, ever-increasing love welled up within. This inner love flowed out towards everything and every creature. I questioned myself: "Is this not possessiveness? Is this not infatuation or attachment? Otherwise, how could I become so attached to these mango trees, as I came to Nagad only recently?" Musing thus, I realised that the feeling of tenderness for trees is a reflection of divine love. God loves all without motive. His love is sublime and impartial. It is utterly different from the ordinary love of worldly people. Mundane love is not true love. It is only a kind of business involving calculation. A butcher fattens a lamb every day, apparently with love. But can it be called love? He is only displaying affection to earn money. Milkmaids feed their cattle seemingly with tenderness. Can we really consider it love or charity? Is it not only a kind of business for more milk? A peasant may appear to love his fields, work hard for them and distribute seeds to them liberally. Is that true love or giving? All these forms of so-called love are only forms of business. How can true happiness exist where there is no true love?

Love is motiveless tenderness of heart. Human love always has a selfish desire lurking behind it. It is not genuine love but mere self-seeking. Divine love alone is pure. Love is God's very nature. Grace flows only from His love. He gives love and receives love. He looks upon the entire universe with the single eye of love. By the light of this divine everlasting love, the universe remains alive. As this sublime feeling bubbles up in an aspirant, he feels love for all. In this state the distinction between the lover and the beloved disappears. Love is nothing but pure compassion, extended to all regardless of merit.

Another marvel occurred during meditation. After the world of masses of darkness, I saw a caparisoned elephant, having seven heads, adorned with heavenly beautiful covers and large necklaces of gold, pearls and precious gems. All these ornaments were irradiated by the morning rays. For a long time in meditation I kept seeing him and marvelling. After coming out of meditation, I read one *Purana* from which I learned that this elephant, called Airavat, belongs to Indraloka, and that this vision is an auspicious sign.

Once again I was engrosed in meditation. I was so excited with curiosity that I wanted to meditate the whole day and night. But this was not possible, because one would not be able to bear the force, heat and impact of such extraordinary experiences and the intense exertion involved in meditation. One should not exceed one's capacity of assimilation. Therefore it is essential to abide completely by the scriptural injunctions as to the purity of food and conduct, celibacy or continence. If a seeker lacks self-control, he cannot reap the full fruits of meditation, namely, extraordinary realisations. A meditator should strive for full Self-knowledge, the knowledge of his own splendour. He must abstain from undisciplined behaviour, excessive merriment or grief, vain talk, indiscriminate eating or pleasure-seeking. He should not let the divine power of grace, which is the reward of great self-discipline, fall on evil days along with him. Otherwise the achievement of the goal of mantra, clairvoyance, the vision of one's chosen deity and worldly prosperity are all hampered.

People say, "Babaji, I have been able to meditate, but without joy." Another says, "I had a certain vision in meditation which turned out to be false." One remarks, "When I sit for meditation, I feel nervous." Another says, "I only become more anxious as a result of meditation." I tell all those who complain, that they have not fully observed the rules of meditation. My dear Siddha students! Slighting the great Shakti who works dynamically within you, is the real cause of all these obstructions. If you sit anywhere carelessly or make friends with an unworthy fellow, the attainment of full realisation will be impeded. If this were not true, why should some

Outside the *sadhana kutir* at Suki

At Suki

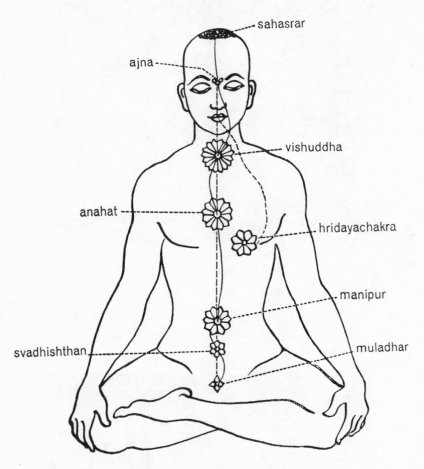

Subtle Centres of Consciousness

aspirants gain more than others, when the Gurushakti which enters them is one and the same?

## The Blue Pearl

While revolving, the pupils of both the eyes became centred on the cranial region. The eyeballs rolled upwards and then downwards. This was followed immediately by a momentary appearance of the tiny, resplendent Blue Pearl, shaped like a sesame seed, which shot out of the eyes like a lightning flash and returned to its seat within. This is a highly mysterious and astonishing occurrence. The tiny Blue Pearl illuminated all the directions for an instant. If I sat facing east, the eastern direction was alight, if south, the southern direction.

Students of Siddha Yoga, how shall I describe the splendour of that Pearl? It moved even faster and more briskly than a flash of lightning. As I beheld it, many expectations were aroused: will Rama, Krishna or my supreme deity, Parashiva, appear within it? Who shall follow Airavat? Although I was eager for a vision of the Divine, my mind was full of joy and contentment. Besides, I began to spend my days in a different manner. After the vision of the Blue Pearl the inner soul was contented, feeling that it had been blessed by the Goddess Kundalini with a supreme gift. I then began to honour one and all in my heart.

My eyes stopped revolving and their vision was fixed upwards. As a result, if I wanted to see something lying below, I felt strain. At times my eyes remained wide open. The acute pain in the space between the eyebrows disturbed my sleep at night. Then a light resembling the flame of a lamp of worship stood still in the two-petalled lotus between the eyebrows. Its radiance and beauty were unsurpassable. As I gazed at it, my vision was blurred. I would fix my eyes on it in a state of self-oblivion. The way to *sahasrar*, traversed by the awakened Kundalini, lies close to that light. This is truly the Siddha pathway, which does not open without the full grace of the Guru. You may be highly devoted, practise most severe austerities and undergo innumerable yogic processes, yet without the Guru's final blessing, this way will not open. There is only one key to unlock this door: गुरुकृपा हि केवलम् । गुरोराज्ञा हि साधनम् । (The Guru's grace alone matters. Obedience to the Guru's command is the only method).

The *chakra* of the two-petalled lotus was also pierced and the prana Shakti began to ascend higher. I was continually envisioning the wickless light resembling a lamp flame. My mind danced in a transport of joy. The spot where I saw this light is the same on which our devout Indian wives daily apply *kum-kum* as a symbol of their conjugal fidelity. The *kum-kum* mark may be made in the name of the husband or as a mere customary sign or to fulfil one of the duties of a woman, but the spot where it is put is the Guru's seat. In this very seat dwells the presiding deity in the form of two seed-letter syllables, *hum* and *ksam*. We owe our existence to It. The above light is only a form of the supreme Gurudev. Our women, in fact, worship God every day by applying *kum-kum*. It is a pity that with the changing times, some of our women are not even aware of this obligation.

I used to gaze at such a divine light. I began with meditating on one light but finally I beheld four concurrently. They emerged one within another, the white within the red, the black within the white and the blue within the black. As I advanced further, crossing different stages of meditation, my joy also multiplied proportionately. Now I was experiencing a new kind of bliss. The visions appearing at this stage were loftier and completely true. Since the vision of the Blue Pearl, the condition of my body, the state of my mind and my insight into things changed and acquired a new character. I rejoiced in my inner Being far more than before. Pure and noble thoughts arose in my mind. I wondered why I could not take any interest in the company of others. Meditation possessed me completely. "What shall I perceive today?"—such was my single hope, single interest and single focus of attention, constituting the fulfilment of my daily duties.

One day as I meditated during *brahmamuhurta*, I saw the flames of a funeral pyre. Who was the woman seated in its midst? She was completely enveloped by tongues of fire, being consumed by them. She was fully absorbed in contemplation. I saw her in that state for a long time, after which my meditation ended.

I intensely yearned for meditation like a greedy person craving wealth. I thought about it constantly like a debauchee obsessed by a young wench. I recollected its experiences like a lunatic trapped by one thought. From the next day onwards, I resolved to start meditating at midnight, because I was moving in such subtle realms that I could not bear the least external noise or disturbance. If someone spoke slightly loud I was disturbed. If someone laughed or a dog barked, my meditation was interrupted. Even the presence of my daily companions appeared to interfere. I eagerly looked forward to their departure. In such a state, I began to meditate, from midnight onwards, in my hut at Nagad.

I did not meditate out of any fear, but with curiosity, faith and zest. I did not meditate to please or derive benefit from anyone, or gratify a sensual craving or some other desire. Nor did I meditate to overcome a physical or mental illness or acquire miraculous powers to achieve personal fame. Nor did I meditate because religion enjoined meditation as a noble duty upon me. Moreover, nobody ever insisted that I should meditate. I meditated only because of my love for God, to explore my true nature and because I was irresistibly drawn towards Goddess Chitishakti. As soon as I sat down I passed into meditation. The presiding deity of each sense organ appeared. I saw a special blended light spreading through the 72,000 nerves with lightning speed. This was followed by the vision of the red, white and black lights. Then the Blue Pearl also made a brief appearance. These lights appeared one within the other, the smaller within the larger, one serving as the subtle cause and also the support of the other.

Now the blue *akasha* began to appear in meditation. Along with that I saw the Pearl possessing infinite power.

As I watched it, I felt as though my eyes would burst. The eyelids stood stationary, neither opening nor closing. This Pearl entranced me completely. I also beheld a new light without. As I slipped into meditation, Kundalini Mahamaya appeared in different shapes. But now whatever form She took, I knew She was Parashakti, the Goddess Kundalini. The Blue Pearl continued to flash repeatedly. Then my eyes moved up behind the eyebrows, as though they had disappeared into the unknown. At this stage, some special work was being accomplished in the cranial region. That process occurred for the purification of the several *chakras* situated therein. Now the focus of my meditation changed from the black light to the Blue Pearl. As I sat in meditation, a quiet movement would occur in my body, followed by fresh impulses of Shakti pulsating in the nerves and then the quaternity of red, white, black and blue lights! I would meditate steadily, gliding at times into profound *tandra* in which I visited different worlds. I could see everything while sitting in my hut. I certainly had some new experience every day. My body became increasingly light, slim, agile, strong and immune to disease. I beheld the full length of the *sushumna*, the central nerve, in meditation. Its colour is silvery with a tinge of gold. It is like a pillar. All the nerves receive motive power from it. Sometimes an aspirant, while meditating, feels pain in the *muladhar* at the back. This is due to the discharge of power currents from the central nerve into others. At times, as a new process took place in my heart, an egg-shaped bright light came into view. This is the vision of the thumb-sized self-effulgent Purusha. He is described in the *Svetasvatara Upanishad* (3-13) as: अङ्गुष्ठमात्रः पुरुषोऽन्तरात्मा सदा जनानां हृदये संनिविष्टः । (A thumb-size being, the inner Soul, always dwells in the heart of all persons).

Meditators must be extremely careful at this stage. They will certainly achieve salvation by virtue of their vision of the Blue Pearl, but they will not be able to have the complete realisation of God and their experience of Him will remain partial. One should be able to pierce through the Blue Pearl to the Self. If an aspirant does not envision the Blue Pearl, his condition will resemble that of an ignorant man who sees the body but not the indwelling Soul. It is, of course, true that the vision of the Blue Pearl gives great peace.

The experience of the inner Self is unmistakable. Sri Tukaram Maharaj, the highly fortunate king of saints, who experienced God in His fullness, says in his immortal poetry:

तिळा एवढें बांधूनि घर । आंत राहे विश्वंभर ॥
तिळा इतुकें बिंदुलें । तेणें त्रिभुवन कोंदाटलें ॥
हरिहराच्या मूर्ती । बिंदुल्यांत येती जाती ॥
तुका म्हणे हें बिंदुलें । तेणें त्रिभुवन कोंदाटलें ॥

Tukaram says in the above verse that the Lord of the universe erects a house as tiny as a sesame seed and dwells in it. He is called the Universal Master as He sustains the entire cosmos. Imagine! The Emperor of the universe, the innermost Self of all living beings, the power of active prana, perceptible to the higher intuition of the yogi, the devotee and the *jnani* possessing omniscience, lives in such a small dwelling. Just as gigantic, sprawling trees grow from minute seeds, so also the Universal Lord, in spite of manifesting Himself in myriad shapes, bodies and forms, resides in a tiny house. In other words, the tiny seed is the source of the huge tree, the tree is contained in the seed; yet the seed exists separately as a seed. Similarly, the supreme Lord, though pervading the entire universe and all beings, lives in a tiny abode. Just as one seed gives birth to countless other seeds that are essentially the same, so the divine seed, while manifesting in innumerable forms, maintains its fundamental identity. The Lord who dwells in the tiny seed, does not lose His integrity or His original power. He remains undiminished and immutable in His essential nature.

This can be clarified further by another analogy. We know that one human being born from another retains all the basic characteristics of his progenitor. A son is born from one drop of his father's semen. The father does not lose his identity though he has produced a son. His nature remains the same as before in every respect. And the son, growing from one drop of the father's semen, comes to possess a full identity like his father. The son resembles the father in his physical appearance and even mental characteristics. We can safely conclude that the father is reborn as the son. Therefore, the son is not a son but the father himself. In the same manner, God, the Source of the universe, Himself creates its myriad forms within His own being, by stirring the Chitshakti in His own Self. He pervades it and yet transcends it. In other words, He raises a house in His own Being and dwells in it. Thus Tukaram's statement is absolutely true, beyond the reach of doubt and controversy.

The *bindu*, as tiny as a sesame seed, is the Soul's abode, inhabited by God. Nay, it is the Self Itself. When you behold the *bindu*, feel certain that your inner Soul is within it. This has been designated as the Blue Pearl, which has a sublime significance. According to Tukaram, this *bindu*, in fact, contains the three worlds. Imagine! Heaven, this world of mortals and hell are all included in it!

The soul is encased in four bodies, one within the other. I have called them red, white, black and blue. The red corresponds to the gross body, the white to the subtle, the black to the causal and the blue to the supracausal. The supracausal is within the tiny Blue Pearl. You can fully realise through meditation how this Pearl embraces the three worlds or the three bodies. Furthermore, Tukaram says that the trinity of Vishnu, Mahesh and Brahma abide and operate within it. Siddha students, now you can judge how sublime, perfect and significant the *bindu* is which you perceive within you in meditation. Within such a minute Blue Pearl, existing within you, lives God, the support of the three worlds.

Therefore, O man, through meditation see God within with reverence. What avails you if you do not seek Him within? By visiting France, England, America and other countries, you see only a small fraction of one corner of His mighty mansion! The supreme Lord dwells within

you with His three worlds. It is not enough to hear about
or reflect on these mysteries. They should be directly
perceived through meditation.

The Blue Pearl is the holiest of holy. Jnaneshwar
Maharaj says:

डोळांची पाहा डोळां शून्याचा शेवट ।
नीळ बिंदू नीट लखलखीत ॥

(The Eye of the eye, even beyond the Void, the Blue
Pearl, is brilliant and sparkling). This scintillating Blue
Pearl can be directly perceived in meditation. O students
of Siddha Yoga! You can certainly envision it, but be
aware that you must be worthy of such a lofty vision.
Your conduct and behaviour should be irreproachable.
Your companions, speech and thoughts, should be filled
with an awareness of God. How noble-souled is he who
has seen the Blue Pearl.

Jnaneshwar says: I shall dwell at the feet of him who
discerns the Purusha living between his eyebrows. I shall
continually meditate on the nature of him who secretly
beholds the divine Blue Pearl. O man! Such a one alone
is truly fortunate and worthy.

The next lines of the above verse of Jnaneshwar, which
I honour greatly, contain the supreme secret for all
travellers on the path of liberation. Furthermore, what
I am going to tell you is the reflection of inner truth,
the criterion of realisation and the key to the secret
mystery of the Guru. For this reason, this verse is as true
as a mantra to me. O dear Siddha students! Listen. Read
it carefully, as it embodies the mystery of all mysteries:

विसावों आलें पातलें चैतन्य तेथें ।
पाहे पा निरुतें अनुभवें ॥ २ ॥
पार्वतीलागीं आदीनाथें दाविलें ।
ज्ञानदेवा फावलें निवृत्तिकृपा ॥ ३ ॥

It means: "O seekers on the Siddha path! That which
opens the inner centre of repose as it arises, is the real
abode of the conscious soul. Look, O brother, this is the
hidden secret of the highest experience. This is exactly
what Parashiva, the primal Lord, told Parvati. Jnana-

deva says that he has seen the Pearl by the grace of his Sadguru Nivrittinath.

Such is the significance of the Blue Pearl which I have also called Neeleshwari, the Blue Goddess. Its vision assures liberation while one is still in the body. But this is not the highest experience or the perfect state or the final goal of the Siddha path. To perceive the Blue Pearl repeatedly means that you are in the *turiya* state. If an aspirant dies at any time after beholding this vision, he will certainly transmigrate to the world of Brahman and achieve ultimate fulfilment by completing his sadhana there.

## My Visit to Indraloka—Heaven

One day in meditation I saw a big city and immediately plunged into a kind of slumber. As a result I could not see or understand anything pertaining to the city. I was delving deep into its waters of love. Piercing through this darkness into Tandraloka, I beheld a chariot coming from afar. It was not a product of human ingenuity, but of divine craftsmanship. It was beset with precious jewels, made not of matter but of consciousness. The chariot was without wheels but had four tiny pillars underneath. It was shedding rays of celestial light in all directions, as though it contained several suns. It moved without touching the earth. I was overjoyed. As the chariot stopped near me, a god in human shape stepped out. He was wearing a white silk cloth. Sandals inlaid with jewels adorned his feet. Around his waist he wore a girdle, not the sort of leather belt used by modern fashionable people, but one beset with countless gems. He had a sacred thread over his shoulder, a necklace of pearls around his neck, and a bejewelled diadem on his head. His heavenly radiance brightened my face and also the neighbouring mango trees. Luminous rings hung from his ears and he held a shining weapon in his hand. The god looked at me, smiled and then spoke in Sanskrit, the language of gods : रथे उपविश (Sit in the chariot).

Although I did not know Sanskrit well, I somehow understood his meaning and arose at once. As I entered, I was surprised to observe that the chariot, which had appeared to be only a ten-foot square from the outside, was quite spacious inside. It was equipped with all facilities, such as pure water, a small bath chamber and several bed chambers. The cushions inside were strangely beautiful, each inlaid with the rarest jewels that lit up the entire apartment. There was one seat which both bewildered and fascinated me.

The god showed me around his enchanting chariot and finally led me into an outer room. Immediately I felt that the chariot was flying with lightning velocity. I sat in one of the seats. The god occupied his seat opposite, whose two shining jewels were throwing light on me. Soon we reached a wonderful city, full of bushes blooming with colourful and divinely fragrant flowers, trees laden with fruits filled with ambrosial juices, beautiful, murmuring streams, exquisite, warbling birds and various kinds of animals. On one side were blue, white, yellow and black regal swans, while on the other, herds of deer, shining with a golden radiance, frisked around fearlessly. Some of those deer sparkled like emeralds, rubies and sapphires. Herds of cows and calves of noble breeds could also be seen. Breezes were wafting a celestial perfume. I was overwhelmed with delight on beholding such scenes.

The chariot landed outside a city and then moved into it. Its every object showed rare craftsmanship. Even the bricks, stones and mortar of its walls were unearthly. The drains were slender and pretty. I soon discovered that I was roaming in Indra's abode. We were actually in heaven! The silvery cool light with which it glowed was different from that of the sun. This region was not tormented by heat. All the leaves on the trees were always green. Even the ones that had fallen to the ground did not fade. There was a palace situated close to the point of our landing. The entire path lying in front was strewn with flowers. On one side of the pathway stood gods with garlands in their hands, while cn the other, nymphs holding gold salvers adorned for *arati*. As soon as the two of us alighted from the chariot, I was greeted with a shower of flowers.

Then I realised that the god who was with me was none else than Indra, the Lord of heaven. He had ascended to his present eminence as a result of his previous meritorious deeds in a human life during which he was a king. In fact, Indra rules all the worlds. Lights were waved to both of us. All the inhabitants of this city were young, free from sorrow and disease and shining with glorious light. Their bodies, though slim, were healthy. Later, when I visited other parts, accompanied by Indra, I was also welcomed there. All the paths were bedecked with flowers. At every place, we were warmly received with *arati* by clusters of young maidens. When I returned to the palace after visiting various parts of the city, I found a band of classical musicians awaiting me. Incidentally, Indraloka is the virtuous realm where sensuous cravings are fulfilled. As it is dominated by pursuit of enjoyment, it can also be called the 'domain of desire.' While I was looking around in wonder, a necklace of pearls and a garland of flowers were put around my neck. At that very moment, the magnificent flying golden chariot appeared opposite. I took it as a signal for departure. Indra and I mounted it and sat in our respective seats. After a short while, when I returned to Nagad, my meditation ceased. (I would like to remind the reader that I was seeing all these sights in Tandraloka, while sitting in meditation inside my hut).

I opened my eyes, but only to behold the same scene. I closed them again and saw the beautiful sight lingering before my inner eye. As I recollected these visions I was struck with wonder. Then I strolled around for a while until the meditative intoxication ended. I sat quietly and reflected on what I had perceived so that I might remember every detail. Thus Muktananda's meditational pilgrimage continued, bringing him countless experiences.

After my visits to heaven, hell and Nagaloka, I developed full faith in the truth of the scriptures. So far I had considered Self-realisation alone valid and rejected heaven, hell, the world of gods and all that as unreal. But now I was fully convinced that the scriptures were absolutely true; only our understanding of them is deficient. The ancient seers could perceive remote regions and events. They composed the scriptures only after obtaining ominscience through yoga. Hence, their writings are unquestionably valid. In fact, when you can acquire some knowledge of the unseen even by insufficient practice, what mystery could remain concealed from the sages and seers whose sadhana was perfect?

## Vision Of My Own Form

I was now blessed with a new experience. In meditation, as the lights appeared, I began to perceive my own form sitting opposite. Even when my eyes opened, I saw it confronting me. I saw myself re-enact in meditation whatever I had done previously. If I took a stroll in the orange grove, I saw my double also strolling there. This was a new marvel.

I began to miss Gurudev very much. I wondered: When shall I go to him? When will he call me? Just then, three of my friends, Nigudkar Guruji, Jeevanji Desai and Babu Shetty came to meet me. I received from them all the news of Ganeshpuri and proceeded there to have Gurudev's darshan. I stayed there for a few days, after which I was commanded by Gurudev to live in the three-room house constructed by him at Gavdevi. Now my dwelling place was quite close to his. I went for his darshan whenever I felt an urge, at least twice every day, morning and evening, without fail. Sometimes, I also spent a whole night at his abode. In meditation I beheld at times my own form and at times Gurudev's. If I meditated on the river bank, I saw my double even there. I told Gurudev about it. He replied, "Hunh! That's good." Then on reading yogic books, I learned that it is called *pratik-darshan*, the vision of one's own form. It indicates that the body has been completely purified.

## More Experiences

Then I perceived a new light, different from red, white, black and blue ones. I saw many worlds in it. It was a soft saffron colour. Countless light blue sparks shimmered within it. Inside the saffron light, a golden radiance also gleamed. It was exceedingly sweet and loving. It arose from within the quaternity of the four lights described earlier. When I beheld this new light, I became fully alert and vigilant because I had clairvoyant visions in it. In meditation, in the same way as I slipped into Tandraloka, so I penetrated to the lustrous seat of this light; I called it Sarvajnaloka, the World of Omniscience.

The seers who attain this state become omniscient. Our great sages of ancient India had risen to this height through the yoga of meditation. They could also tap this omniscient centre at will during their waking hours. A meditator occasionally reaches this state by grace of the divine Parashakti. Whenever my mind was stabilised in Sarvajnaloka, I could visit many remote worlds. These visions are completely authentic. Sometimes I also foresaw accidents in the outer world, such as a mill catching fire and suffering considerable damage, or a river in flood. These mishaps came to pass without fail. I could not see all this at will, but only by penetrating to Sarvajnaloka in meditation by the grace of Goddess Chiti. In this manner, I saw marvellous scenes in meditative visions.

Some yogis acquire extraordinary powers at this stage. It does not take long to obtain these through meditation. But a true seeker longs only for perfection, being a true child of his Guru. He does not attach any importance to supernatural powers, nor would he reveal them to others.

Each day I meditated on the Blue Pearl and saw many visions in it. When I began to experience bliss during these, strains of celestial music reverberated in my inner ears. At first I heard them in the left ear. In certain books it is stated that if one hears *nada* in the left ear he will die shortly. Several friends warned me solemnly. I replied that death occurs only at its proper hour, appointed by destiny. I continued to meditate longer. I was lovingly meditating on the Blue Pearl. Together with the melodies, I began to hear a very subtle sound in the left ear. My meditation now was deeper than before, because I beheld the lights and I heard music. I enjoyed the mellifluous strains of the *veena*.

One day I wanted to ask Gurudev about *nada*. I always went for his darshan at a fixed time, but that day I went at an irregular hour. I stood before him. I knew that the great, omniscient sage would ask me with a flourish of his head, "What is it?" This is exactly what happened. He then uttered 'hunh' and nodded. I said, "Babaji, they say that it is a premonition of approaching death to hear *nada* in the left ear." Babaji said, "This distinction between the right and the left . . . utterly meaningless, both . . . belong to Rama. Yes, both . . . His. In fact, *nada* does not originate in the ear but . . . inner *akasha* of *sahasrar*." The distinctions of right and left, or front and behind are quite irrelevant. It is the sweet celestial music, the sound arising from *chidakash*, that reverberates within. It cannot be an inauspicious foreboding of death. *Nada* leads to God-realisation. It is an expression of *pashyanti*, a mantra inspired by Chiti. By this *nada* alone, meditating yogis and *jnanis* track the source of their existence. Jnaneshwar Maharaj says नादाचीये पैल्तीरीं, तुरीयाचिये माझे घर। (On the yonder shore, across *nada*, there is situated my abode of *turiya*). Such sublime and auspicious *nada* cannot be an omen of death. It is, on the contrary, a herald of immortal life.

Now I was seeing inner miracles within the Blue Pearl and also hearing heavenly strains. I meditated daily. At this stage I could not take interest in anything except meditation. Once during meditation my eyeballs rolled upwards. Then they became inverted and rested in that position. I saw a firmament full of white lights and heard divine melodies all around. My mind became focussed on this. Immediately, I beheld a gloriously beautiful, luminous Blue Star which was not the Blue

Pearl. Its brilliance was unparalleled. It was similar to the familiar planet, Venus, which shines sometimes in the west in the evening and sometimes in the east before daybreak. This beautiful Star is located in the centre of the upper *akasha* of *sahasrar*. I continued to watch it until my meditation ceased. I came out of *tandra* and began to stroll outside. I went on the hill behind the Gavdevi temple, wondering what that Star was. While I was sitting there a star descended from the sky and then vanished into thin air. It looked exactly like the one that I had perceived in meditation. I could not resolve the mystery. When I meditated again, waves of rapturous delight and love began to stir. That Star and the firmament came into view again. The Star shone steadily.

I now began to see a luminous ball of light repeatedly. This radiance surpassed all the other lights. While perceiving such divine lustre, I made further progress in sadhana. The four lights appeared first in meditation as before. When the Blue Pearl appeared, my mind would converge on it for longer periods and experience immensely joyful repose. The respiratory movement became steady, slowing down progressively. The outgoing breath measured only two finger-lengths from the nose, while the incoming breath reached only the throat, no further, not even the heart. However, I did not pay any special attention to it lest my meditation should be disturbed. I took great care to keep my mind focussed. In this process I inhaled different divine aromas. These were so sublime that in comparison, the perfumes brought by my devotees, even the best ones, paled into insignificance. No external scents can ever compare with these supersensuous smells. I became intoxicated by these fragrances. My mind was submerged in joy. I continued to have this experience for a long time. While inhaling these aromas, my outgoing and incoming breaths became considerably shorter; in other words, their movement slowed down greatly. At that time, a special kind of *pranayama* took place spontaneously. While prana moved gently, such sweet and beautiful love would arise that it felt like a direct, true revelation of God. Love is, indeed, God. For this reason *Narada Bhakti Sutra* (51) says: अनिर्वचनीयं प्रेमस्वरूपम् । (This love can never be adequately described).

The experiences of the subtle levels increased my enthusiasm for meditation all the more. I was in such a wonderful state that I had ecstatic and high experiences in meditation one day which were surpassed by those of the next day. I discovered that inner joy is boundless. Love is ever-growing. One can never reach its utmost limit. With this, I also knew within me that still more lay beyond.

Sometimes, while meditating, I suddenly tuned into a different experience. My eyes gradually rolled up and became centred on the *akasha* of *sahasrar*. Instead of seeing separately, in the state of *bindu-bheda* they saw as one. What a gift of Siddha Yoga! How mighty the power of Kundalini! What one comes to understand only intellectually through the study of the scriptures is directly realised through Siddha Yoga.

## My Visit to Siddhaloka—
## The Realm of the Perfected Ones

The Blue Star appeared again and stood motionless. While gazing into the upper regions of *sahasrar* I visited several worlds. The large Blue Star served as my vehicle. This was not the blue light or Blue Pearl but the Blue Star. Though appearing small, it was large enough to contain me. It transported me to a far-off region. What a beautiful world! Oh! How exquisite! This was the most enchanting of all the worlds I had visited so far. Its beauty is beyond my power of description. In fact, to describe it in words would be a mockery of it. In this sublime world, where the Blue Star had taken me, I saw uncommonly attractive paths. There were forests, caves of varying sizes, flowing springs of pure water, white, blue and green deer and white peacocks. How tranquil its atmosphere! This realm was filled with a soft light, somewhat like that of the rising sun seen through

a blue glass. It had neither a sun nor a moon. Blue light
was spread all over of its own will. The climate of this
region was entirely wholesome and the light enchanting.
As I alighted in this world I experienced such powerful
impulses of Shakti that I intuitively knew I was about
to have the splendid darshan of ancient seers. I began to
move there with the speed of thought! Lo! This was
Siddhaloka! As soon as I arrived there, I began to know
everything.  I saw innumerable Siddhas absorbed in
meditation! Everyone was seated in a different *mudra*.
Some were just sitting quietly. They did not even look
towards me. Some of them had matted locks, others
clean shaven heads, yet others pierced ears.  Some sat
under trees, some on stones and others inside caves. Each
had his own cave, hut or small house of unearthly design.
I saw and recognised those greet seers and sages whom
I had read about in the *Puranas*. As I went a little
further, I saw many yoginis who were sitting steadily in
their *mudras*. I saw Sai Baba of Shirdi. Nityananda Baba
was also there, though in his physical form he was still
at Ganeshpuri.

I roamed about in Siddhaloka for a long time watching
the yoginis and Siddha saints. I was intensely fascinated
by this realm. I had not liked any other realm as much.
It would be wonderful if I could live there. I did not
want to leave. Then I saw a vast lake where golden
lotuses were blooming. As I was returning from there,
I saw the seven sages in a group. On seeing them, I felt
peace, happiness and love. Then I entered a very beautiful forest. I could not recognise the trees growing all
around. While beholding the Siddhas, I also felt a desire
to sit in meditation in the lotus posture.

As soon as I sat down, the Blue Star reappeared. I did
not know why I felt compelled to board it. Who was
controlling me? Immediately, the Star flew me back to
my place of meditation at an enormous velocity.

When I arrived back, the Blue Star pierced into my
*sahasrar*, burst and spread through its vast region. There
was no star before me any longer. Only a honeyed white
light remained. I then passed into Tandraloka, which

was quite close. An unfamiliar Siddha from Siddhaloka appeared and said, "What you saw a short while ago was Siddhaloka, where the liberated saints reside. It is free from hunger, sleep and what you consider to be wakefulness. There one eats joy, drinks joy, dwells in joy and continuously experiences joy. All its objects are joy in different forms. Just as a fish lives and sleeps in water, eats and plays in water, likewise, the inhabitants of Siddhaloka abide in joy. No one can reach there without a Siddha's grace. He alone can go there whose way is the Siddha way, who belongs to the Siddha tradition and who is going to attain full Siddhahood. The Blue Star which took you there, is the only means of transport to that region. It is also the vehicle which carries you to other worlds." After saying this and blessing me, the great saint departed.

I was in Tandraloka in an ecstatic state. I was also highly inspired. Meanwhile, flowers were showered on my head from above. This drew my attention upwards. I saw the same Siddha saint, throwing a huge golden lotus, measuring about two feet in diameter, from the lotus pond towards my head with great force. I was watching the lotus in its descent. It was coming down to the accompaniment of the chant of *Om*, the *udgitha*. It landed on my head with a forceful thud. As I heard the sound, my eyes opened. I was still in Tandraloka. It seemed as if someone had slapped me violently on the head. I saw the golden lotus lying on the floor where it had fallen after striking my head. How entrancing! It was superbly well-formed and what divine fragrance emanated from it! I continued to behold it with surprise and curiosity. I was congratulating myself on my great fortune and also praising the splendours of Kundalini. Then I suddenly became aware of Gurudev's grace. I immediately closed my eyes and bowed to him inwardly. When I opened them again, the lotus had disappeared. O, how strange! What an astonishing occurrence! I can still feel the impact of the lotus striking my head. I unlocked my posture. That session of meditation had ended. I went out and took a stroll. I looked towards the sky once and knelt reverently to the direction in which my Gurudev lived in Ganeshpuri. I sat calmly in the garden, closed my eyes and recollected the meditative experiences, visualising the sights seen in meditation.

After this, as I sat in meditation, some physical movements would take place at first. This was followed by the red aura. If I do not refer to this light sometimes, the reader should not forget it. As day begins at sunrise, so does meditation at the rise of the red aura. It became brighter than before and now shone brilliantly. I felt that the light of the Blue Star that had burst in *sahasrar*, had commingled with the red aura. Or else it was due to the vision of Siddhaloka. This is not improbable. If I went to Kashi, I earned some merit. If I went to Dwarka or Rameshwaram I did not return empty handed. If I went to Ganeshpuri, I experienced bliss. How, then, could my visit to Siddhaloka remain unfruitful? Then the golden lotus had also fallen on my head. The increased brilliance was perhaps due to its touch. Within the divine red aura twinkled countless sparks of the exploded star. By its light, I could see all my nerves, excretory system, gall-bladder and all my inner organs. Then I saw a beautiful light within the red aura moving with great momentum, which was the light of my Sadguru's power of grace. As I gazed at the red aura, it was followed by the thumb-sized white flame, which also shone brighter in the new radiance. Then the black light appeared, with an equally increased glow. Finally, the Blue Pearl appeared, emitting new rays. It was still blue but its brilliance had increased greatly and continued to increase even more. My mind became fixed on its intense radiance. A stream of pure love flowed in my heart. This love was as pervasive as the blue light spreading through all my nerves. Like the blue rays, its waves and eddies leapt and frisked about in the nerves. It also thrilled my sense organs. Along with the Chiti beams, rays of bliss spread through my entire body. While meditating in such blissful love, I passed into Tandraloka.

One day on entering Tandraloka, the significance of my visit to Siddhaloka flashed vividly on me. The

Siddhaloka to which I had journeyed was genuine.
Whoever attains perfection will inhabit this realm
regardless of his religious affiliation. The golden lotus
falling on my head was a gift of its grace.

The Blue Star which had transported me, is situated
in the *sahasrar* of every creature. Its light may vary but
its size is the same in all. Using it as a vehicle, the
individual soul transmigrates after leaving one physical
form. It does not change at all even when the various
physical forms inhabited by the soul are burned, buried
or destroyed. It leaves the dead body along with prana
but stays for eleven days in the place where death occurs.
Afterwards, according to the writ of destiny, it carries
the soul to different worlds with its sinful and virtuous
impressions. This Blue Star is the self-propelled auto-
mobile of the embodied soul. It accompanies the soul
through its reincarnations. But my Star had exploded,
putting an end to births and deaths. How can you be
transported without a means of transport? This pheno-
menon is also known as the piercing of the knot of the
heart. I learned in Tandraloka that all the karmic
impressions of my previous innumerable lives had been
obliterated. As I came upon such knowledge, my state
changed. It is important to note that these experiences
were not under the control of my will but of the inner
Shakti—and the Shakti is supremely free.

### Pitruloka—The World of Ancestors

While describing my experiences, I left out one which
I must relate here. This is my visit to Pitruloka, which
is situated between heaven and Siddhaloka. The same
Blue Star that took me to Siddhaloka carried me to
Pitruloka. I would like to remind you again that I am
not referring to the blue light or Pearl but the Blue Star.
O Siddha students! You and I live in a world of
mortality. Just as our world actually exists, so does
Pitruloka. This I am stating from direct personal
experience.

That is a world of its own kind. There are various

orders of ancestors in that realm. I have actually seen them. In the worlds of heaven, serpents and the moon, all the inhabitants are equally provided with pleasures. This equality does not hold here. We find the same inequalities as those prevalent on earth, namely class divisions of more and less rich, more and less virtuous. Nevertheless, there is more happiness in that world than in ours. Here I saw some old men, acquaintances of my childhood.

It is undoubtedly true that the funeral rites such as *tarpan* and charitable distribution to others which we perform, subtly affect the state of our ancestors. For they eat what we offer them from here. That they partake of our deeds of nobility and charity and bless their descendants is also entirely true. Therefore it is necessary to please the inhabitants of Pitruloka through ceremonies like *tarpan*. O Siddha students! You should not doubt this even in the least. The foods that we offer them in such rites certainly reach them through the power of mantras, but in subtle forms. Chitshakti, which is one throughout, transports them from here to there by means of mantric vehicles. I shall illustrate this by an example from our modern life. Suppose, you have a friend in America. Although America is far away from India, he says to you over the telephone: "I have remitted so many dollars to you through my bank. You can get them from its branch in your city." And you receive the dollars, beyond a shadow of a doubt. This is a merely material transaction carried out through physical sound over the telephone, a material instrument. You never question this. Why should you then doubt that the offerings made on earth are delivered in finer forms to your ancestors in Pitruloka by means of mantras?

In this context, I am reminded of a story relating to Eknath Maharaj. I once doubted its authenticity. In fact, it is not at all desirable to question the characters of great men, their noble qualities and extraordinary actions. My doubt was an infection caught from others. One should not doubt the ways of Siddhas. Do not judge their actions by the criteria of vice or virtue. Each action of theirs is sacred, being divinely inspired. Sri Eknath Maharaj looked upon all with perfect equality. He had fully realised God. He saw one Principle pervading forests and multitudes, the high and the low, the acceptable and the rejectable, saints and sinners. Siddhas do not recognise the distinctions of name, form and shape, seeing only the true reality everywhere. I shall first illustrate this by another story.

There was a shepherd called Ramja. He was fabulously rich. He possessed gold statues of his deity, Khandoba, and His mount for worship. The mount of the deity was a horse, much bigger in size than the deity. The saying of great saints that Laxmi, the goddess of wealth, is inconstant, is true. Nothing endures here. Times change. Ramja's condition also changed. He lost his wealth and was reduced to beggary. Metaphorically speaking, one may say that wealth and destitution are real brothers, two sons of the same mother. Similarly pleasure and pain, fame and notoriety live together, being brothers. They love each other greatly, so much so that they never like to separate or forget each other. What happens is that sometimes we are greeted by the elder and at other times by the younger brother. When the elder welcomes us, we obtain wealth, power, riches or a kingdom. But when the younger tells the older, "Sire, please take a rest for a while. Let me serve in your place," we are visited by want, beggary, misfortune and misery.

This is exactly what happened with Ramja. The elder brother went away to take a rest and the younger came to greet him. Ramja became utterly poor. He could not even make both ends meet. The people said, "O brother Ramja! Why must you suffer such privation? Why don't you sell your gold images after begging forgiveness of the Lord for it? Purchase sheep again and run your business. You can earn money once again and get new statues. You may then install them, worship them and hold an open feast for all the *brahmins*, *sadhus*, saints, and all the poor, the blind and the lame. If your business runs well, you will be able to perform noble deeds."

Even one's thoughts become mean in poverty. One

becomes poor not only in gold or money but also in noble thoughts. Ramja accepted the suggestion. He picked up the images of Khandoba and His mount in his cloth and went to a jewellery shop. The jeweller asked him, "O Ramja brother, what's the matter?"

Ramja took out the images of Lord Khandoba and His horse and said, "I have come to sell these. I am forced, O wealthy sire, to do this, since I am in need of money. How much will you give me for them?"

The jeweller weighed them. While the statue of Lord Khandoba weighed only one pound that of His horse weighed three pounds. Those days, one pound of gold cost only one thousand rupees. The jeweller said, "Ramja brother, I shall give you Rs. 1,000 for your God and Rs. 3,000 for His horse."

This enraged Ramja. "Oh, you rich fool, have you gone out of your mind?" said Ramja, reddening with anger. "You are valuing my Lord at only Rs. 1,000 and His horse at Rs. 3,000. Have you lost your senses?"

The jeweller said, "Oh, Ramja, you are being very stupid. You might look upon the statues as the Lord and His mount, but to me, they are both lumps of gold and I am valuing them according to their weights. If you want to sell them, I will buy them. Otherwise, be on your way."

Sri Eknath Maharaj, a high Siddha, had this equal vision. He was aware only of gold, not its different forms. For him, one God pervaded everything in the universe. He was not conscious of the differences of high and low, old and young, caste, community or status. "The Lord is the universe," was his view of life. He practised complete equality. One day an untouchable girl came to him and said with great love and devotion, "O Baba! They say that God Himself draws water for you, but I can neither see nor call Him. O Eknath Baba! You are my only deity. Please come to my hut to partake of our plain and simple fare. I have listened to your stories and in one parable, you say that great saints are as holy as gods. Please, Baba, please eat with us today. I have come to invite you." She thus made her humble request.

Eknath Maharaj accepted it. He went to her house to take food and ate the simple *chapatis* cooked by her. All the villagers noticed this. They began to discuss it heatedly, as was to be expected.

They said, "Did you see that? That Eknath fellow, in spite of being a *brahmin* and devotee of the Lord, took food at a sweeper's. How shocking! He is defiled. From now on, no *brahmin* must visit such a fellow who has fallen from his duty." And all the *brahmins* ex-communicated Eknath Maharaj!

This did not at all affect him. He was as blissful as ever. His attitude was that one should always welcome prosperity or misfortune equally. He remained even-minded and unruffled. The villagers became hostile and began to persecute him with curses and insults. Eknath did not take it ill at all. This saint had an outlook of perfect equality in spite of being a householder:

ममता नहीं सुतदार में, नहिं देह में अभिमान है।
निन्दा प्रशंसा एक सी, सम मान अरु अपमान है॥
जो भोग आते भोगता, होता न विषयासक्त है।
निर्वासना निर्द्वन्द्व सो, इच्छा बिना ही मुक्त है।
सब विश्व अपना जानता, या कुछ न अपना मानता।
क्या मित्र हो क्या शत्रु, सब को एक सम सन्मानता॥
सब विश्व का है भक्त जो, सब विश्व जिसका भक्त है।
निर्हेतु सबका सुहृद सो, इच्छा बिना ही मुक्त है॥
माया नहीं, काया नहीं, बंध्या रचा यह विश्व है।
नहिं नाम ही, नहिं रूप ही, केवल एक ईश ही परिपूर्ण है॥
जो ईश्वर है वही जीव है, वही सब जग का परमात्मतत्त्व है।
ऐसा जिसे निश्चय हुआ, वह इच्छा बिना ही मुक्त है॥

(Unattached to his wife and children, not identifying
    Self with body,
 Accepting praise or blame, honour or insult equally,
 Enjoying pleasures, as they come but not seeking
    them, not a sense-slave,
 Without craving or conflict—such is the liberated one.
 Either accepting the entire universe or nothing as his
    own,

Honouring everyone, friend or foe, alike,
Worshipping the whole universe, worshipped by the
   whole universe,
Wishing everyone well without selfish motive—such
   is the liberated one.
Neither *maya* nor the body is. The universe is unreal,
   as a sterile woman's child,
Names and forms do not exist. God alone unfolds His
   fullness.
The individual Self is the same as the Universal. God
   is the divine Essence of the world.
Holding this conviction, such is the liberated one.)

Thus Ekanath Maharaj was always full of joy. At his
home, each day he conducted religious discussions,
devotional singing and meditation. He sat in bliss, moved
in bliss and slept in bliss. To him the whole world was
an expression of bliss. God is bliss. The universe created
by Him cannot be otherwise. The eye that can perceive
the world as an unfolding of divine joy can only be
obtained by the Guru's grace. In this manner, Eknath
Maharaj used to live joyfully.

In a few days, the time of the year sacred to the
ancestors came. I have already told you that our offerings
do reach our ancestors living in Pitruloka. It is necessary
to perform the various rites related to them, as we, the
descendants of our forefathers, owe a great debt to them.
We must never forget that our parents give us their vital
fluids, blood and even their food. They eat insufficiently
so that their children may have their fill. They sacrifice
their sleep to ensure that their children enjoy sound
sleep. If some delectable gifts come, they first serve them
to their children and take only the little that is left over.
What sacrifices do parents not make for their children?
Therefore, we shall always be indebted to our ancestors.
It is essential for a wise son to make ritualistic offerings
to his ancestors. According to religious tradition, on such
an occasion, *sannyasis*, *brahmins* and other guests are
invited, feasted courteously, and offerings are made to
the ancestors. Eknath Maharaj also invited all the
*brahmins* to a feast on the day consecrated to his

ancestors. But not even one turned up because Eknath had taken food at an untouchable's. So then he invoked their ancestors. They all actually came from Pitruloka to partake of the feast! How amazing! After seeing my own ancestors in Pitruloka, I became convinced of the truth of the story. Pitruloka actually exists.

In this manner, I visited numerous worlds. Each day, I had new experiences in meditation. As my mind stabilised on the Blue Pearl, I would regain Witness-consciousness. This can be considered to be the state of *samadhi*, but in it one remains fully conscious. The respiratory movement slows down without ceasing completely. This is the *samadhi* on the Siddha Path. It is not a state of dark, ignorant, inert absorption, lacking awareness, but the one in which the Witness-consciousness is continually present. The realm of consciousness is that of knowledge. Therefore, there should be the Witness-consciousness in true *samadhi*.

I always began my meditation first by bowing to the four directions, considering them to be forms of Parashakti as well as the Guru. I sat down on my seat, regarding it as the abode of Shakti and also that of the Guru. Never did I take the mat or velvet sheet underneath for what it merely appeared to be. I felt that Chiti pervaded above and below—everywhere, in fact. I bowed inwardly to all things and creatures and then sat. While meditating thus, I continued to sway in divine bliss. As meditation ceased, I would regain my external consciousness. Relaxing my posture a little, I would gently rub my legs with my hands. When I rose up from meditation, I reverently touched my seat and bowed to it. Then I would take a stroll.

Even on coming out after meditation, I continued to bask in the radiance of love which had spread in meditation through my 72,000 nerves. I was highly intoxicated. This light, charged with great energy, was romping blissfully in each of my blood corpuscles. This was a new madness, the madness of love, different from other kinds of madness I had experienced before. It seemed as if the currents of love, by flowing throughout my body, were showing me that I had been blessed by Parashakti.

I continued to meditate like this every day. I would meditate in the morning, at noon and again in the evening. One verse of Tukaram would come to my mind: तुका म्हणे दिनरजनीं हाचि धंदा। (Tuka says that this is his only occupation the whole day and night). A businessman, an officer, a servant—each follows a daily routine: waking up in the morning, taking a bath, breakfast, going to his office with his lunch packet, office work, closing the office after finishing work and returning home. If he were asked what he did, he would reply: the same as I do everyday—going and returning, working, eating, drinking, and sleeping at night. The case was similar with Swami Muktananda. He meditated in the morning and meditated in the evening. When meditation ceased, he would work in the garden, watering the plants. He meditated again at night and then retired for sleep.

## Nadaloka—The Domain of Celestial Melodies

Now I attained a new state in meditation, which is known as Nadaloka. There are many kinds of *nada*, some of which resemble the rumble of an ocean, the roll of thunder, the murmur of a brook, the rattle of a fast-moving train, the drone of an airplane coming from a distance and the crackle of a funeral pyre. I began to hear all these various sounds. At different times I listened to the full-throated singing of the divine name by a large group of devotees, the battering of kettle drums, the beats of a *mridang*, the echoing strains of a conch, the sonorous peals of large bells suggesting the *udgitha* chant, and the sweet, resonant vibrations of a *veena* and other stringed instruments. Off and on I heard the buzz of insects such as beetles and bees, the cries of peacocks and the songs of cuckoos echoing in a forest after sunrise. Sometimes the melodies which I had perceived in Indraloka and various other worlds re-echoed. And at other times many different indistinct sounds reverberated in the *akasha* of my heart.

Now I began to apprehend all ten grades of *nada* :

'chin-chin,' 'chini-chini,' peals of bells, strains of conch,
quiverings of *veena*, clash of cymbals, lilt of flute, beats
of *mridang*, roll of kettle drums, and roar of thunder. I
would float on the waves of this new musical ecstasy.
Because of this, at times I could not sleep for a whole
fortnight. It appears that sleep and *nada* are somewhat
incompatible. It was, perhaps, for this reason that sleep
turned away from me. But I did not feel any consternation at this loss nor was my mind perturbed. Usually
insomnia affects the mind or body adversely, but nothing
of the kind happened in my case. In spite of the loss
of sleep I remained active and joyful as before. I did
not seem to need sleep. However I was eating much less.
My body also looked somewhat slim.

During this phase of heavenly music, a yogi acquires
the art of dancing. Sometimes I danced at night on the
hill for hours on end. How divine my feeling then! I
would be the sole witness of my own dancing. I did not
let anybody else see it because I felt quite shy. The
artistic dance movements increased my appetite and
loosened my limbs. I wondered how boys and girls, men
and women, could dance shamelessly in public. I had
still not overcome my modesty. Did this indicate a
deficiency within me?

While enjoying the divine sounds, I also examined them
carefully. Some seekers think that *nada* arises in the
right or left ear. But the fact is that these rapturous
sounds do not originate in the ear but in the *akasha* of
*sahasrar*. From there they can be heard in either ear.
There arose a divine freshness in the *akasha* of my head.
My memory was enhanced to such a degree that I
distinctly remembered all those who came for darshan
and the different offerings they made. Sometimes I
thought that if students could gain such retentive power,
they would not need to take elaborate notes.

I recollected one verse of Jnaneshwar, a perfect Master
of Kundalini Yoga: हेचि आत्मप्रभा नित्य नवी । (This light of the
soul is ever-new). Muktananda says similarly, the light
of meditation is ever-new. I had innumerable experiences.
Though I meditated every day, I did not feel in the least

bored nor did my sadhana pall. On the contrary, I
applied myself with greater zeal and earnestness. I
behaved like a man who begins to run when he finds his
destination quite close. I was hearing countless celestial
sounds each day. Several times I listened to the sweet
flute strains. How enchanting and magical! I had heard
some songs about the irresistible appeal of Lord Krishna's
flute. One milkmaid says: "O Lord! Stop playing on
your flute. For your tunes absorb me so much that I
cannot attend to my work. I do not even remember my
children. I lose the will to return home. O Master! We
have to go home. O! Why can't you put your flute away
for a while? The notes are so sweet and entrancing that
our legs do not turn homeward. I have to go and feed
my children. Please stop playing! I have to serve food
to my husband. My parents-in-law must be waiting for
me. Please, O, please stop playing on your flute." In this
humble manner the milkmaid entreats the Lord.

My dear Siddha students! When I listened to the flute
strains in *sahasrar* I lost consciousness even of Tandraloka. I did not know where the inner Witness vanished.
Nor did I know in which region I lost myself or what
happened while hearing the sweet tune. Is it surprising,
then, that the milkmaids forgot themselves when they
actually heard supremely blissful Lord Krishna playing
on His flute? You should not have the slightest doubt in
this matter. The milkmaids, who really heard the divine
flute, were themselves love personified—rays of the sun
of Lord Krishna—the love which should be remembered
every morning. When a yogi can become so engrossed in
the flute notes echoing in his *sahasrar*, what must have
been the condition of the milkmaids?

I sometimes danced, sometimes swayed, and sometimes
became lost in the *nada*, being intoxicated with love. The
*nada* is indeed the Absolute Reality. It forms a kind of
sound-body of Sri Guru Nityananda. It is the vibrating
current, set in motion by Kundalini. About the *nada*,
the scriptures say: आदौ भगवान् शब्दराशिः । (God originally
manifested Himself as sound). I perceived God with
these sounds. They represented the last phase of my

dynamic Kundalini awakening. Thus while hearing *nada*, my mind would converge on its source. I witnessed the centre which, activated by *nada*, emits divine sparks. All my senses were drawn towards it. Even my tongue rushed in that very direction. My body responded to whatever variety of *nada* I heard with a corresponding quiver that was mildly painful. Sweating profusely, I felt as though I would collapse. My head trembled violently. I felt as if a gentle fire were burning in my body. Sometimes a tiny drop of nectar dripped from the upper *akasha*. At other times different sensations of taste were released from there—salty, sour, bitter, and astringent. Sometimes, ambrosial milk trickled through my palate from Nadaloka. It entered my gastric fire and then flowed to my 72,000 nerves. Consequently, many subtle ailments of the body vanished. However hard I might work I did not feel tired. While enjoying these unearthly melodies and knowing that they are *Shabda-Brahman*, I directly experienced It in them. My dynamic Kundalini felt delighted on meeting Her husband in the form of *nada*. The currents of Her joy flowed through my entire body. And Muktananda would begin to dance. As the waves of *nada* played within me, my mind also became sharp and agile.

While listening to the Lord's melodious flute tunes, I began to comprehend mysterious matters. I was hearing *nada* for longer durations. I heard it even while engaged in routine activities. In fact I perceived it at all times— coming, going, sleeping and eating. When I felt angry, *nada* became louder! The longer I listened to the flute strains, the richer my voice became. Thus I would hear various kinds of *nada* and benefit from their characteristic effects. When I heard the thump of a kettle drum, I would obtain clairvoyant vision and see distant things. At times, while sitting in my own room, I could see what was happening in another. Sometimes it happened that I entered a room just in time to catch somebody redhanded while he was indulging in some secret activity, as though I had been informed of it. However, I would tell him I had been called by such and such a person. In this manner my meditation grew like a waxing moon, as I heard the beats of a kettle drum and imbibed its influence.

Finally, I heard the ultimate *nada*, namely the rolling thunder, which is the most significant and powerful. It is the celestial cow which grants the desired fruit to a yogi. When it emerges, the upper *akasha* trembles with its impact. For a few days, the aspirant is not himself on account of this continually thundering sound. This is the *nada* which leads to *samadhi*, the goal of yoga. From within it alone, a yogi can hear the *udgitha*, the *Om* chant. Then he discovers that *Om* is self-begotten. It is not the mental product of a sage, like sectarian mantras. Nor was it composed by the head of a monastery. It is born of itself, arising of its own accord in the *akasha* of *sahasrar*, not under alien inspiration. As the yogi hears this heavenly chant he is transported with delight.

Sometimes I disregarded my rule of secrecy and spoke to people about it. They heard me with love; but to feel grand and important, they passed it on to others, saying that Swami Muktananda had heard this or that *nada*. They even communicated it to Baba Nityananda. This was enough to infuriate him. The next day, when I went for his darshan, he spoke thunderingly: "What a fool! . . . Should . . . talk like this? . . . Remember . . . disclosing such secrets . . . yogi loses what he has attained . . . suffers. . . ." Such words of displeasure would retard my progress for several days. I have told you repeatedly that in Siddha Yoga, the Guru's grace alone matters. Obedience to the Guru's command is the sole significant factor. The Guru's displeasure impedes sadhana and delays attainment of perfection.

In this manner, I progressed in meditation each day. Now my mind was completely centred on the Blue Pearl in meditation. I had penetrated through the different bodies, through the red aura to the white flame, through the white flame to the black light and now through the black light to the Blue Pearl. I beheld a golden halo, mingled with saffron, surrounding the Pearl. As I meditated more and more, its brilliance increased pro-

portionately. The next day I would find it more luminous
than on the previous day. Despite the steady increase of
its glow and my joyful and enthusiastic response, I felt
that perfection was still some distance away. My inner
heart told me that there was still more to experience.
Though peaceful and contented, I felt that I had still
further to go.

Now I want to emphasise a fact so that a meditator
may have unshakable faith and believe with his whole
being in the power of Chitshakti and the actual presence
of Gurudev within him. He should think that just as his
nose, ears, eyes, tongue and face actually exist, so also
his Guru actually dwells within him. Dear Siddha
students! Ponder this truth carefully. Have full faith in
the Guru and the divine power of grace. Think it over.
When a doctor gives an injection, the injected medicine
spreads throughout the entire body. You may have
sometimes received injections which immediately heat up
the blood. The small pill of an *ayurvedic* physician expels
a certain ailment from the body. Consider how potent
is its influence, which can permeate each of your bodily
nerves and cells and eradicate traces of disease from
them. This is your everyday experience. Similarly, when
the Sadguru initiates you through his look, word, thought,
company or physical touch, he himself enters your being
directly or indirectly with Parashakti that sports in
supreme bliss and uproots ignorance, the basic cause of
all afflictions. He dwells within you from head to foot,
entering your seven bodily components, ten sense organs
and five sheaths, assuming their respective characters.
When this is so, it cannot be difficult for you to receive
guidance from within and attain realisation. If you turn
away from the wisdom and love of the Guru, from faith
and obedience to him, you are actually denying him.
Muktananda says truly that the Guru is yours without
reservation, but you haven't become fully his. He is not
at all far from you, but you withdraw from him. For this
reason, the ever-new inner visions are delayed.

I had unswerving faith in my Guru. Wherever I went,
I did not forget to take his photo. If I went for a walk,

it was with me. If I sat to eat, it was with me. If I slept, it slept with me. Not only this, but I even kept one in my bathroom, regardless of people's opinion.

I received a message from Gurudev or the inner light, in other words from Sarvajnaloka, described earlier: "O Muktananda! Even though you have become liberated as a result of your vision of the Blue Pearl, and experienced transcendental bliss, you have not yet achieved perfection. For this you will have to penetrate the Blue Pearl!" To me this was a true command of Goddess Chiti. I began to meditate more intensely. The Blue Pearl stayed for longer durations, during which its radiance increased steadily. It would also reveal its ever-new ways and miracles. Numerous questions arose in my mind: What is the real nature of the Blue Pearl? Is it just blue light or is it the Blue-throated One? Is it blue-complexioned Sri Nityananda, or the Blue Goddess, Uma Shakti Kundalini? I perceived the Pearl approaching closer. As it expanded and increased in radiance, so did Muktananda rise higher and still higher; Muktananda opened, Muktananda was transformed, Muktananda became pervasive and realised what he really was. As the Blue Pearl varied its rhythm, so did Muktananda in unison. Now my faith in it became still firmer. Just as one feels in relation to the parts of one's body: 'They are mine,' or even 'They are me,' I felt so in relation to the Blue Pearl.

## The Vision of the Lord in His Blue Form

O my dear Siddha students! Now a new event took place. Listen to me with love. Do not ignore what you hear. One day I was meditating joyfully. I worshipped Sadguru Sri Nityananda, who is one with Mother Kundalini Shakti: "O Gurudev! You are in the east, you are in the west, you are in the north and in the south. O Sadguru! You are above and you are below. O dear Sri Guru! You are in my eyes, you are in my ears and nose and mouth. O grace-bestowing Lord! You are in my throat and arms and chest. You are in my back and abdomen. O Mother! O Father! You are in my thighs

and legs and feet. O my beloved Baba! You are in me.
I am in you. It is you alone who determine the difference
between our forms and shapes." As I invoked the Guru
the red aura arose, shimmering in its splendour. Other
lights followed. The white flame—the black light—the
Blue Pearl. My heart throbbed with joy. In *sahasrar*, the
thundering *nada*, the great friend of yogis, rolled and
roared. And then a most wondrous miracle occurred. I
should not talk about it but my Guru is urging me. At
this time I am unable to write. My hand does not move.
My pen has stopped. It is difficult to even keep my eyes
open. Only my lips and tongue are moving. Perhaps
Nityananda is moving them by force. As I am not
allowed to talk about it, Bhagawan Nityananda himself
is speaking. My dear Yande is writing. He has surrendered himself to Baba Nityananda. For this reason he
is writing.

Lo! The glorious shining Blue Pearl, as it moved closer
to me, began to expand with its innumerable lustrous,
inner rays. It became an oval and continued to grow into
a human shape. I was beholding its expansion with
amazement. The oval finally assumed a human form.
Supernal radiance shone forth from it. For a while I lost
consciousness. Who knows what hapened to Tandraloka?
Where did Sarvajnaloka disappear? The intuitive intelligence, which had so far disclosed all the secrets, also
vanished. Muktananda no longer knew who he was. As
self-awareness vanished, he also lost awareness of others.
When there is no seer, sights dissolve. When there is no
listener, sounds melt. Smells evaporate in the absence
of an inhaler. For a while I was conscious of nothing.
However, I was still in meditation. My lotus posture,
facing north, was firmly locked. Once again I saw a
shining human form in place of what was an oval. As
Muktananda regained self-consciousness, Tandraloka returned. Intuitive intelligence returned. My extraordinary
memory, always reporting on my inner states, also came
back.

The oval-shaped Blue Pearl stood before me. Its
radiance began to wane. Then I discerned a blue human

figure within it. How enchantingly beautiful! His blue form shimmered and sparkled! His body was not a product of human fluids, the seven components. Nay, it was composed of the blue rays of Chiti which, according to Tukaram Maharaj, condense into the eye lotion that grants divine vision. He was a mass of pure Awareness, the Life of Muktananda's inner life. He was the inner essence of Nityananda. He was the same as the playful, conscious Mother Kundalini. The Divine Being stood before me shining and scintillating. What a marvellous form! How captivating His eyes! Ah! How sharp His nose! How fascinating His ears and earrings! What tresses of hair! What a noble forehead! He had no beard. He wore a crown inlaid with the rarest jewels, made of Chiti, not of matter. How long and manly His arms and fingers and nails! All these were blue. How beautiful and soft His clothes! How long and shapely His legs! How well-formed His toes! I continued to gaze and gaze at Him in sheer amazement, head to foot, foot to head, without blinking my eyes.

He came close to me, uttered an aspirated sound and made a gesture not quite intelligible to me. "Say something," said He. What could I say? I was absorbed in beholding Him. He went round me once and then stood again. He looked towards me and made a sign with His eyes. Finally, He spoke, "I can see with any part of my body. I see with the eyes, also with the nose. I have eyes on all sides." He lifted His foot slightly and added, "I can also see with this foot. I see all things in all directions. I have tongues everywhere. I speak not only with tongues, but also with hands and feet. I have ears on all sides. I can hear with the whole body." Thus He was speaking and I was listening raptly. "I walk with the legs and also with the head. I can walk in any way. I can traverse any stretch of distance in an instant. I walk without feet and hold without hands. I speak without tongue and see without eyes. I am the farthest as well as the nearest. I am the body in all bodies, yet I am different from the body." Having said this, He uttered something more that was heard by Nityananda and cannot be written here. "This very path is the Siddha path, the true way," He added. He upraised one hand in the gesture of blessing. I was utterly astounded. Right before my eyes, the blue oval which had expanded to a height of six feet, began to shrink. It became smaller and smaller until it was the Blue Pearl again.

Waves upon waves of utter bliss were soaring within. As I recollected the grace of Gurudev Nityananda and divine Chiti Kundalini, I floated into Tandraloka, where I at once understood that I had beheld the Blue Person who grants the final beatific vision. He is also called the Unmanifest Being by whose blessing one realises the highest Truth. After bestowing His benediction on me, He merged into the Blue from which He had emerged. And then my meditation ceased.

How wonderful the innumerable visions seen in meditation! How sublime man's worth! How glorious the Blue Pearl! How bountiful the Lord of meditation! Man is a magnificent being. Man is exalted. O Muktananda! You are sublime. You are infinite. You are marvellous. As I thus congratulated man and visualised once again what I had seen, I was beside myself with joy. Now the conviction that 'I am the Self' became firm as a rock. I was blessed with full faith in 'I am That' or 'That am I.' God is in me, I am in God—this truth began to be realised.

I felt certain that the Blue One was the Divine Person described in the *Gita* (XIII-13) :

सर्वतः पाणिपादं तत् सर्वतोऽक्षिशिरोमुखम् ।
सर्वतः श्रुतिमल्लोके सर्वमावृत्य तिष्ठति ॥ १३ ॥

(He had hands and feet everywhere. He has eyes, head and face on all sides. He has ears everywhere. He knows all and exists, pervading all).

सर्वेन्द्रियगुणाभासं सर्वेन्द्रियविवर्जितम् ।
असक्तं सर्वभृच्चैव निर्गुणं गुणभोक्तृ च ॥ १४ ॥

(*Gita*, XIII-14)

(He has all the qualities of the senses and yet is without

any of the senses, unattached and yet supporting all, free from the three attributes of manifestation and yet enjoying them). He dwells in *sahasrar* subtly performing all sense-functions. Though He is apprehended by the senses, He is beyond them. He is, in fact, devoid of senses. Although, while in the body, He identifies himself with it exclaiming, "I am Muktananda, I am, I am," He remains perfectly detached. He supports all. By taking care of every cell of the 72,000 nerves and imparting vitality to vital fluids, essential nourishment to blood, He sustains all. He transcends the *gunas*, yet enjoys them while residing in *sahasrar*. If He is given food, He eats it. If He is offered flowers, He receives them. If clothes, He wears them. If one bows to Him, He accepts the obeisance. In spite of the devotees' wrong notion, "We are giving to Baba," He takes the offerings.

बहिरन्तश्च भूतानामचरं चरमेव च ।
सूक्ष्मत्वात्तदविज्ञेयं दूरस्थं चान्तिके च तत् ॥ १५ ॥

(*Gita,* XIII-15)

(Without and within [all] beings, the unmoving and also the moving; because of Its subtlety, unknowable; and near and far away is That). He is not comprehended because He is subtle, though He pervades the outer and inner being of all movable and immovable creatures— men and demons, birds and animals, insects and germs. Though it is thought that He dwells far far away, He lives in the centre of *sahasrar* which is so close. This Supreme Person appears to be different in different men, races, actions, names, forms, times and spaces, yet remains undifferentiated. He lives as man in man, bird in bird, cow in cow, horse in horse, male in male and female in female. In short, He becomes all and yet remains above all. He gives His strength to all beings like a mother, maintains their lives and finally gathers them all into Himself. He is the Light of lights; all lights derive light from Him. He is absolutely free from darkness. He knows everything. If it were not so, how could Muktananda recognise the Blue Person? In fact, I had envisioned in the Blue Pearl, Blue Mahadeva, Blue Nityananda, who is the supreme object of knowledge, attainable in higher states of meditation only by Kundalini's grace. He is accessible only to the superior insight of Sarvajnaloka. The Blue Person dwells in His fullness within *sahasrar* and within the heart.

O aspirants! He exists within your Blue Pearl. But do not imagine that you have attained perfection just by your vision of the Pearl. The Unmanifest Being is the supreme mystery, the goal of the Siddha way. This is not a topic that can ever be expressed in speech or writing. By His grace alone comes the final realisation. Siddha students would, perhaps, know why I have recorded the inexpressible. I have been driven to speak about it and dear Yande has taken it down.

In spite of all these experiences, I fell slightly short of utter contentment. Now I had risen to a still higher stage of meditation. The Blue Person, perceived for a short while, is also known as the ball of light. Yogis apprehend Him who contains the entire world within Himself, within the Blue Pearl in meditation. I was now meditating on Him alone. I remembered only Him. He was the sole dweller in my mind. I meditated at all hours. In meditation, I beheld the same Blue Pearl, ambrosial and radiant, in manifold variations. I was becoming more absorbed in it, since its lustre became more dazzling each moment. I was meditating in *sahasrar*. I was also hearing the roaring divine thunder. This *nada* overwhelmed me with joy to such a degree that the various former cravings of the mind were scattered and ejected into the unknown. While enjoying this music I would for a moment attain oneness with the Pure, the Absolute.

An aspirant should bear in mind that after his Kundalini Shakti is awakened by the Guru's grace, She attends to all his needs. She is the treasure of inner knowledge, with Her seat in *muladhar*. The more he seeks refuge in Kundalini and in the Guru, the greater their protection of him. He should remind himself again and again how important it is to submit exclusively, without the least reservation, to the Guru and the Shakti. When I call Her the divine power of grace, he should take it to mean that

She is Kundalini, She is the Guru and also Parashiva. Just as the sewing needle pierces cloth and moves along upwards, likewise, Kundalini Shakti moves upwards from *muladhar* into the *brahmarandhra*, piercing all the *chakras* in the *sushumna*. She permeates all his 72,000 nerves. Then the aspirant certainly experiences in his body Her soft, tender, joyous, divine touch. This touch can also be felt as hard, depending upon his temperament. In that case, he will feel as though his entire body were on fire. Nevertheless, both the softness and the hardness of Her touch are equally divine.

As meditation in the *sahasrar* becomes stabilised, accompanied by rolls of thunder therein, the tongue curls upwards into the soft palate and remains there. As a result, the seeker begins to sip divine juice. Sometimes, while the tongue is in this position, the cool dew of the moon is released. As he enjoys it, he is filled with wonder. He practises sadhana with greater zeal in order to drink more of the nectar. There are many varieties of this fluid, tasting like butter, milk, ghee, buttermilk and honey. This flow begins when the seeker's mind is merged in the *ajna* chakra and he perceives his own soul as the wickless flame shining in the space between the eyebrows. It destroys many internal diseases. If the prana becomes stabilised on the same spot, divine aromas issue. As he inhales them, he ascends to loftier planes.

After the vision of the Blue Person, my mind would converge on the upper *akasha* in meditation, where I discerned glowing vapours enfolding the Blue Pearl in their centre. This brightness intensified each day. It is said that the radiance of *sahasrar* is derived from the Blue Pearl. Each time in meditation, the awareness, "I am the Soul" arose. Sometimes I found that the Blue Pearl kept moving in and out of *sahasrar* for a short while.

### Fear Of Death

I saw a new marvel in meditation. I would pass into a state in which my eyes rolled upwards. Both my eyelids were drawn up. My pupils were focussed above on the Blue Pearl in the centre of *sahasrar*. My neck tilted backwards. The ball of light already described, lies in *sahasrar*. One day, its light was suddenly released. And lo! Not one or two thousand but a million suns blazed. The brilliance was too dazzling for me to endure: I lost my self-possession. It was no longer in my power to stop meditating or rise up from my posture. Nor could I open or close my eyes at will. The brilliance had enthralled me! While staring at it, I became unconscious. As I began to recover, I exclaimed, "O Mother, O Lord Sadguru, save me! Save me!" I was terrified of death. My prana ceased. My mind functioned no longer. I felt that my prana was passing out of my body. "O Lord! O Sadguru!" While exclaiming thus and chanting *Om* . . . *Om* . . . , I lost all power over my body. Like a dying man, whose mouth is agape and arms outstretched, I emitted a strange noise and collapsed on the floor. In a moment, I involuntarily passed urine. I lost consciousness completely.

I lay for some time in that unfamiliar state of unconsciousness. Then, like a man awaking from sleep, I got up after about an hour and a half and felt amused, saying to myself: "I died a short while ago, but I am alive again!" I stood up feeling deep calm, love and joy. I realised that I had experienced death and become immensely terrified while confronted with the blazing glitter of a million suns. Now that I knew what it meant to die, death ceased to have any more terror. I became completely fearless. This is the state of emancipation from individual existence. Since then my courage has multiplied a thousandfold and I have not known what fear is. Now I am not afraid of anyone. I have no anxiety as to what may happen, nor do I anticipate anybody's actions or reactions. The very centre of fear has been annihilated. I have attained supreme fearlessness.

## The Eternal Blue Of Consciousness

Full awareness of Self began to spring spontaneously

from within. Formerly, the thought "I am the body" had
dominated, but now I was becoming increasingly conscious that "I am Shiva." My joyous ecstasy became more
intense. Memories of the vision of the Blue Person and
His blessing pulsed in my mind. I felt more and more
that He is within me; nay, "I am verily He." I rejoiced
in being drunk with ethereal music, in the intensity of
love permeating my entire being and in the fearlessness
bestowed by the ball of divine light. I advanced in
meditation, experiencing the Self more and more. Yet
intuition said that still more lies beyond and I felt a
corresponding lack, which I could never have overcome
myself. The only alternative was total surrender to
Gurudev, who is the inner Shakti. However, I continued
to meditate. Each day I saw the ball of divine light and
the Blue Pearl within it and listened to the thundering
*nada*.

Sometimes, the omniscient Blue Person flashed like
lightning. Each day I became firmer in the attitude: "It
is the light of my own Soul that pervades the entire
universe." Though I could not directly see the inner
Self, I saw It in the repeated visions of the Blue Person.
By the infinite grace of Lord Nityananda, I was realising:
it is my own Self of the Blue Form that dwells within
the inner being of all. It pervades the entire universe
and activates all. Though it is the One without a second,
non-dual and undifferentiated, it vibrates into myriad
forms. It revels by becoming many from one, and one
from many. The same Self is Sri Krishna, the eternal
blue of consciousness of *Srimad Bhagavatam* and its final
goal. It is the Life of the milkmaids, the Soul of yogis.
This same inner conscious blue is the Absolute of *jnanis*,
denoted by *So'ham*. It is the chosen deity of the devotees
which floods them with the elixir of love. The same blue
is Sri Guru Nityananda, the beloved deity of Muktananda.
It is the divine power of grace, blessing Siddha students.
Owing to our ignorance we are unable to see that this
universe arises in the Absolute Being, the supreme God.
But on becoming enlightened as a result of the unfolding
of Parashakti Kundalini, we look upon this universe as a

divine game.

I began to realise that That, by whose favour *maya* is seen as the supreme Lord in action, is the blue of consciousness, my inner Self. The blue consciousness that spreads through the entire universe, which is the supreme, pure Witness of all, immutable, infinite, everlasting and true and which has bestowed true knowledge on me, is my inner Self.

A cloud cannot permanently hide the sun and a blind man cannot see it, though clearly visible. In the same manner the blue consciousness, the seer of all, though apparent, cannot be perceived without the Guru's grace. That is the same as my inner Self. It plays hide-and-seek. In fact, it is manifest, though concealed. That which takes care of all my needs, which was realised by our ancestors, which will also reveal itself to future generations, by whose grace the world is no longer seen as merely the world, is my inner Self, the Satchidananda. I began to have this firm conviction.

That, which is the Light of all lights and is manifest even in matter, without knowing which knowledge remains incomplete, but by knowing which everything becomes easily known, is the blue radiance of Sri Guru Nityananda's grace. I began to firmly know this from within. The firmer such knowledge, the more vivid the feeling that there is still more to realise. The supreme Kundalini, along with deepening my meditation, bestowed the knowledge of the Absolute.

### The Supreme Knowledge

In my musings following meditation, I truly began to comprehend the purport of the Vedantins. That, which is perceived as the immutable Witness-consciousness by them, in which higher intelligence merges itself while probing It and thus fulfils Vedanta, became clear to me in meditation.

That unchangeable Soul, which apprehends the external world as 'this' during waking consciousness but remains different from it; which keeps awake during the dream state and perceives the dream world as 'this,' without the aid of the physical senses and discursive mind; and which penetrates the dense darkness of deep slumber and watches its void, is the highest goal of meditation. Such knowledge dawned.

That Witness-Self, which seated in the eyes, sees sights; inhabiting the ears, hears sounds and interprets them to the appropriate organs; which, activating respiratory rhythm, lives motionlessly behind it, is the goal of Vedanta. Such knowledge spontaneously arose within.

Man says in ignorance, "I ate, I drank, I took, I gave," but in reality, the inner Self, the unchanging Witness, the Absolute, is the enjoyer of everything. Being thus awakened, when I was confronted with the various worldly people who cried and complained, I began to wonder whether they were stating the truth or a falsehood. I looked upon them as embodiments of the same inner Self.

Just as a painter draws varied images on the same canvas with a single brush, a single set of colours and a single conception, likewise, the same One appears in various forms and colours of the universe. In other words, unity underlies diversity. Such knowledge began to arise.

In this manner, I was continually becoming more enlightened but that did not prevent meditation or slacken my practice. As I meditated, my vision became fixed more and more on *sahasrar*. Both my pupils were drawn towards it. And then a new event occurred which is beyond words. I do not know how I am still talking about it. My dear Professor Jain is taking it down. The inevitable does come to pass. The will of Lord Hari prevails. It is true: "Rama, the Lord, governs all."

### Final Realisation

My meditation approached its culmination. The final destination of my sadhana, my spiritual pilgrimage, was quite near. I came quite close to the inner fulfilment, thus fulfilling my Guru's command. This is the highest realisation or the summit of man's fortune. Here the vehicle of sadhana carrying a spiritual aspirant comes to a permanent stop. And then one may see nothing, yet everything becomes known. The unshakable conviction that one has attained the most sublime state spontaneously arises within. After this, one sits in bliss, sleeps in bliss, roams, comes and goes in bliss. He dwells blissfully at an ashram, his actions are blissful, he eats and imparts bliss. "Now I have crossed the ocean of worldly existence." This is what he actually experiences. By virtue of this realisation he is not agitated while engaged in any activity; his heart becomes serene like an ocean and his mind, with all its afflictions dissolved, is transmuted into Chiti. "That which is dear to all, being their inner Soul, I verily am, I verily am, I verily am." Such a voice reverberates within.

Once again I watched the Blue Pearl, the Satchidananda, whose vision grants joy free from conflict, knowledge free from duality, experience free from doubt and equipoise free from agitation.

My own, my dear Siddha students! Now I was meditating as before. Lord Nityananda suddenly administered an inner jolt. Immediately, the rays of the red aura gleamed in my 72,000 nerves and innumerable blood particles. The white flame appeared along with its support, the black light; and then the dear, the beloved Blue Pearl, the ground of all! Immediately my meditation became more intense. My vision focussed upwards. While I was gazing at the tiny Blue Pearl, it began to expand in all directions, spreading its blue radiance. The entire region from the earth to the sky became irradiated. It was a Pearl no longer, having enlarged into the shining, sparkling infinite Light. This has been designated by the scriptural authors or the seers of the highest Truth as the conscious light of Chiti. I actually saw the universe arise from this expanding light like clouds of smoke from a fire. The cosmos appeared in the conscious light and the conscious light in the cosmos like threads in cloth and cloth in threads. Just as one seed grows into a tree, shooting forth twigs, leaves, blossoms and fruit, similarly the selfsame Chiti becomes, in Her own being, birds and

animals, germs and insects, angels and demons, men and
women. I perceived the refulgent, divinely beautiful
conscious light calmly throbbing as supreme bliss on all
sides, within and without, above and below. Though my
eyes were open, I was in meditation. Just as a diver
descending into water finds himself in the midst of water,
surrounded by water and water alone on all sides, so also
was I completely enveloped by that conscious light. In
this state, the universe vanished and I beheld only pure
effulgence surging all around. As the sun-god spreads
his infinite kinds of glistening rays on all sides, so the
blue light was spreading its countless luminous rays all
around me.

I was conscious of the world no longer. I was in a
sublime state. And lo! I beheld in the midst of the
spreading blue rays Sri Gurudev, my worshipful deity
Nityananda, standing with one arm uplifted to bless me.
When I looked again, Nityananda had melted into Parashiva holding his trident. What an enchanting form!
Composed solely of blue light! His hands, feet, nails,
head and locks were all masses of blue radiance. While
I was gazing, Parashiva also dissolved as Nityananda
had and this time it was my own form, the form of
Muktananda, my double that I had earlier envisioned.
Muktananda too stood in the midst of the conscious blue
light, his body, his shawl and his rosary of *rudraksha*
beads being all made of the same blue rays. Muktananda
dissolved into Shiva into Nityananda. The blue light
was still unaltered. What brilliance! What colour! How
entrancing! I was seeing Nityananda in the sparkling
radiance of consciousness. And then he merged into it.
Just as ice melts into water, camphor evaporates into
air, likewise Nityananda dissolved into the all-pervasive
blue light. Now it was only a shimmering mass of Glory
without name or form. And then all the spreading blue
rays converged from all sides into the Blue Pearl, tiny
as a lentil seed. The pearl merged into *sahasrar* from
where it had emerged. At once Muktananda was bereft
of consciousness and memory. The distinction of the
"inner" and "outer" evaporated. He was no longer aware

of himself. Here I have not revealed a supreme secret, because my Gurudev does not permit me, God does not wish it, and the Siddhas do not urge me.

I was immersed in inner *samadhi* for some time. Then as the Witness-consciousness began to return, the blue light, called सत् चिन्मय नीलिमा । (the eternal blue of consciousness), by Shankaracharya, appeared again. My mind was fixed on it. I felt myself entering the Blue Pearl—the basis of all—in the centre of *sahasrar*. Once again I perceived the universe stretching on all sides. I looked around. All men and women, high and low, young and old, each had the same Blue Pearl within him that I had seen within me. I fully realised that it was truly the inner Self dwelling in everyone's *sahasrar*. Then I emerged from meditation, returning to the normal state. Though I had fully regained body-consciousness, I was still beholding the Blue Pearl with the inner eye. It drew my attention forcibly towards itself. Through this process I attained perfect peace and equanimity.

I meditate these days also. But I feel certain that there is nothing more for me to see. The certitude that I have attained the highest arises spontaneously in meditation. For the extremely subtle, tranquil, all-pervasive, conscious blue light that followed the three visions within the Blue Pearl has not altered or vanished and still bathes the external universe. Even with closed eyes I perceive it glowing and shimmering, softer than the soft, tenderer than the tender, subtler than the subtle. When I open my eyes, I see the blue rays all around. Whenever I look at anyone, I first see the blue light and then him. When I look at an object, I first see the honeyed, subtle, conscious rays and then the object. Regardless of where my mind is directed, I perceive the universe within the lustrous mass of light.

The manner in which I see all things, whether large or small, demonstrates the truth of the aforesaid verses of Tukaram. In other words, the lotion of blue radiance has been applied to my eyes, granting me divine vision.

## Divine Sport

These days when I am absorbed in meditation, I apprehend the blue rays of the conscious light and the Blue Pearl within it. I constantly see the soft conscious mass of light trembling delicately and shining in all conditions —whether I am eating, drinking or bathing. It surrounds me even during sleep. I have transcended the dual as well as the non-dual, as That pervades both. Differences of space, time and substance no longer exist. The blue light subtly pervading the whole universe also permeates my Soul. I even see that which is invisible to others. Just as by applying magic fluid to the eyes, one can see the hidden treasure; similarly, the blue lotion, the invaluable gift of the Guru's grace and of the Goddess Kundalini, has granted me the divine vision which penetrates the unseen, the subtlest secrets of life. Now I know fully that my own Soul is pervading everywhere as the universe. In fact, the cosmos does not exist; it never existed. For what we regard as the universe is only a conscious play of Chitshakti. Such is my firm conviction. I spontaneously perceive the inner meanings of *sah* and *aham* which combine to make *So'ham*. The Absolute bliss, attainable through the Vedantic contemplation: 'Thou art That,' is, in fact, my own Self vibrating subtly within me. To support this I would quote one passage from *Pratyabhijnahrdayam*, which describes the cosmic view of Shiva, the supreme Lord:

...श्रीमत्परमशिवस्य पुनः विश्वोत्तीर्ण-विश्वात्मक-परमानंदमय-प्रकाशैकघनस्य एव-विधमेव शिवादि-धरण्यन्तम् अखिलम् अभेदेनैव स्फुरति; न तु वस्तुतः अन्यत् किंचित् ग्राह्यं ग्राहकं वा; अपि तु श्री परमशिवभट्टारक एव इत्थं नानावैचित्र्यसहस्रैः स्फुरति!

It means that for Lord Parashiva, also called Parashakti by us, there is no such thing as the universe. He is true, eternal, attributeless, formless, all-pervasive and perfect. He apprehends the whole range of manifestation, from Shiva to the earth, including the movable and the immovable, the visible and the invisible as identical with His own Self, being saturated with the blissful light. As a matter of fact, anything other than Him is simply imaginary. The distinctions of the seer and the seen, the perceiver and the perceived, the individual and the universal, matter and consciousness are unreal. It is supreme Shiva who pulsates into various innumerable forms. I now see that the universe is the body of the Lord, and that Parashiva Himself is projecting it in His own limitless Being.

The last two verses of Jnaneshwar's poem which forms the basis of this work, describes the pure blissful consciousness, the source of the Blue Pearl as:

तयाचा मकरंद स्वरूप तें शुद्ध । ब्रह्मादिका बोध हाची झाला
ज्ञानदेव म्हणे निवृत्तिप्रसादें । निजरूप गोविंदें जनीं पाहतां

(Its very essence constitutes the true nature of God. This alone is the experience of all sages and seers from Brahma onwards. My innermost form, envisioned by the favour of Sadguru Nivrittinath, is verily Sri Govinda, the supreme Lord. I see Him in everyone).

The statement of Vedanta that nothing but the immanent Lord exists, is true. In fact this very knowledge of God is the essence of life, by obtaining which we can make our daily life ambrosial. Man has the greatest need of such knowledge. It can be acquired only through Shaktipat. All the saints have realised God within themselves by the grace of the Siddhas. The experiences of Jnaneshwar, described above, are truly representative of those of all. The inner Self, explored by the seers such as Janak, Sanak and Narada, is indeed the very essence of the blissful knowledge, handed down through spiritual tradition extending through the ages. That verily is Govinda, full of supreme bliss, who dwells in all hearts. He is present in everyone, from the enlightened to the ignorant, from the stupid to the insane, because lunacy and ignorance are only conditions of the mind, whereas the Soul is perfectly detached and pure. The purest Person, transcending the sixteen *kalas*, abides forever in *brahmarandhra*, in the centre of *sahasrar*. He is also known as the 'Seventeenth,' the Soul. One whose vision has been completely purified, discerns it in the Blue Form in *sahasrar*. Jnaneshwar says that only the Sadguru's grace has enabled him to reveal the most mysterious Truth.

The greatest fact is that this universe is a divine sport, a bursting forth of Chitshakti. It appears to be material owing to our ignorance of Chiti. When the knowledge of Chiti is attained, matter will vanish and one will see only Chiti everywhere. Vasugupta Acharya says truly:

इति वा यस्य संविक्ति: क्रीडात्वेनाखिलं जगत् ।
स पश्यन्सततं युक्तो जीवन्मुक्तो न संशय: ॥

(*Spandashastra*)

(He, who continually perceives this entire universe as a sport of the Universal Consciousness, is truly Self-realised; he is liberated in this body, beyond any doubt). This entire world in which we live is a play of the self-luminous Universal Consciousness. To one with this vision, the universe is only an unfolding of divine Shakti. For him there is neither bondage nor salvation; neither means nor end; neither contraction nor expansion. For his eye of knowledge has been opened by the Guru's mercy. The veil of differentiation that creates dualities has been rent. But for the Guru's benevolence, the divine, playful Chiti will not sharpen perception and reveal the true nature of the universe. When She enters a Siddha student by the Guru's grace, She saturates his whole body and purifies him completely. She remoulds him in Her image and takes seat in his eyes, heart and mind: then he perceives this universe as a glorious game of Chit-shakti. This is the true insight. This is also said by Vasugupta Acharya: the universe is nothing but a play of Universal Imagination. Chiti is absolutely free and self-effulgent. She holds the triple power of creation-sustenance-dissolution within Her. Being the funda-mental cause of everything, She Herself is the means of happiness for all. Though She is above space, time and form, She voluntarily assumes these limitations. All spaces, times, and forms are Her expressions. Chiti main-tains Her unity and identity in spite of Her manifesting as the universe. She is omnipresent, ever-full and ever-radiant.

When mighty Shiva wishes to create, Chiti expands Herself of Her own accord, differentiates Her own Being and manifests into innumerable forms. Chiti expresses Her own creativity by unfolding as the external universe, which is Her immanent aspect. Despite appearing as the cosmos, She remains pure, self-illumined and untainted in her transcendent aspect. Similarly, as the conscious Self of man, in Her outgoing movement, She takes on countless forms, which comprise his being from head to foot, including the gross, subtle, causal and supracausal bodies, five sheaths, the four states, the four psychic functions, the 72,000 nerves, the seven bodily components, the ten organs of perception and action and their objects, the five facets of prana and their functions and the five basic elements. She projects Herself as happiness, sorrow, fear, disease, impurity, childhood, youth, heaven and hell. Yet Her purity and and transparency remain ever un-sullied. Remaining unaltered, She revels in the external universe. In Her transcendent aspect, She is always detached from waking consciousness and from the good or bad actions of its physical organ, from all the activities of the dream state, and from the void of deep sleep. She expresses Herself in supracausal *turiya* while remaining above it. She appears as the entire universe, while transcending it as pure consciousness, its never-perturbed Witness.

Chiti resides within the Blue Pearl, blissful and honeyed. She has no parallel. In Her unity, in Her role as a pure Onlooker, She is supreme Consciousness, supreme Shiva, absolutely alone. Nothing else precedes, concurs with or succeeds Her. This is also called the transcendent Shiva, 'the formless, attributeless Absolute' of the Vedantins.

Siddha students, reflect on it. When, on obtaining the Guru's grace, you dwell for a while in *sahasrar*, absorbed in your own bliss, you are not conscious of anything other than yourself, nor does anything else appear or exist. You are alone in your fullness. You yourself enjoy your own bliss, the ecstasy of the Guru's grace, in your own being. This is known as the heightened state in which

one experiences one's own perfection. This is where
Siddha students should repose. Here you perceive your
own Self within your own being. This is the true *aham*
or 'I.' If someone asks you about Its nature, say that
this very 'I' is the Absolute, Shiva, Rama, Shakti, or
Kundalini, and also constitutes your own identity. When
this 'I' comes out of the supreme transcendent state, It
becomes 'this'—the universe. It passes into deep sleep
from *turiya*, into dream from deep sleep, into waking
from dream, assuming a universal form. In this state, It
plays in the field of the three *gunas.* It manifests of Its
own accord right from *turiyatita* to waking. Even when
It becomes the universe, It neither forgets Its essential
nature, takes on an alien form, nor despoils Its integrity.
Thus of Its own free will, within Its own being, It makes
the universe.

Chiti appears as the perceiver and the perceived. The
whole assembly of outer existence included in "this" is
the perceived, whereas the inner Shakti which knows
different objects separately as "this pot" or "this cloth"
is the perceiver. The entire universe is the field of the
known, while the Universal Soul is the knower. The
perceived is in perfect accordance with the perceiver and
meant for him to enjoy. The all-powerful Chiti, that
performs countless marvels, unfolds Herself as the knower
and the known, as the Universal Soul and the universe.
This is, indeed, Her splendid play. Kashmir Shaivism
says:

शरीरमेव घटाद्यपि वा ये पट्त्रिंशत्तत्त्वमयं
शिवरूपतया पश्यन्ति तेऽपि सिध्यन्ति ।

It means that the Siddha student who looks upon this
body as a form of Chiti that comprises the 36 constituents,
nay, as that of supreme Shiva Himself, attains all realisations, according to the laws of Siddha science. In fact,
Chiti is conducting Her own sport in Her differentiated
and undifferentiated aspects. Just as the same man
passes through his own four different states, likewise
Chiti embodies Herself as the universe, which is in no
way different from Her.

All the scriptures proclaim that the Absolute is Satchidananda. This world, originating from the Absolute,
is none other than It. The divisions such as "I," "you"
and "this" are all counters in Its game. The supreme
Lord is unity in diversity and diversity in unity. This
is true. Just as the numberless water drops, bubbles,
waves and foam of an ocean are in no way different from
it, similarly, the countless names, forms, and qualities of
this universe are not at all different from Chiti. As the
cool feel of water is nothing but water, so this conscious
universe-play of Chiti cannot be alien from you. Just
as from the logical standpoint, cloth is nothing but cotton,
cloth cannot come into being without cotton; in the same
manner, from the spiritual standpoint, the universe is the
Absolute, the universe cannot exist without the Absolute.
The cosmos is an expansion of the Absolute, only another
name for the sport of Universal Consciousness. Such a
viewpoint is the true worship of Parashakti, the true
knowledge received from the Guru.

Those who are ignorant of this *Chitshaktivilas*, the
divine play of consciousness, and consider the universe
to be essentially different from Chiti, suffer in diverse
ways because of this delusion. But those who apprehend
this Chiti-filled universe as Her game, themselves become
Chiti. This is the Vedantic doctrine:

> है ब्रह्म सच्चा, जगत मिथ्या, यह मात्र सिद्धांत है ।
> ब्रह्मात्मा को जाने बिना, होता नहीं दुख का अन्त है ॥
> जो जानता सब में एक को, वही नर पाता शान्ति है ।
> जो ब्रह्म है सो आत्म है, यही कहता वेदान्त है ॥

(The Absolute is real: the world is unreal. Such is the
truth.
But for Self-knowledge, suffering does not cease.
He who sees the One in all, alone attains peace.
The Absolute is the individual Soul—such is the
Vedantic teaching.)

Therefore, Siddha students should contemplate the
following supreme mantra and thereby achieve Self-
awareness. A true Indian leader, who identifies himself

with his own country and people, continually dwells in the spontaneous national awareness: "I am the soul of India and India is my soul," though engaged in different activities such as sitting, standing, coming or going. A member of a respectable and large family, consisting of one or two hundred people of varying ages, fully identifies himself with each one, in spite of his own personal world comprising his wife, sons, daughters and grandchildren. My dear Siddha students! In the same manner, let your mind throb spontaneously with this constant thought: "Shiva is mine. I am His. The universe made by Him is He. All its activities are His movements. He is the same as I."

यह विश्व शिव की वाटिका, है सैर करने के लिये ।
ना राग, ईर्ष्यां, द्वेष, चिन्ता, वैर करने के लिये ॥
यह विश्व शिव की मूर्ति, शिवभक्ति करने के लिये ।
विश्व शब्द का बाध कर, शिव-ध्यान करने के लिये ॥
यह विश्व शिव-अवतार है, न जान धोखा खाय है ।
शिव से विलक्षण जान कर, व्यर्थ अतिभय पाय है ॥
यह विश्व शिव-दर्पण भवन, शिव बन जो भीतर देखता ।
सर्वत्र ही शिव एक उसको, बिम्ब प्रतिबिम्ब भासता ॥

(This universe is Shiva's own garden, meant for a
    joyous stroll,
Not for attachment, jealousy, aversion, anxiety and
    hostility.
This universe is Shiva's own image, meant for His
    worship,
For destroying the concept "universe" and meditating
    on Him.
This universe is Shiva's own incarnation. Ignorance
    of this betrays one.
Considering it to be other than Him, one becomes
    unnecessarily terrified.
This universe is the mansion containing the mirror of
    Shiva. He who looks into it feeling one with Shiva,
Sees His own images and reflections, sees one Shiva
    everywhere.)
Now I give you another mantra to ponder its truth:

सर्वो ममायं विभव इत्येवं परिजानतः ।
विश्वात्मनो विकल्पानां प्रसरेऽपि महेशता ॥

(*Ishwarpratyabhijna*)

(He who knows all this glory of manifestation as his own,
who realises the entire cosmos in his Self, is divine, even
though thoughts may play in his mind.)

Dear Siddha students! Fully realise this mantra by
dwelling on it, reflecting on its meaning and acting in
full harmony with its spirit. He who continually contemplates his identity with this assembly of 36 elements
called the universe, which is directly perceived by the
senses and is the support of his life, realises that it is his
own splendour. He will continue to dwell in his perfection. His divinity will remain undisturbed by his mental
tendency that creates differences where there are none.
Just as the Pacific Ocean does not lose its serenity
even when it breaks into waves, similarly, you will
realise your Godhood without fail, despite your inclination
to see the universe as alien from yourself, provided you
are constantly aware that it is your own glorious treasure.

O Siddha students! The universe belongs to you. You
are its Soul. Different levels of manifestation arise from
you. They are your own forms. You are perfect in your
aspect as the Universal Spirit. Remain continuously
aware that the universe is your own splendid glory. This
is the Guru's command, the teaching of Parashiva, the
Siddha mode of perception. This is the easy and natural
means to liberation, the holy sacrifice to please Parashakti, the supreme mantra assuring merger in Chiti.
This is, indeed, Self-knowledge, the true meditation on
the Guru. And this is, according to Muktananda, the
noble sacrifice fulfilling one's most sacred duty.

The Hut in the Orchard at Nagad

At Nagad

Baba Muktananda

Baba Muktananda

# BOOK II

# TEACHING OF
# THE SIDDHAS

# 1

# THE COMMAND OF THE SIDDHAS

Dear Siddha students! I have something important to tell you. Our way is the Siddha way. Our principles are Siddha principles. We belong to Siddhaloka where the beloved Gurus of our tradition dwell. We live our lives under their protection. We follow the path shown by them and our goal is Self-realisation. Our aim is to live in a perfect state and finally to dwell in Siddhaloka. All our actions bear full fruit, for the grace of a Siddha never fails. It is bound to have its effect.

Fish fry possess all the characteristics of fish and naturally live under water. Lion cubs are lions in every sense of the word. Calves of elephants, though without tusks, are still elephants, showing all the qualities of their species in their vital fluids, blood, teeth, bones and flesh. In the same manner, you possess the perfection of your perfect Father. Therefore you should not become worried or anxious. A child grows up in natural course, following the laws of different stages of growth. "Why are my ears small? Why don't I have teeth? Why don't I have the powers of adults?" Such questions arising in a child's mind are futile. As you grow up each day, your father's seed will realise all its potentialities in due course. One grows from childhood to full-fledged youth in a spontaneous manner. It is stupid and confusing to worry about this process, as this will only inhibit growth. Therefore, you should not lose your patience, steadfastness and strength through anxiety. Always remember that a disciple of a Siddha cannot remain in bondage.

Lion cubs can never be like donkey foals. Their heads, nails and all other parts are lion-like. However, if a lion cub spends too much time with donkeys, he will lose some of his valour, and the donkeys will begin to regard him as one of them. In their company he loses his radiance, his real nature and ways, and gradually acquires asinine qualities. He even begins to roar like an ass. He eats filthy things like his companions, bathing in dirty street pools. After a length of time he resembles a lion only in his external form, but not in inner characteristics. Gradually he becomes shorn of his prowess, daring and love of forest solitude, forgetting his majestic origin, brave habits and leonine ways. He begins to live in crowded streets in a town or village. Meanwhile, a washerman comes along looking for a donkey to carry the load of dirty clothes of the whole village. In this manner, the lion too has to carry dirty linen to the washing place, along with his companions. That poor cub does not know that he has shrunk from a lion into a donkey. On the contrary, he exults in being progressive, imitating donkeys who are in the majority!

Progress implies that an ass grows into a lion, but not the reverse. You should not wander like an ignorant seeker from door to door, meeting slight and scorn. Your realm, the realm of the Perfected Ones, is the noblest, possessing great power. Compared to it, the worlds of Indra, the moon, the sun and others pale into insignificance. You belong to a noble family. Countless Siddha yogis and yoginis of your tradition are standing behind you, protecting you. For this reason do not waste your time among petty-minded devotees or renunciants. Remember that you have to attain Siddhaloka.

Your innumerable predecessors dwell in Siddhaloka. All Siddhas, from the supremely perfect primeval Lord and the seven sages, to the countless seers from time immemorial to the present day, inhabit Siddhaloka with full powers; they bestow Shakti on you, activate your yogic sadhana and are ever ready to protect you and fulfil your needs. Do not think that you have only the power of your Guru behind you. You are the rightful descendant in the line of the perfect inhabitants of Siddhaloka, though you may not be aware of it. When you visit Siddhaloka, you will gain full knowledge of your lineage. In this line, from Shiva, the primordial great Lord, conscious and blissful, through the divine sage Narada, the great seers Vyasa, Shesha, Shukadeva, Yajnavalkya, Kakabhushandi, Suta, Shaunaka and Shandilya; Bhishma, King Janaka, all the perfected milkmaids of Vraja; kings such as Prithu, Ambarish, Bharata; Prahlada, Dhruva, Sanaka, Hanuman, Akroor, Uddhava, Vidur, Sanjaya, Sudama; Kashyap, Sutapa, Prishni, Manu, Dasharatha, Kaushalya and Vibhishana, to Sai Baba of Shirdi, my beloved Zipruanna of Nasirabad and your supreme Master, Bhagawan Nityananda, are all extend- ing protection to you from Siddhaloka. Therefore, do not falter or hesitate, but stick to the Siddha path with exclusive fidelity and absolute devotion.

Young Siddha students should follow their parents' advice. It is essential for them to submit to authority. They must be regular and disciplined, otherwise they will not reap full benefits. Their spiritual practice will become feeble. They will fall short of perfection. Their progress will be obstructed. Their merger in Chiti will be delayed.

You are forced to look hither and thither because you are ignorant of your own potentialities of perfection. You must have unswerving faith in your principles, the Siddha path, the yoga of meditation and Siddha mantras. The Siddha's grace is there to support you like a strong mountain. Our mantra is a perfect mantra. When such is the case, why should you become inconstant, enfeebling your exclusive loyalty? For a faithful wife, her husband constitutes her sole world: she loves only him; devotion to him is her highest duty; her needs are met when her husband's are; she rejoices in him alone; he is her sole delight; loyalty to him is her true mantra repetition, knowledge, meditation and sacred bath; she surrenders her intellect to him; love of her husband is her life-long vow; she is addicted only to him; she is helpless without him. Similarly, students of Siddha Yoga should be bursting with love for the Siddha path, delighting solely in it.

Do not worry that you have achieved nothing. A

Siddha can open you in a moment. If you possess full devotion and reverence, unshakable faith and readiness for total surrender, you cannot remain far from a Siddha's grace; nay, you will be blessed at once. When great Siddhas grant their favour, you become not only realised and liberated but also a full Siddha. You cannot remain in bondage. Keep Siddhaloka constantly in your mind. Be aware of the divine potency of Siddhas that can bring the impossible within your reach. Continually remember the light shining within you and repeat the *chaitanya* mantra that will raise you to the Siddha status. You should always bear in mind that the great Shakti, which freely performs myriad functions, is active within you. Never forget that the divine, effulgent, great Shakti dwells within you. Understand your true worth and organise your life accordingly. Do not feel anxious about what your sadhana will lead to, when it will bear fruit or whether your attainment will be full or partial. Remember that a lion cub is not different from a lion. Pay special attention to this. This is the Guru's word. This will constitute obedience to his command. After Arjuna listened to the entire philosophy of the *Gita* from the Lord, he only said, "I shall do Thy bidding." Carry out the Guru's command fully. Imbibe the Guru's teaching. Traverse the path shown by him. This is the boat that will take you across the ocean of worldliness. The quality of your achievement and the pace of your progress will be directly proportional to your reverent and loving acceptance of the Guru's authority, orders, instruction and way. Do not slight the Guru. This will drive you away from the path and delude you.

By hostility and jealousy towards brother disciples, by false talk and violation of the code of conduct prevailing at the Guru's abode, and by disturbing your mind with petty quarrels, particularly during the time of meditation or study, you will gradually lose the Shakti. Weeping, grumbling, conceit, and hurting another's feelings are not the signs of one who serves the Guru. If my Gurudev called me just once, from whatever distance, I used to respond immediately, repeating thrice, "Yes, Gurudev," and rush to him. If he asked me anything, I would reply at once because I did not want to cause him trouble by compelling him to ask me again and again.

Remember that your inner, expanding, dynamic Shakti is indeed the Guru. Be careful about the company you keep to maintain the purity of your sadhana. Bad company is highly injurious, even fatal. Take a firm pledge to keep away from it. Through unworthy company all the vile qualities and tendencies to degrading behaviour are automatically fostered. All your noble qualities are destroyed. Kaikeyi, who was full of love, affection and modesty, caused immense grief to King Dasharatha and all the inhabitants of Ayodhya, and had to lose the love of her own dear son, Bharat, owing to the evil influence of her maid Manthra. Just as even an ocean of milk is spoiled by one drop of sour curd, like-wise, bad company easily brings all the wicked tenden-cies. One begins to indulge in deplorable things such as discussing everyone, talking ill of others, indiscretion, arrogance, enmity, impurity, misconduct, vulgar movies and plays and impure hotel foods on account of bad influences. Siddha students must avoid undesirable company; otherwise the inner Shakti will not gather momentum.

The divine Chiti continuously flows out from the body of a Siddha student. Therefore, O Siddha students, whatever place you meditate is turned into a temple. Your dwellings become highly sacred. You lend holiness to holy places. You impart living force to a mantra. Various postures, *mudras*, and kinds of *pranayama* of external yoga are automatically performed by those who are touched by you. Your outgoing and incoming breaths are invaluable. Always remember you are emitting Chiti rays from every cell of your body. Therefore you should be aware that you are the abode of Chiti, who promotes your highest good and operates within you with all Her dynamism. The Guru is seated with you as the divine power of grace. Do not consider yourself ordinary or ignorant, or too young or dependent on others. The divine Chiti, to whom we owe this universe, who Herself

appears as the universe, is manifested within you. Therefore, you are the holiest of the holy places, the mantra
of mantras, the god of gods and the purity of worship.
You should be conscious of your own worth, keep silent
as much as possible and ennoble your life with good
conduct, purity of mind and vigilance. Do not become
entangled in showy, corrupt ways.

In the West, young boys and girls do not mind coming
into contact with each other's body. They keep chatting,
moving, laughing and playing together unnecessarily.
By this mode of living, they are losing their potency.
Do not follow such ways. Your inner Shakti will become
angry with you. You should also remember that it is far
better to discharge faeces than semen. This applies not
only to celibates, *sannyasis*, and *sadhus*, as they have,
in any case, renounced women and worldly life, but also
to those living in the world. Live in the world and live
joyfully. Love each other, O husband and wife, regarding
each other as divine. Increase your radiance. Just as
you save each penny, save each drop of semen. All of
you should remember that one drop of semen can
produce a radiant human being. Hence remain aware of
its immense value. It is the seminal fluid that imparts
lustre to you. If you lose this native glow, not even the
best rouges, powders and creams can brighten your skin.
This fluid is the vehicle of Chitshakti. You purchase
Chiti by it, as it were. It is a necessary agent for
activating Kundalini and the highest means to stabilise
the *samadhi* state. Minutely examine the condition of
one who has wasted away his semen.

My dear Siddha students! Listen to my advice. Become aware of your own true importance as living
embodiments of Chiti and keep yourselves pure. One ray
of the Light which shines within you gives rise to the
sun, the moon and the stars. You have acquired such an
influence over only a short period of sadhana that Shakti
now flows into others by your touch or company. When,
after practising sadhana only briefly, you are able, by
the Guru's grace, to transmit vibrations of Shakti into
your neighbours, you can imagine how infinitely greater

your worth shall be, if you pursue this path with full seriousness for a prolonged period. Why should you not, in such a case, be worshipped in the world as an ideal father and mother?

Here is a warning for Siddha students. It is creditable, indeed, that you have stored up Shakti over a short period through meditation and purity of character. But this Shakti may easily be lost before the attainment of perfection. Therefore, take good care of it. Remain alert while sitting or standing, coming or going, giving or receiving, or engaging yourself in any other activity. Increase your store of Chiti instead of decreasing it. Do not undermine your sadhana by listening to the perverse comments of an ignoble man who commits base actions, leers maliciously, or indulges in bad conduct and corrupt ways.

The divine Chiti dwells within you as your best friend; She brings a universe into being on opening Her eyes and dissolves it on closing them. Even a slight association with the beloved Chiti makes the universe lovable. She is working within you. Isn't it a pity that you should mix with unworthy persons instead of making friends with that Chiti and delighting in Her? You yourself can imagine how deleterious such company can be. This injunction, inspired by Chiti, dear to Her, pleasing to Her, emanating from Her, is permeated by Her. If you carry it out, you will attain Chiti.

# 2

# THE LIBERATED LIFE OF SIDDHA STUDENTS

Dear Siddha students! I have been telling you repeatedly that the universe is nothing but a sport of Chiti. When Chiti gives joyful expression to Herself in the form of consciousness, She appears as the world, vibrating into innumerable forms—चिदेव भगवती स्वच्छस्वतन्त्ररूपा तत्तदनन्तजगदात्मना स्फुरती । When a Siddha student attains this knowledge of Chiti through the yoga of meditation, he sees the entire range of manifestation, inner as well as outer, as Her play; he feels Her vibration throbbing in each action and therefore continually experiences bliss in all his work and activities. He remains constantly aware of Chiti's pervasiveness. He knows that all the movements in the universe are Her quiverings; nay, they are Chiti Herself. With the conviction that whatever *is*, is divine Chiti, he looks upon the inner satisfaction, even arising from outer activities such as eating, drinking and merry-making, as a throb of Chiti's bliss, and becomes blissful himself. With a mind purified by meditation on Chiti, he realises that the pleasure of sensuous enjoyments, corresponding to his stage in life, is the same as the joy emanating from Chiti. Not only this. As he remains satiated and joyful in sensuous enjoyments, so he relishes Chiti's bliss even when he is without them. Such a yogi, living in the world, sees Chiti's activity in all his daily activities; he knows that Her bliss pulsates in them and thus he becomes fully contented within. He consolidates this state by the force of contemplation on Chiti, as a result of which his mind gradually sheds all concepts and imaginings and becomes illumined by the inner Light of bliss. The *Vijnanabhairava says*:

182

जग्धिपानकृतोल्लासरसानन्दविजृम्भणात् ।
भावयेद्दरितावस्थां महानन्दमयो भवेत् ॥
गीतादिविषयास्वादासमसौख्यैकतात्मनः ।
योगिनस्तन्मयत्वेन मनोरूढेस्तदात्मता ॥
यत्र यत्र मनस्तुष्टिर्मनस्तत्रैव धारयेत् ।
तत्र तत्र परानन्दस्वरूपं संप्रकाशते ॥

(When one experiences the expansion of the joy of the
savour arising from the pleasure of eating and drinking,
one should meditate on the perfect condition of that joy;
then one would become full of great bliss. When a yogi
mentally becomes one with the incomparable joy of song
and other objects, such a concentrated yogi attains
identity with that joy; he becomes one with it. Wherever
the mind finds its satisfaction, let it be concentrated on
that. In every such case, the true nature of the highest
bliss will shine forth.)

In fact, lack of awareness of the all-pervasive God is
suffering, whereas awareness is joy. Dear Siddha
students! You are conscious, omnipresent and perfect.
The universe is not at all distinct from you. What do
you want to renounce? What are you running after to
grasp? Nothing other than you exists in the world. You
alone permeate the entire universe. You are the perfect,
imperishable Substance. There is no difference between
you and the world. From the non-dual viewpoint, you
alone fill the whole world. You truly are the tranquil,
undiminishing and pure Kundalini which is the light of
consciousness. Ignorance never could and never will
penetrate your innermost being. You are the sporting
Universal Consciousness. You are neither *rajasic* nor
*tamasic*. No alien element can influence you. You are
attributeless and with attributes, untainted, the pure and
playful Chiti who always maintains Her unity. Just as
different ornaments like bangles, bracelets and anklets
are nothing but gold, likewise, this universe originating
from the unfolding of Parashiva's Shakti, is nothing
but Chiti. The effect cannot run counter to the cause.

My dear Siddha students! Whatever you see anywhere

is your own Light. Nothing is other than you. You
pervade all. The thought that you are here but not there
should not be entertained. Continually contemplate the
thought that you are everywhere, the Self of all. None
else except you exists in this world. The *Shivasutra* says
स्वशक्तिप्रचयोऽस्य विश्वम् । (The universe is the expansion of
one's own Shakti). The illusion called the universe has
arisen in you on account of your impurities. Worship
Goddess Chiti. As your impurities are removed, you will
discover that the world itself is Chiti's seat of repose.
You are pure consciousness, pure Being. The whole
visible universe is your expression. Why do you complain
for nothing? Everything is saturated with Chiti. You
alone were real in the beginning, you are real now and
will remain real forever. You are free from birth and
death. When there is no bondage, where is the question
of deliverance? Chiti is the Creator of all. How can you
be the experiencer? You are Nityananda, present everywhere in your fullness. Do not allow your mind to be
trapped or troubled by thoughts and imaginings. Merge
them in Chiti, considering them to be Her vibrations.
Understand that though you appear to be imperfect,
perfection is concealed within. Dissolve your desires in
Chiti and live free from craving. Know that the object
of meditation in the heart is all-pervading. The soul is
eternally perfect. Understand this and realise that the
meditator is the object of meditation. When none but you
exists, on what else will you meditate? See your own
splendour stretching forth on all sides and fill your mind
with peace.

You may continue to reflect on the words of the
scriptures throughout your life, teach the six schools of
Indian philosophy day and night, or even give sublime
sermons; but if you do not become one with Chiti you
will never overcome fear. Only when you consume the
differentiating notion of "I and mine" in the fire of
meditation, will you attain imperishable bliss. You may
continue to perform noble deeds till eternity, enjoy
sensuous pleasures or achieve concentration a million
times, but as long as you see yourself as different from

Chiti you will never find release from bondage. But when you merge yourself in Chiti you will attain indestructible bliss. Be free from all conflicts and tensions. Discard bigotry. Relinquish desire, even the desire for liberation. Give up all props and enjoy repose in Chiti. You will then obtain independent peace. You will enjoy eternal happiness. A renunciant renounces sensuous objects but becomes antagonistic to them, while a sensuous person embraces them and becomes attached to them. Dear Siddha students! Neither cling to sensuous objects nor repulse them. Then you will become a *muktananda*, enjoying the bliss of freedom, disentangled from conflicts and dualities. You will obtain everlasting peace.

As long as you oscillate between possession and renunciation you will remain chained to the world. If you rise above both you will reach the other shore. Neither renounce the duality of possession and renunciation nor possess it. Rejoice in your own inner nature. Continue to enjoy eternal peace, looking upon the universe as Chiti's revelry. The glories of Chiti are infinite. He alone will accept this as true who has experienced it personally. How can idiotic people, with their sensibilities impaired, minds corrupted and hearts afflicted, comprehend the mysterious divine power of Chiti? What is there that cannot be effected through the Guru's agency by the Mother who, without any concrete materials, creates such a beautiful, unsurpassable universe in the void? He who is continually aware of Chiti while hearing, seeing, touching, smelling, eating, drinking, sleeping or waking, will never become listless or indifferent. Such a Siddha student is ever-liberated. The wise man who always remains unattached like the sky and does not become agitated even for a moment, has perfected meditation, since he is one with Goddess Chiti. Such a Siddha student is supremely fortunate. He who is asleep to the outside world but remains ever-awake in Self-contemplation, always enjoys bliss. He who remains filled with Nityananda has achieved perfection. He is truly great. He is a supremely holy centre of pilgrimage who remains immersed in his own Self, having known his true nature. He delights in his own being, having discovered the source of contentment therein, and feels neither uneasy among multitudes nor happier in the forest solitudes.

The world is merely illusory. From the spiritual viewpoint it is Chiti's sport. The eternal, everlasting principle of Shiva is throbbing in the whole universe. The Siddha student who knows that the light of consciousness is shining everywhere with its red, white, black and blue components, is a living embodiment of Chiti. He has perfected his sadhana. He has renounced the differentiating mentality. He has attained the goal of hearing, reflection and contemplation. He has achieved awareness of the presence of Mother Chiti in his heart. The enlightened man, to whom the identity of the Absolute and the individual soul is self-evident, is the true Siddha student. He is fulfilled. He is worthy of worship by the whole world, since he has achieved the knowledge of his own Self appearing in diverse forms. He does not look upon the body as a mere body or the mind as a mere mind. To him all are manifestations of Chiti. He is truly wise, ever-free, and he secures the bliss of the Absolute. Such a Siddha student is liberated while still in the body. It is said in the *Skanda Purana*:

कुलं पवित्रं जननी कृतार्था
वसुन्धरा पुण्यवती च तेन ।
अपारसंवित्सुखसागरेऽस्मिँ—
ह्लीनं परे ब्रह्मणि यस्य चेत: ॥

(One whose mind is merged in the highest Brahman, the ocean of limitless divine bliss—by him the family becomes sanctified, the mother has her life fulfilled and the earth becomes holy.) The entire family of the seeker in whom Chiti expands, becomes sanctified, since She purifies everyone. The mother of such a son or daughter has fulfilled her role. The earth on which he walks also becomes holy. Only that family is truly noble in which such exalted children are born. The homes of the men and women, the boys and girls whose inner Shakti has been activated, are undoubtedly sacred and worthy of worship. The mind of the aspirant, whose inner Shakti is expanding more and more, finally merges in the limitless Universal Consciousness, the Absolute, the infinite ocean of bliss. All the holy waters unite where the students of the yoga of meditation live. In fact, they themselves are sacred whose darshan is uplifting. He lives with his family without being attached to them. He treats praise as well as blame equally. He enjoys sensuous objects if they come his way but does not become entangled in them. His mind is free from craving. He sees Chiti everywhere. Such a one is liberated while still in his body.

He does not regard the world as real, considering it to be Chiti's play. He sees the light of Chiti in foes as well as in friends. He worships the entire universe as God Such a one is liberated though he lives in the world.

He is so possessed by Chiti that nothing else can attract him. He remains absorbed in his own joy, contented in his own company, rejoicing in his own being. The Lord says in the *Srimad Bhagavatam* (XI-14-24).

वाग्गद्गदा द्रवते यस्य चित्तं
रुदत्यभीक्ष्णं हसति क्वचिच्च ।
विलज्ज उद्गायति नृत्यते च
मद्भक्तियुक्तो भुवनं पुनाति ॥

(His mind melts with choking words. He weeps every moment, sometimes he laughs. He sings loudly and dances without shame. One devoted to Me sanctifies the world). Divine love is manifested in him whose inner Shakti is aroused by the Guru's grace. His voice becomes so charged with joy that when he speaks, he scatters it in an unlimited measure in all directions. His heart melts with love each moment. Drunk with this love, he cries again and again, sometimes laughs, sometimes sings loudly and dances without any sense of shame. Such a seeker of Siddha Yoga grows into a great devotee of the Lord and sanctifies the three worlds. As Chiti, whose nature is blissful love, becomes active and the Blue Pearl reveals itself, pure love bubbles up within. This uprush of love makes the voice joyous and thaws the heart. Such a Siddha student purifies all his four bodies through meditation. Wherever he meditates becomes holy. He purifies even the holy centres with his contact. He is living proof of the absolute truth of the scriptures. In fact, hearts like his, inspired by Chiti, are poured out in sacred works. He is liberated forever, though still in the body.

He leads his practical life like others. All his actions are noble and salutary since they are activated by Chiti. He appears to be mad, but enjoys profound inner peace. He does not cling to attachments or shun aversions. He is free from all the *gunas*. He loves all. Such a one is easily liberated while still in the body.

He does not become nettled by afflictions, nor does he crave pleasures. He never gives up the noble path, nor takes to the ignoble one. His mind always vibrates with Chiti's impulses. He is profound, steadfast, pure and detached. Grace, love and compassion flow from him. Such a Siddha student is liberated while living in the world.

He is not scared of the phantom of either *maya* or the body. This world is a garden of Chiti to him. He knows God is the individual soul as well as the universe. Such a wise Siddha student finds undisturbed repose in Goddess Chiti. He has fulfilled his human birth. There is nothing left for him to accomplish or attain. He has obtained what he set out to obtain. On realising that the only mystery to be unveiled was his own Self, he finds Shiva within. He is the veritable Vaikuntha and also Mount Kailas. He is Badrinath and Kashi—all the places of pilgrimage, in fact, lie within him.

# 3

# PRETENCE OF MEDITATION

Dear meditating Siddha students! Your meditation should be genuine. You should not try to cheat or become hypocritical in order to secure praise or satisfy your vanity. If someone behaves like this, he is only deceiving himself. He picks his own pocket as it were. What's the use? When a pretender is tested it will be difficult for him to get through it.

It is good that many movements occur during meditation. It is essential to be full of intense feeling. But this should not be affected. Meditating yogis! Value the wealth of your inner Shakti far more than external success. The inner Shakti is conscious and omniscient. She knows that when She activates you to perform movements, you become intoxicated. She possesses full knowledge of past, present and future activities and events. She is not different from Shiva who is all-knowing. The *Spandakarika* (3-48) says: सेयं क्रियात्मिका शक्ति: शिवस्य पशुवर्तिनी । (It is indeed the Shakti of supreme Shiva that is active within a person.) The same Shakti dwells within Sri Nityananda, the supreme Guru. O Siddha students! Take care that your path of sadhana is right and authentic, for the dynamic Shakti witnesses all your activities as your inner Self.

Many people say to each other, "What a wonderful meditation I had! What an intense feeling! How wonderful! How remarkable!" These words are uttered only to receive applause. They meditate not for Self-realisation, but for approbation. The wise ones call it pretentious meditation.

A heron keeps standing in water for long hours with closed eyes as if he were meditating. Sometimes he even stands in the midst of a running stream in the medita-

tional posture. He spends his entire life in this manner—
standing each day for long periods apparently in meditation. Yet he does not receive Shaktipat, nor envision
lights, nor realise God. For he is concentrating not on
God but on fish; not for inner peace but for filling his
stomach.

Similarly, there are pretenders in the field of yoga.
They do not meditate on Sadguru Nityananda, nor on
the divine power of grace, nor on the nature of their own
soul. They are only concerned with fish, which they
surely get., He who meditates on fish always catches fish,
eats them and lives at peace with himself as well as
others! Tell me, how can you attain God or behold lights
by meditating on fish? Isn't it remarkable that you should
want to pass into *samadhi* while your thoughts dwell on
snacks and cookies and movies? Practitioners of meditation! This affected meditation will not take you to
Vaikuntha. You obtain only what your mind dwells
upon.

To avoid such false meditation, meditating Siddha
students should know how the Guru's Shakti, which
induces meditation, works in them in five forms. In the
*Tantrasara* this topic has been discussed as follows:
प्रकाशरूपता चित्शक्ति: । स्वातन्त्र्यम् आनन्दशक्ति: । तत्चमत्कार इच्छाशक्ति: ।
आमर्षात्मकता ज्ञानशक्ति: । सर्वाकारयोगित्वं क्रियाशक्ति: । That means that
this Chitshakti enters you from Sri Gurudev with Her
discriminating light and independent joy; of Her own
free will She performs innumerable miracles. She is
conscious of all your toughts, be they significant or
insignificant. She knows which movements are necessary, which ones should occur in your particular case,
and She causes them to happen. Thus the supreme
Shakti of the One Parashiva, whom we call Chitshakti
Kundalini, the Guru's power of grace, or the Guru's
spiritual power, dwells within you in Her five aspects:
consciousness, bliss, will power, knowledge and dynamism. She lives in equal fullness in the immanent Shiva
as well as the transcendent supreme Shiva. She also lives
within your Gurudev in the same measure. And what is
within your Gurudev passes into you easily. If you

remain faithful to him, the Shakti will also remain faithful to you in a corresponding degree.

Showy meditation cannot release this Shakti. This Shakti does not depend on any other factor. She is self-effulgent; She freely enjoys Her own bliss without any other support. She is the indomitable will power that can perform any miracle. She is the power of knowledge that acts in the knower as well as the known. Finally, She is the dynamic power emitting vibrations which create innumerable objects. This fivefold Shakti dwells within God and also within the Guru, adapting Herself to his disposition. The same Shakti passes into the disciple according to his worth. This five-faceted single Shakti pervades the disciple, the Guru and God, maintaining Her unity. This being the truth of things, you can imagine how Gurudev knows the quality of your meditation and the feelings of your heart. Therefore, I urge you to avoid pretence of meditation.

Although herons keep standing with their eyes closed in a lake from morning to evening, they do not obtain the light inherent in that power of consciousness; the independent joy of that power of bliss; the fruits of that discriminating power of knowledge; the impulses of that marvellous power of will; or the direct vibrations of that power of dynamism. Why don't they experience all this? Because their meditation, despite its outward resemblance to that of a yogi, is directed only towards fish. What results do you expect from your meditation? What do you contemplate? You may be meditating for a while, but what does your mind actually love? You cry because someone else cried, but without knowing why. You laugh because someone else laughed, without knowing why. If someone moves one finger, you move all ten. But you do not know why he moved one or you ten. If another wheels about just once, you wheel twenty-five times. But you do not know why. You have only mimicked him. He is activated by the inner Shakti, whereas you are activated by your external mind. This is known as pretended meditation.

Muktananda cheers both! He expresses his approbation.

Just as a heron eats fish to his fill as a result of his day-long exertion, likewise you receive applause ten times as a result of your laughing a little, crying a little, and performing a few movements. What more do you want? A heron meditates for fish while you for applause, not for the love of inner Shakti. He gets fish and you get applause. Why didn't you and the heron attain Vaikuntha? You never meditated on it. One receives what one contemplates.

There are many ashrams which grant you fruits according to your desires. About twenty years ago there was an ashram not far from my dwelling, housing the Samadhi Shrine of a Siddha saint. For this reason many pilgrims visited that place and I, too, frequented it. On reaching the shrine, I would go round it to realise the inner Self and meditate peacefully in a distant corner. My mind would contemplate the Self and thus obtain the reward of its effort. A certain couple also came; they had no child. They received some instructions and finally were blessed with a child. In the same manner, one came for winning his case in a court of law, another for getting through his college examinations, yet another for overcoming a disease. One contemplated there for wealth, another for sensuous enjoyments. Some visited the shrine only for fun. Then there were some love-birds who could not find a rendezvous in Bombay and came to meet each other in solitude under the pretext of visiting the shrine.

Thus all kinds of people, including Swami Muktananda, visited the shrine. They say, "Swami Muktananda acquired supernatural powers, but others received nothing from the shrine, that is, from the patron saint." They also ask me why I gained so much and others practically nothing. I explain to them that others also received full gains. I obtained what I yearned for: knowledge, meditation and devotion. I longed to have a deep personal relationship with God and that was granted. Those who desired a child got one. Those who wanted to become learned received knowledge. Another who wished to win his court case, won it. The patient that prayed for recovery from his disease was cured. The boys and girls who wanted to pursue an affair also had their wishes granted. Whatever desire each one had was fulfilled.

Your reward will vary in kind and quality according to your approach, mental make-up, faith in your Guru and knowledge of him, trust in the inner Shakti and knowledge of Her ways, the manner of your meditation and above all, your motives. If you are only shamming meditation, a flying chariot will not come down from Kailas. However, you can have fish. Therefore, meditators should meditate with care and noble aspiration.

You should see what your mind stabilises on and how much you are entangled in other things. When Muktananda used to meditate, he directed his mind to his only deity, Bhagawan Nityananda, who was his only brother or sister disciple. His Guru was the sole focus of his loving emotions. What's the point of finding new brothers or sisters after discarding real ones? Can you have such relationships without impure and twisted motives? In fact, all the men and women of the world are one's brothers and sisters. Why then become attached to one and averse to another? As far as Muktananda was concerned, Nityananda was his only dear relative, his sole dear friend. He did not form connections with anyone else. Nor did he cheat anyone under the cover of affiliation to Nityananda. He constantly meditated on Nityananda, his thoughts continually dwelt on him; he rejoiced in Nityananda alone. He obtained full contentment, peace, relief, joy and Self-knowledge only from Nityananda.

A young yogini was meditating the other day. I happened to go into the meditation room and I found her laughing heartily, with her eyes closed in a charming *mudra*. I asked her why she was laughing so much, and she replied, "I have observed people sham meditation in their attempt to impress and deceive you, thinking that you are simple-minded. But the fact is that you are neither impressed nor deceived. However, you pretend to be ignorant of their motives and bluff them. For this reason I am laughing."

I said, "Dear daughter, that is true. I give them what they want."

O meditators! You may be meditating deeply, performing vigorous movements, plunging into intense, intenser and even the intensest feelings, but remember that the conscious power of knowledge keeps watching you, reporting your true inner state to me. It was this power that revealed the above secret to that girl. Therefore she had good reason to laugh and what she said was true. I have a sort of secret 'meditation meter' that nobody will ever be able to see. From this meter I detect the quality of your meditation and measure your true worth. Be careful, therefore, whether your inner and outer movements are genuine or not. Towards what object are your actions directed? How strong is your inner faith? What does your mind cling to or seek refuge in? This will indicate your real motives, though all of you may be visiting the sacred shrine—whether you are seeking children, cure for a disease, employment or a high grade in a college examination. Whatever be the desire behind your pilgrimage, it will be fulfilled. Fully examine your motives for meditating. When your thoughts centre on the north, isn't it absurd to ask why you don't see Rameshwaram? Rameshwaram is situated in the south. Turn about. Direct your thoughts to the south. You will certainly see Rameshwaram.

In this context I will narrate the story of Laila and Majanu, taken from the discourses of Swami Ram Tirth. Laila was the daughter of a king and Majanu was the son of a labourer. They fell in love, but could not get married because of the differences in their social status and background. However, they loved each other intensely. Their love grew with the passage of time. Laila would climb into the highest tower of the palace and call out, "Majanu, Majanu!" Majanu would wander through the city streets calling out, "Laila, Laila!" His mind became completely one-pointed. He had only one desire, one succour, one hope. Laila was the sole object of his thoughts. He only wanted to be united with her. He was not inconstant. His mind turned to none else than Laila. When Majanu's father found his son so mad about the princess, he became afraid that the king would punish him. But true love is afraid of no one.

The king was also overcome with anxiety about the pathetic plight of his beloved daughter. He tried different means for the recovery of her health. He put her under the care of physicians, experts in mantras and Tantras and astrologers, but to no avail. If he asked her to go to the theatre to divert her mind, she asked, "Will I meet Majanu there?" If he suggested a trip to a far-away resort, she would refuse to go because Majanu would not be there. Laila and Majanu pined for each other in this manner.

Muktananda is of the view that you should either pursue an object with such selfless intensity or not at all. A selfish pursuit is of no use, nor does it take you to God. Majanu and Laila had forgotten themselves while dwelling on each other. Laila had become Majanu by constantly remembering him and Majanu had become Laila. If a meditator does not merge himself completely in the object of meditation, he is a thief. The more he withholds himself the worse his thievery. Majanu's condition became identical to that described in a verse:

खटका नहीं है खाने का, चिन्ता नहीं है पाने की ।
ममता नहीं है देह की, परवाह नहीं है प्राणों की ॥

(He is not worried about his food, nor anxious for any gain, nor attached to his body, nor clinging to life itself.)

With the single hope of union with his Laila, he wandered around in a state of complete self-forgetfulness. The people of the city took him for a lunatic. The king was moved to pity on seeing him in such a condition, for he was convinced of the truth of Majanu's love. Majanu had made an offering of himself to his beloved through self-effacement, like an earring melting into gold. He saw his beloved everywhere. He had transcended the distinction of "you and I," being conscious of Laila alone. So the king had it proclaimed in the streets that all were to give Majanu food and drink, clothes and shoes and send the bills to the royal treasury.

The news spread like wildfire. Majanu had obtained everything through his contemplation of Laila. The needy, sluggards, parasites and the destitute of the town also heard this. They thought it would be profitable to become a Majanu. The Majanus multiplied. Everyday a new Majanu appeared on the scene. Whoever pretended to be a Majanu received free shoes, free cloth and free board, and all the bills were sent to the royal treasury. The king learned with dismay that Majanu's bills amounted to more than several thousands. When he investigated the matter, he was told that the number of Majanus had risen to more than a thousand! Naturally he became concerned. His feeling of pity was proving quite expensive. What should be done now?

His Prime Minister was extremely shrewd. He said, "Your Majesty, if you delegate full authority to me, I shall handle this matter to your satisfaction."

The king agreed. Now the Prime Minister sent the crier around to proclaim that on the seventh day from that day, Majanu would be hanged at midday because he had sullied the fair name of the princess by claiming to be her lover.

How can I describe the condition of the fake Majanus? One threw his new clothes away, another his shoes, yet another his cap. They ran away to hide in distant corners. One found employment in an office, another began to work as a domestic servant and another as a watchman. All the Majanus were busy concealing their identities, because they were mortally afraid of the hangman's noose. They all disappeared. Only the genuine Majanu was left. He was of course prepared for any eventuality. It did not matter to him whether he was hanged or burned alive. He was ready to lay down his life, for he set his own life at naught. He valued only Laila. He had merged himself in her; he had become one with her.

My dear students of meditation! Only when you are put to a true test in meditation will your worth be judged. This test is very similar to those held in other fields. Through this, a genuine Majanu or meditator attains Laila or God. Otherwise he has to discard his cloth, shirt and shoes and run away. True meditators resemble Majanu. Therefore, do not pretend, but actually meditate. You will attain true joy.

Hail the fivefold Shakti within, dwell on Sri Gurudev and merge yourself in him. He who effaces himself in meditation, becoming one with his deity, like the earring melting into gold, attains the transcendental state and thus fulfils himself. His parents are also fulfilled. He alone achieves everlasting life. From a mortal he becomes immortal. Only when a devotee realises the emptiness of the world and sees his own Self pervading all beings from Brahma to the tiniest insects, does he become filled with devotion within and without, in each cell, as it were, and truly enjoy it. The one whose devotion has reached such a peak receives the true knowledge from the Guru. Chiti revels in him all the time. Such a Siddha student is truly worthy, since he is aware of the glories of meditation. As he continually honours the Guru-Shakti revealed within him and sings the Guru's praises, all his tears cease. Muktananda says that he comes to embody Nityananda fully.

Truth is rewarded with truth and falsehood with false-hood. Decide then what you are going to choose. Meditate genuinely for genuine attainment. Supreme peace is not far away; it lies within your own Self. But for this you must totally purify yourself.

# 4

# THE SECRET OF RENUNCIATION

It is entirely true that supreme peace follows renunciation. In fact, renunciation itself is the highest attainment. There are, however, innumerable varieties of renunciation. Some people renounce their homes but continue to weep for want of peace. Some relinquish religion but do not find contentment. Another discards his clothes, smears his body with sacred ash and becomes known as a renunciate, but he does not obtain peace. One gives up cereals, but drinks milk and takes pride in it. Some abandon women, some their families and some even speech. Still all of them remain hungry for peace. They do not know where to find it. The Lord's statement that peace lies in renunciation is true. त्यागाच्छान्तिरनन्तरम् (*Gita* XII-12). But the question is: what should be relinquished? And how? Affectation is on the increase in the name of renunciation. Worldly people have become fed up with this and also frightened. They are repulsed by practices such as piercing the ears and plucking the hair.

There are many who think that peace is not accessible to those living in the world. A common conception is that peace can be obtained only by living in a cave, a forest or a mountain cavern. Worldly people think that their insipid worldly enjoyments, families and households exhaust the scope of life; that meditation, renunciation and yoga are reserved exclusively for *sadhus* and renunciates who have relinquished their homes. But Muktananda says: yoga, meditation and detachment are meant precisely for those for whom worldly life, wives and children, factories, business and industries, household and wealth are important.

There is no doubt that renunciation is essential. But what does it mean? Countless renunciates are roaming

198

around as beggars, feeling proud that they have abandoned everything. One wonders how so many sects manage to survive by advocating and wearing the label of renunciation for all to see. Yet they also lack peace. Renunciation is, indeed, indispensable for peace, but it should be reasonable. Meaningless forms of renunciation should be avoided.

In India, there are many so-called perfect renunciates who eat only when they are offered food right in their hands, but not otherwise. There are even others after whom one man has to keep running from morning to evening, holding their food, which they may eat in the evening if they feel like it. Somebody once said to me, "Swamiji! Look what a great renunciate he is! He eats only when he is fed. Four to six people are engaged to make arrangements for him to eat."

I said, "Look, brother, I take my food punctually with my own hands. I have renounced the half-dozen people who are held up for the sake of one. Isn't it a mockery to be considered a renunciate but hold up six men from their work? I help myself. Don't you consider it renunciation that I am not depending on six persons to feed me?"

Thus there are countless forms of so-called renunciation. We should ask ourselves what is the advantage of practising self-denial and why is the peace spoken of by the Lord not experienced? It is the height of foolishness to eat food or drink water only if it is offered. Renunciation should be based on knowledge and understanding of truth. Otherwise, what's the point? One relinquishes one home only to build another in an ashram or forest. One discards white cloth to wear saffron. Thus only the colour of cloth has changed. Only the outer form has changed.

In this context, it would be useful to reflect on the example of King Sikhidhwaja. His story occurs in the great work, the *Yoga Vashishtha*. It is the story of the true awakening that quietens the mind and imparts supreme peace. King Sikhidhwaja was a great seeker of liberation, possessing genuine curiosity for true religion.

He was very keen to realise the highest truth. As days passed, his aspiration became more intense. He used to meet great saints, seers and sages and hold satsang with them and he also practised sadhana. His eagerness to realise the truth increased day by day. After practising different kinds of disciplines, he finally thought that realisation was impossible without renunciation. He decided first to abdicate his throne, handing his sceptre to the queen and retiring into a forest.

He sent for his beloved queen, Chudala, and opened his heart to her. He said, "I cannot live without inner peace. My ignorant mind is constantly frightened of this world. I live with the pride of 'I am a king.' But the fact is that I sleep like a commoner and I eat like one. Who, on the face of the earth, has not been devoured by time? Yet I expect to live forever. Am I not being stupid? Why shouldn't I relinquish this perishable and fleeting life right now, when after all it has to perish one day? O Queen Chudala! You are my beloved wife. You have done me many good turns. Do me one more favour. Kindly sit on the throne and rule the kingdom so that I may be free to seek peace and quench the thirst of my soul."

The queen was fully aware of the king's mental state. Through the practice of yoga she had attained the knowledge of past, present and future. She could see that the king was deluded by a wrong notion of renunciation. He would not see reason if she discussed it frankly with him. With clear insight into his character, she allowed him to leave.

The king retired into the forest solitudes of the Himalayas, raised a hut in an uninhabited region and began to perform sadhana, practising meditation, concentration, mantra-repetition and austerities. As he followed severe restraints, his mind became more unsteady and uneven. The truth is that a man can find peace and joy in that way of life which corresponds to his disposition and upbringing. If it goes against his grain, he will feel unhappy even in the most favourable environment.

The king had lived for a long time in royal grandeur. But now he wore rough bark, stayed in a straw hut and slept on a deer skin. He took cold baths and subsisted on roots, tubers and fruits, living austerely. His mind became more troubled and restless each day. He had come to find peace, equanimity and bliss, but instead, he became increasingly more agitated, disquieted and dejected. Yet he perservered, for he was a true seeker. He continually thought in terms of renunciation. What more should he give up? Peace immediately follows renunciation, but he was still far from it. He thought he had not renounced enough.

Queen Chudala was a great yogini having the gift of omniscience. Moreover, she was a modest and faithful wife. To her, the universe was Chiti's outward expansion. She had her cave of equanimity right in her palace. She was constantly aware of the supreme Lord while engaged in any work. As she looked upon all things as vibrations of Chiti, having renounced the differentiative tendency, she was a perfect renunciate, in the scriptural sense of the word. She had not relinquished her home, but the sense of difference that alienates one from one's own Self. Therefore she was free from anxiety in her worldly affairs to a degree corresponding to her inner quietude in meditation. Not only this, but by the power of yoga, she could travel anywhere she liked, with the Blue Pearl as her vehicle. She could assume any physical form. She had many times spoken to her husband about the true nature of the inner Self, but the king had regarded her merely as a wife and therefore had not benefited from her instruction. The queen, being highly intelligent, patiently waited for the right opportunity to bring her husband round, for it does not avail to reason with a person before his time. Through meditation, she kept herself fully informed of the king's condition. By means of her inner vision, she could see what he did and what he left undone.

The king practised renunciation more vigorously. He emaciated his body by reducing his food to an exclusively fruit diet, taken, first, once in two days, then once in

three days and finally once in five days. The queen felt
troubled about such excesses. She could not wait any
longer. By the power of yoga, she took on a new form
and a new name and appeared to the king as a seer called
Kumbha. The king was astonished to see an unfamiliar
seer there. He welcomed him respectfully, offering him
a seat. Kumbha inquired after his condition. The king
told him about his inner plight and added, "O venerable
seer! I have not obtained peace as yet. Kindly show me
some method by which I may attain it."

The seer said, "Your Majesty, there is only one way
to peace: renunciation," and with that he vanished.
When the king heard this, his surprise was even greater.
He began to ponder: "What exactly should be renounced?
What more can I abandon? I have discarded my throne,
wealth, possessions, power, glory, comforts—in fact everything. I have given up attachment to near and dear ones,
acquaintances and friends and now live in a straw hut
in a mountain forest. Yet the seer Kumbha says,
'Renounce.' What does it mean? What more is left for
me to abandon?"

He was oppressed by doubt. He thought he would give
up his hut, deer skin, water bowl and even the bark.
Meanwhile, Kumbha turned up again and said, "O king!
Are you happy? Have you obtained peace?"

The king replied, "Venerable seer! I am still as far
away from peace as ever. I am pining for it."

The seer said, "Your renunciation, it seems, is not
complete as yet," and vanished.

The king again brooded on what more he could
abandon. He carried his renunciation to its utmost
extreme. He resolved that he would discard whatever he
had, including his body. He thought: "I shall light a
pyre and throw all my things into it. Then, finally I
shall jump into it myself. When this body is consumed,
I will certainly attain peace." He collected dry logs from
the forest, made a big pyre and lighted it. He recalled
his associations with each of his objects and put them in
the fire one by one, saying, "O dear hut! I have lived
in you for many many days, but without peace. Now I

offer you to the fire. O dear water bowl! I drank water from you for many many days, but without peace. Now I offer you to the fire." He threw his deer skin and also his bark into the fire. Whatever he had was on fire. Now he was left with only his naked body. He circled the pyre thrice and then said, "O my dear body! I gave you various delectable savoury foods to gratify you, but I did not find joy. I bathed you in various perfumed baths but I did not find peace. I gave you many beautiful maidens to enjoy but I did not obtain contentment. I washed you so much, fed you so much and adorned you so much, yet I remained without tranquillity."

As he was on the verge of jumping into the fire, the seer Kumbha appeared. He caught him by the hand and said, "O king! Wait, wait! How unjust! What is this horrible act?"

The king replied, "O seer! After renouncing every possession, I am now relinquishing the body, offering it to the fire. This will certainly bring me supreme peace."

Kumbha said, "O king! If the cremation of the body could give peace, everyone would surely do it. How can you experience peace by burning the very body that is essential for finding it? How will you obtain peace if the body is consumed? O king, you don't understand what you should relinquish. Look, the body is made of flesh and blood. Its inner structure is most marvellously framed. It is the product of the union of the father's sperm and the mother's ovum. What in it is specifically yours that you may abandon? O king! This body is formed from the generative fluids of the parents which are the quintessence of the food eaten by them. Food springs from the earth. Now tell me in what way your body is your exclusive possession that you may abandon it? Man eats the food growing from the earth, spends his days on its surface and finally merges into it. Therefore, this body is really made of earth. Now is it justifiable for you to renounce the body, which is given to you by others and consider it to be renunciation of something belonging to you? In fact, for him who has attained true knowledge by the Guru's grace, what is there to discard except his sense of 'I' and 'mine'?"

On listening to the seer's words, the king realised that he had no right to abandon the body which was not his but a gift from God. Is it wise to slight the body, or endanger its health by irregularity or enfeeble it through lack of restraint and discipline? One should think intelligently about this. In fact, *abhinivesha*, the source of all miseries, is what should be relinquished. *Abhinivesha* has been defined in the scriptures as follows: 'To regard something as ours that does not belong to us and to identify ourselves with that which is not the Self, is *abhinivesha*.' The ego, the sense of a separate existence, gives rise to all our afflictions. This is responsible for reducing God to a limited, individual self, happiness to sorrow and One to many. If this 'I' sense could be annihilated and replaced by *So'ham* there would be nothing left to renounce. The world is nothing but Chiti.

The forms of renunciation which are neither necessary nor sanctified by the scriptures, bestow confusion instead of peace. In fact renunciation is the most entangling enjoyment, while discriminate enjoyment is the highest renunciation. Why did God create the world? For whom was the world created? For what object? If a seeker thoughtlessly takes to the forms of renunciation not enjoined by the scriptures, he is unworthy. Man is in misery on account of his ignorance of the true nature of the universe. If one could fully realise that the world is Chiti's sport, one's worldly life would become spiritualised. The world created by God is in no way different from the Self—it is, indeed, His embodiment. This is a true Vedantic principle, that the effect cannot be different from the cause; in fact, the cause is hidden in the effect.

It is a perverse, differentiating mentality which looks upon Chiti contrarily, while living in the world that is full of Chiti. It is, of course, true that as long as a man himself is sour, false and cheerless, the world would appear equally so to him. This proposition is self-evident: one sees the world as one is. Whether one is a householder, a renunciate, a monk or a mendicant, the world only reflects one's own state. But the one who has received the Guru's grace, awakened his inner Shakti, and witnessed Chiti's sport in his own heart, will also find Chiti unfolding and vibrating without. I am reminded of a couplet:

श्रीगुरुचरणाम्भोजं सत्यमेव विजानताम् ।
जगत् सत्यमसत्यं वा नेतरेति मतिर्मम ॥

(He who knows the Guru's lotus feet as the sole reality does not care whether the world is real or unreal.) Whether the world is real or imaginary is simply a matter of scholastic controversy, and controversy yields nothing. Only when the mind becomes free from controversies can it perceive Chiti's playfulness. Then the universe is seen to be God Himself. Anyone who has had a vision of God will never see this world as empty or joyless, but as His glory.

Renunciation is not that of home, caste, community, duties corresponding to one's stage of life, food, body, or selfless action in the world, but renunciation of differentiation, of *abhinivesha*. As we give up *abhinivesha*, the truth hidden in us and in the external world reveals itself. Then a seeker sees one Chiti flowing through sense organs, actions and outer objects. At this stage, misery ends once and for all. He begins to look after his everyday affairs with ease, reverence and devotion, seeing God underlying them all.

As King Sikhidhwaja completely discarded *abhinivesha* according to the teaching of the seer Kumbha, his outgoing mind became introverted at once. He descended into his inner depths until he penetrated to the Self. He was immersed in the *samadhi* state—aware of only Oneness. He transcended the distinctions of inner and outer, dual and non-dual, and attained peace. He resembled an insomniac who glides into a long and profound slumber on being caressed by gentle breezes at a cool and pleasant water-spring. When the mind, that has been turbulent for a long time, actually finds peace within, it discards mentation and becomes one with the Soul. The king, having attained what he was searching for, became absorbed in bliss. When his attention finally turned to the outside world, he found it pervaded by the same bliss. He had uprooted his own differentiating mentality. He saw his inner joy reflected outside as well. The king fully realised the truth of the principle that God is everywhere. His attitude was changed. He renounced his wrong conception of renunciation. He abandoned multiplicity, embracing unity and awoke to the inner Soul. The non-differentiative vision of unity put an end to diversity. He perceived the Lord of the universe everywhere. He began to see the opposition of solitude and society as a merry product of delusion. His veil of distinction was burned up in the fire of knowledge. He neither preferred forests and uninhabited regions nor denounced towns and cities as the habitations of vulgar and busy commoners. He fully attained the knowledge that He who is in forests, caves and solitary regions, was also in the palace. Upon this awakening, he felt an urge to return to his palace and actually did so. After receiving the Guru's grace and knowing that the world is a manifestation of Chiti, he began to look upon the world, his family and subjects as helpful and congenial, enjoying Chiti's play in them. Remaining established in the inner Self, he ruled his kingdom and accepted gladly whatever destiny brought him. He experienced Chiti vibrating far and near, in hunger and thirst, hope and despair, justice and injustice, contentment and avarice, anger and agitation.

Though he accepted differences for practical purposes, in his heart he was only aware of undifferentiated unity. He had fully realised the Truth. He beheld the light of his own soul illuminating his ornaments, food and drink, wood and stone, animals, gods, human beings, sages and seers. He perceived one God permeating all names, forms, qualities and elements of this animate and inanimate universe.

Dear ones! Possession and renunciation have meaning only so long as one is not fully realised. But on knowing the Truth, one finds that none but one's own Self exists. One's own beauty pervades everywhere.

One thing is certain: whether you are enlightened or

not, you have to bear the consequences of your past actions. An ignorant man suffers them, weeping and grumbling, in slavery to the differentiative mentality, while a wise man, with his eye of knowledge, sees the world as Chiti's sport, as the light of his own soul and enjoys it innocently. Both the ignorant and the enlightened have to live their lives, but one remains occupied with the enjoyment of outer sense objects, while the other, with Chiti's inner play. As the latter carries immense merit, accumulated through innumerable lives, he will also be chased by beauty and material wealth. Yet he will not be born again. Nor will he become entangled in sensuous delights. For he lives blissfully, transmuting sensuous pleasure into spiritual joy. Such a yogi does not rejoice in sense stimulation, but in the soul. Though he appears to be worldly to the worldly, from the spiritual viewpoint he is a great yogi who has become one with the Absolute. That which is a mere assemblage of gross elements to the ordinary man is the Supreme Being to the yogi. This constant awareness is his meditation. His meditation is therefore not interrupted when he attends to practical affairs.

For ordinary people, there is a cleavage between sense enjoyment and the spiritual goal of meditation. To extinguish his craving for enjoyment, the average meditator feels compelled to direct his mind towards a purely spiritual object. But the yogi who has become one with the Absolute is constantly in meditation, whether bathing, eating, drinking, coming, going, dressing or wearing ornaments, since all these activities are for him expressions of the Divine. This is, according to me, the meditation that continues uninterruptedly for all hours of the day and night. In this state, inspired by Chitshakti, a Siddha yogi can outwardly be a king and live in splendour, be indifferent and indrawn like Jadbharat, become a naked *avadhoot* like Rishabhdeva, or behave like a foolish, mad, devilish creature. All this is, however, determined by destiny. Chiti, who imbues us with Shiva-consciousness, may bring us honour or infamy, prosperity or adversity. We should accept all as gifts of Her grace.

As these conditions are determined by the will of Shiva, we should experience only His love in them. But this attitude can be developed only by those who have been blessed by the Guru's grace. The ones who are not so blessed will feel miserable even in the most favourable circumstances.

The differentiating outlook is the sole cause of man's fear and restlessness. Referring to those who consider distinctions to be valid, the *Brihadaranyaka Upanishad* says: मृत्यो: स मृत्युमाप्नोति य इह नानेव पश्यति (4-4-19). (Such a one goes from death to death. He secures nothing else either in this life or the next.) The *Taittiriyopanishad* says: उदरमन्तरं कुरुतेऽथ तस्य भयं भवति (2-7). (If one sees even the slightest differences, one is subjected to fear.)

Truth, equality, awareness of the Self of all and faith in the Guru's teaching are the best paths to fearlessness. Just as a fish remains thirsty in water, likewise, a man without the Guru's grace finds this blissful world barren and savourless. Such a deluded person imagines a serpent in a rope and falls prey to fear. Similarly, he superimposes impure concepts such as 'matter,' 'insipid,' and '*maya*' on this conscious universe in which Chiti is revelling and makes himself thoroughly miserable.

If we see ourselves truly, we shall discover that we are neither denizens of hell, animals, human beings, nor gods, but pure perfect souls in our innermost nature. Dwell on this thought again and again until you imbibe it fully.

The mind remains active only as long as the world is seen as different from the Self. This activity of the mind divorced from the soul constitutes worldly chains or bondage. When one's own soul is perceived as pulsating in the world of the movable and the immovable, the mind discards mentation and merges in Chiti. The person whose mind is one with Chiti sees the Self on all sides. Then concepts of body, *maya*, duality and distinction all dissolve into the non-dual consciousness. The pure One, the goal of the scriptural authors, called Satchidananda, appears in all names and forms. The world is as one sees it. When the soul irradiates the eyes, the entire universe is perceived as Self. Just as on sunrise, what had appeared as darkness appears as light, likewise, in the dawn of Self-knowledge, the world appears as Self.

The differentiative tendency is at the root of all miseries. It has condemned everyone to the round of duality, causing ceaseless affliction. Although distinctions are not real, they appear to be so. When the Guru's grace lifts the veil of duality, a seeker realises God within himself. This is the state of *jivanmukti*, or the state of spontaneity—a worthy destination for man. This is a benevolent gift of Chiti. Inner awakening is essential for attaining it, which can only be effected by the Guru. To deserve this, we should be devoted to the Guru, meditate according to his instructions, following the path shown by him.

Dear seekers! Equipoise is that which we should possess, and disharmony that which we should renounce. As one begins to dwell on equality, distinctions fade. Awareness of one Life is the true nature of all. It is, indeed, the Absolute. This is the message of all saints.

# 5

# THE PATH OF LOVE

The path of love is a noble path. Love is also devotion. It is a dynamic throbbing of the heart which is highly inspiring. Love is the very nature of God, called Supreme Bliss or Satchidananda by the scriptural authors. It dwells in its fullness within man. Even if he does not experience it, it resides in full splendour within him. A blind man who has never seen light may remark, on hearing others talk about it, "Light does not exist; I have never seen it; I cannot even imagine it." But the fact is that light exists, only he does not have the eyes to perceive it. Similarly, love may not be experienced, but it lies embedded in the heart. If you do not make any effort to discover love or follow its path, how can you hope to attain it?

Love is pure nectar. Love is immortal. The milkmaids of Gokul realised God through love alone. Love is the light of the secret inner cave. It flows from within through different senses. It is the inner stream of love that rises into eyes, lending charm to whatever is seen; that flows into ears, imparting melody to sounds; that bathes the tongue, pouring its sweet essence into the juices. Love is the supremely blissful soul whose emanations make sensuous objects enjoyable. If the soul were to stop pouring love through the senses, they would become sterile, insipid and joyless. In fact, love is the digit that gives value to zeros in a number by preceding them.

Man should learn to love in his everyday life. But this love should be pure, independent and desireless; it should be given for its own sake. If love has desire in it, it becomes a mere commodity of commercial exchange. One may imagine it is true love, but it is not. Love is free

from craving and the notion of 'yours' and 'mine.' Love
is selfless, being nothing but love.

There is so much love in the heart that it is enough
not only for one man, but for the whole of mankind.
Unfortunate people do not have access to it because of
desire, unnecessary mentation and anxiety. It is only
when one becomes completely selfless that the inner
spring of ambrosial love is released.

Your love should not be directed towards sense gratification or selfish ends, for then it loses its divinity and
degenerates into attachment. Attachment is undoubtedly
impure. It cannot lead man to God. Love increases by
giving, not by receiving. The idea of 'yours' and 'mine'
obstructs it. Love should be extended equally. Let it be
your unique possession.

One Guru had an attendant who was utterly devoted
to him. Someone asked him, "Brother, how are you?
Tell me about yourself. How is life in your ashram? Do
you suffer from heat or cold?" The attendant replied,
"Sir, I feel neither the heat of summer nor the cold of
winter. I am a mere servant who only knows how to
serve his Master. My Guru alone knows whether I feel
hot or cold, happy or miserable." What a noble attitude!
He had immersed himself without the least reservation
in service to his Guru. Your love should be equally lofty,
being entirely free from impurities, egoism, strain and
desire. Such love will lead you to God, making you
divine.

Do not torture yourself by repeating that you are
impure, joyless, unreal, ephemeral, born only to suffer.
Several poetic works, communities and religions consider
the body to be pathetic and malignant, depriving it of
all value. How unjust! How unfairly you treat the body
that becomes divine through devoted worship and
remembrance of God, meditation and love for the Guru!
Sant Tukaram says: ब्रह्मभूत होते काया च कीर्तनीं (the body becomes divine by repeating God's name). I have seen
many aspirants who ill-treat their bodies to such an
extent that they end up suffering from disease. Dear
Siddha students! Your conscious body is the sacred

temple of Goddess Chiti. Treat it with due respect by being pure and chaste, eating good wholesome food and by wearing simple, neat, clean and beautiful clothes.

O Siddha students! You are in search of inner peace but you hate your body and senses. You long for inner joy but develop hostility towards the body which is a means to that joy, as though it were your most formidable enemy. Do not forget that you attain salvation by means of this very body. If you know your inner being, you will realise that the body is not illusory, but a significantly beautiful temple; by loving it your inner fount of love will be liberated. Consider that the ever-new joy that reveals itself during meditation dwells in the heart as a free, vibrating force. If you wish to become one with God and with your beloved Guru, and tap the inner source of love, you must first love yourself. Develop love and let it flow from you to others.

Dear Siddha students! To attain love it is essential for you to have the right knowledge of the body, which is the seat of love. You must know its component elements and their functions and take care of it with pure, friendly and courteous affection. The human form has been your companion through many lives. It has shared the joys and sorrows of your various pursuits for a prolonged period. It is a means of sadhana, a ladder to the city of liberation, a glorious temple of the inner Self. The Lord of love, the supreme Master, dwells in the innermost sanctum of this shrine. Hence, Muktananda says that the awakened student, who has realised the truth of the body, will not distrust it, treat it with vile antagonism, engage it in ignoble acts, nor degrade it through corrupt, wicked and undesirable ways. Those who regard this body as a mere means of pleasure like a hotel, club or cinema, vitiate its purity and enfeeble it. They treat it unjustly, disrespectfully and insultingly. Those who are unkind to their pure and friendly body, suppressing it violently and tormenting it mercilessly, fill their hearts with tears instead of love. They pray to the Lord to deliver them from the prison of the body, yet the fault does not lie with the body.

THE PATH OF LOVE 213

The body is the dwelling of your soul. It is a means of experiencing joy and sorrow. It is your servant always obedient to you. The body is ready to go wherever you want to take it. If you want it to ride a mount, gourmandise or give it plain fare, it accepts all these conditions uncomplainingly. You may adorn it with the most precious jewels or cover it with a loin-cloth or tattered rags; it is equally happy. The body is such a servant, such a friend as can be excelled by nothing else in the wide world.

Consider the five fundamental elements comprising your body. How beautiful the earth is! What variety of grains grow from her, the mother of innumerable beings! How pure the water that supplies sap to grains, fruits, flowers, trees and creepers! How full of love! It cleanses and sustains all. Or the fire that resides in all beings according to their needs and assists them equally. Inside the human body it digests food as gastric fire. It lives in wood and stone, in fact, in all objects, in keeping with their various natures. What an ideal example of all-pervading selfless love! Next, the air. It constitutes the prana, the very life of man. It equally permeates all beings, whether animate or inanimate. It imparts movement to the whole world. Without prana the body is reduced to a worthless corpse. Finally, the ether. It seems to remind us of the ever-detached soul. Activities are only possible due to the space provided by it. These five elements compose the body. The conscious Spirit pervades its each and every cell. Fully realise the value of so beautiful and chaste a vehicle, and love it as God.

Think about it. Is it not sheer madness to become furious with the eyes and injure them or pull them out if they are filled with greed and burn with jealousy, anger or avarice while looking at another's wealth and beauty? Is it reasonable to punish the innocent eyes in the name of renunciation or disillusionment? The poor things are your constant friends. They become neither attached nor averse to anyone. They only help you to see. You may utilise your senses in any manner, as they are always at your disposal. Whatever task you may

assign them, they always perform it willingly. This body
co-operates with you whether you are being loving or
violent. It adjusts itself according to your ambition or
aspiration. It faithfully reflects your inner feelings.
Therefore, understand your body properly. Selflessly
love the sun and the moon situated in your eyes, and the
deities of your other senses and the other parts of your
body such as hands and feet. Know and worship the
transcendental Being performing the functions of your
different sense organs. This worship should not be
mechanical but should abound in pure and desireless love.
Of course, self-control is essential and mastery of the
senses is equally essential. All that I am pleading for
is that the body should not be tormented or sickened
under the pretext of renunciation or self-discipline.

Your body is a wondrous work of divine art, impregnated with great secrets. A mine of knowledge exists
within it. Only by means of the body can you visit God's
court, Vaikuntha, Kailas or the immutable city. What
would you do if you discarded your body? You can know
your own Self through meditation only within this body.

Various kinds of powers inhabit the sense organs,
muscles, nerves and the brain of man. Begin to know
them. They cannot work against you. They are neither
beneficial nor harmful, neither good nor bad, being
entirely detached. They only act according to the dictates
of your mind. The same divine inner Shakti, assuming
the forms of desire, anger, infatuation, greed and so on,
becomes active within you, using one or another of your
sense organs as Her medium of expression. Muktananda
exhorts: Meditate! Kindle love! As love begins to pulse
in all your senses, renunciation, yoga and knowledge will
arise within you spontaneously. At present, your mind
seeks love in the outer world through senses and objects
of enjoyment. If man could love himself as God, his mind
would not wander in the external world. What is there
in it after all? True love is released in meditation. A
pleasure-seeker torments his body with pleasurable excitement until it becomes enervated. Finally he begins to
spurn it and becomes miserable. A renunciant torments

his body with constant animosity, wasting it away with unwanted rigorous austerities and craves for the joy of liberation! Tell me truly whether it is not sheer idiocy to fight against this invaluable body continually, instead of rising above it. What kind of renunciation is it that hates instead of loves the body? It is a divine gift, meant for becoming inundated with the innumerable rays of ecstatic love which glow in *sahasrar* and for ardently loving one's inner and outer being. If, on the contrary, one sacrifices one's body for poisonous, impure, unworthy sensual enjoyments, is he not the prince of lunatics? Dear Siddha students! Value the bodily chariot in which you have to conduct your journey of deliverance. Learn to keep your body in order. Look upon it with love and respect. Do not desiccate your body, but drench it in the nectar of love. That alone will unite you with God.

I once read an authentic account of the last moments of an enlightened saint. The saint had foreknowledge of his death. On the eve of his final departure, he bade a loving and grateful farewell to everyone, asking for their forgiveness and blessings. Then he bowed to all the directions, the five basic elements, and the knowledge-bestowing Guru. Finally, he expressed gratitude to his body—the body in which he had consummated his spiritual journey, realising the Divine. Singing its praises, he addressed his body with folded hands, saying: "O my dear body! I have been able to attain God by your generous assistance, your bountiful grace. I thank you most heartily. I don't know how much I must have tortured and agonised you, but you have always helped me. I am deeply indebted to you. I have attained the highest *nirvikalpa* state in meditation through you. O my beloved body! You bestowed an alert and perceptive intelligence upon me. Therefore, my friend, I shall always remain grateful to you. I have committed sins against you wittingly and unwittingly, but you have always been good and kind to me. You did not take revenge on me for my unjust treatment, but stood by me as a faithful friend. But for you I could have neither performed

spiritual sadhana nor realised God." Having thus spoken
to his body, the great saint merged with the Absolute.

I want to ask my dear Siddha students: have you ever
looked upon your body with such selfless love? Have you
ever showered it with affection by Self-contemplation,
meditation, hymns, chants, harmonising the repetition of
*So'ham* with your breathing.? Have you ever thanked it
by observing sacred vows and restraints, taking sweet and
pure juices and serving it agreeable food conducive to
longevity? If not, what an ingrate you are! What could
be more deplorable than to be so discourteous towards
your beloved friend?

Dear Siddha students! Cultivate an enlightened attitude towards your body. Extend courtesy, honour and
love to it. As I recollect that loving address, "O my
beloved body," heavenly joy wells up within me. If you
could also respond in a similar manner to these great
words of awakening, it would not take you long to
experience supreme bliss.

Dear seekers! Become aware of the full significance
of your body. Develop a selfless relationship with it.
Look after your body according to the rules of the health.
He who has realised the value of the body will direct
it towards yoga, love and meditation.

Do not be angry with the different parts of your body.
If you have to feel anger, be angry with anger, not with
the body. Neither torment your friendly body by listening
to the prattle of the ignorant, nor become insensitive or
hypocritical towards it. Dear aspirants! You reap the
fruits of all your actions in this body. It is in the body
that you practise austerities. By its means men have
achieved greatness in different fields. Great sages, seers,
kings, brave warriors, poets, actors, painters, athletes,
women of exemplary purity, Jesus Christ and Lord
Buddha all lived in the body. Keep such a valuable body
unsullied. A body that is not industrious is of no use.
Regulate your body by regular work, *asanas, pranayama*
and meditation. Keep it neat and pure like a temple.
Regulate your diet and recreation. Let this be your only
aspiration: that by its means you may envision inner

lights in meditation. Let this be your sole expectation: that your body and senses may become reasonable and disciplined and radiate inner love.

You complain that your mind pushes your body around by its thoughts and fancies, and that it imposes its dictates on your body and senses. Is it justified to punish your body in order to control the mind? What purpose would it serve to punish Peter if you are angry with Paul? I agree that the mind is fickle and unsteady, and it does cause trouble. All spiritual disciplines aim at controlling the mind. Yogis learn different techniques only to restrain the mind; yet they become proud, conceited and ease-loving. They find neither love, inner happiness nor contentment. All of them lament that the mind is not stable. I also repeat the same. But have you ever provided the mind with a worthy object? If you offer it a congenial support it will hold onto that joyfully, without roaming here and there.

Once upon a time a Swami stayed at a small village. He lived in a plain and simple hut, feeling rich in the midst of poverty. One day the wealthiest man of the neighbouring town came to his hut for darshan. The Swami happened to be out at that time. His disciple asked the millionaire to sit down but he did not want to. He began to pace up and down under a tree. This behaviour surprised the disciple. The Swami soon returned. The disciple told him everything in a tone of surprise. The Swami said, "We are mendicants after all, my brother. We have no suitable place for him to sit. It was for this reason that he was roaming about."

This is true for the mind as well. If it finds an agreeable hold, it will stop wandering. Dear brothers! You are also in the same boat. Your mind is always craving something pleasant.

O mind! What is it that you would not do for your pleasure, self-interest and peace? Yet you remain sad and distracted. You take to the path of knowledge but only become apathetic. After mastering some elements of yoga you feel elated for a while but fall into dejection again. You madly seek love among sensuous objects but to no avail. You become addicted to sensuality yet remain discontented and unsteady. You are continually haunted by nightmares of disquiet.

Learn a new lesson now. Love all with motiveless, unsurpassed and unlimited love. If you have not loved anyone, how can you find peace? Remain pure, untainted and independent, without antagonism. There is nothing in God's creation that hates you or takes a hostile stance against you. You should learn to make the most of the objects created by God. Do not consider the mind to be your enemy. The mind possesses great powers but you will only be able to utilise them if you know this. Descend into your inner depths just once. Then your mind will not move away from there. There are some *sadhus* who can perform miracles by virtue of ordinary mental powers alone. If you come to know your mind fully, you will discover what a wonderful worker it is. It is endowed with enormous creative potential.

You may give your mind the most pleasurable objects to enjoy but it will not be fully contained by them. It will flit from sights to tastes, from smells to sounds and then elsewhere. This inconstancy, this exuberance of the mind is a sign that it is looking for an exalted state. If the mind did not fluctuate so rapidly, an angry man would be stuck in his anger, an avaricious fellow trapped by his greed, a deluded one engrossed in his delusion, and a lascivious person held by his lust—forever and ever. A wealthy man would be fully satisfied with his wealth and an artist with his art. But this does not happen. Everyone seems to repeat that peace does not lie in wealth, art, beauty, sensuous enjoyments or any other thing. Your mind keeps wandering here and there, remaining unhappy. Finally, the instability of your mind makes you desperate.

Muktananda says: dear Siddha students! The mind yearns for true love, equanimity and unity with God; in fact, a worthy pursuit to occupy it. It is for this reason that it is so restless. It leaves agitating occupations behind and moves further on. Just as a beetle flits from one flower to another to drink their juices or a bee to gather honey, likewise, the mind continues to roam for some reason. Remember that there is a deep purpose behind the unsteadiness of the mind—it seeks perfect repose. So long as it does not fully absorb itself in meditation on the Self, it remains fluctuating and inconstant. If, by the grace of Kundalini, it becomes engrossed in meditation and illuminated by the inner light, it overcomes its restlessness and becomes still. Remember that the mind will not let you rest in peace until it has found repose in the soul. If it stabilises completely on the Self in meditation, it will overflow with supreme bliss. Then the direction of your life will be changed and you will be utterly transformed. The pure spring of peace will begin to flow within you.

The mind cannot enjoy full contentment in anything but God. If it could find God, it would obtain everything and become centred on Him. Then it would not move away even if you tried to divert it. Thus we see that it is the restlessness of the mind which compels you to seek peace and truth, by being dissatisfied with lesser things. The mind can rest only in God. It is this very nature of the mind that takes us towards peace. In this manner, the mind is really kind to us. The mind's unsteadiness is a great boon. It is this restlessness which has driven you to the great knowledge of Siddha Yoga. Its instability is a positive factor that has increased your interest in meditation. It has brought you a Siddha's grace. You should, therefore, honour the mind for its benevolent kindness.

My dear seekers! Bear in mind Muktananda's words of actual experience. One may declare proudly: "My religion is the greatest," but if the mind does not find peace therein, that religion cannot reflect God. However much a certain mantra may be praised, if it does not satiate the mind, it has nothing to do with God. However exalted a sect may be, its head may perform astonishing miracles, or may scrupulously observe religious rites such as sipping holy water, applying sacred ash and worshipping gods and goddesses, but if the mind does not obtain repose, God is not there. If the mind is able to rest for only a short time but then feels agitated and obliged to wander again, it has not yet attained quietude. If the mind is repelled by a certain occupation, it will keep running away regardless of your earnest efforts to hold it there. It continues to roam in search of happiness. It may be held briefly by an illusion of peace, but later it becomes even more restless.

Instead of doing violence to the mind in different ways, lovingly lead it in meditation towards the flowing stream of the blissful Self. Take it gently towards the cool shade of Self-love, towards the radiant light of true happiness. Just turn your attention to the supremely blissful soul; your mind will impatiently rush again and again in that direction. If you try to quieten it by force or power of will or rigorous austerities, it will become even more agitated and antagonistic. As soon as it attains complete joy, it will give up its fugitive tendency and rest content. Therefore, soak your mind in love. Let it be absorbed in the love of the Self. Love your mind. Do not consider it merely as the mind; give up your animosity towards it and make it your intimate friend. Then persuade it to move towards the inner soul. This is the process of meditation. If you consider the mind to be Chiti and fill it with love, you will win it over. But if you regard it as something ordinary and become inimical to it, it will conquer you. If you wish to completely triumph over the mind, love it. Love is the mantra of victory. Love is, indeed, the magnet that draws God. It is the noble sacrifice that transports the mind with ecstasy. It has immense power. Love realises the impossible. Love alone can make the mind whole, can prevent it from scattering its energy. Stop thinking of yourself as a pathetic helpless creature. Instead, saturate your heart with love, and then you will realise your own greatness.

Dear meditating yogis! Only through meditation can you find the precious inner treasures. Without it, you are utterly destitute. Meditation alone is your true wealth. Therefore, first love yourself and then meditate with love.

Once a Siddha lived in a forest. An aspirant came to

him and said entreatingly, "Venerable sire! I want to see God. What method should I follow?"

The saint examined his inner condition and asked, "Whom do you love?"

The aspirant said, "Isn't love an impediment on the way to God?"

The saint said, "No, love can never be an obstruction. It is desire and infatuation which are the obstacles. Love is the true nature of God. Widen the embrace of your love for yourself and for your dear ones to include all. Such love alone can lead to God. Therefore, love everyone."

Love can achieve everything. A lover sees God by love. Through love he easily attains Him who is supposed to be difficult of attainment. Other ways are not so simple. It is only the path of love that is so natural, for love is not unknown to you. You do not have to obtain love from outside by difficult practices, as its springs lie within. Let your heart overflow with love. Let your love be all-encompassing. If you continue to give love, more of it will be released from within. The more you give, the more you will have. He who gives love is greeted everywhere by love.

I have seen so many people who only hate in the name of love. True love will never hate anyone. It is above distinctions of high and low. I have seen so-called devotees who declare in angry, metallic tones, "As we are followers of Vishnu, we shall never visit a temple of Shiva!" If love is attended by such anger, I wonder whether it is love for all. Is it not sheer barbarity? Divisions based on caste, community, race, religion and status cannot be sanctioned by love. Love, on the contrary, bestows intense awareness of undifferentiated unity.

Love is present within you, giving you ever-new experiences. Think about the peace of deep sleep. Find out from where this supersensuous contentment arises. What is the source of the joy of meeting a friend? Where does the pleasure of beautiful sights originate? From where does the spontaneous sense of fullness spring when your mind is at rest? If you contemplate these questions you will find that sublime joy, also called supreme bliss, lies hidden within you. That, truly, is love. Therefore, worship love. Show only scenes of love to the Witness behind your eyes. Let your behaviour be full of love. Let your love for cows, dogs, trees, flowers and fruits grow each day, as love is the basis of all.

Love is a kind of nuclear power of transformation. Do not let your heart become arid. Do not look upon yourself as a loveless creature by listening to someone's stupid talk. Man does gross injustice to himself when he ignorantly considers himself to be a petty sinner and begins to infect others with such a deplorable outlook. Once I went to the confluence of the three rivers at Allahabad for a holy bath. As I sat down, a priest came and asked me to make a wish. He insisted in spite of my refusals. He brought flowers and other things and said, "Swamiji, say, ' I am a sinner.'" I retorted at once, "You are a sinner, not I, since your tribe has not given up its practice of befooling pilgrims even in a sacred place. I shall proclaim, 'I am noble, I perform noble deeds, I am without desire.'" Hearing this, the priest slunk away. Because of evil influence a man begins to regard himself as joyless, false, destitute or perishable, and does not allow the love within him to bloom.

Dear seekers! Scholarship without love is futile; so is yoga. Any discipline lacking love can never lead you to the soul's bliss. Love your own Self fully and give love to others, but your love must be without desire, craving or attachment. It is the only weapon which can vanquish the enemy of delusion. It is not necessary to read much of the scriptures, for all thoughts come from God. Here the question is not that of knowledge, but of love. Do not exhaust your life in controversies about possession and renunciation, neither of which has much significance. Self-awakening alone matters. Yoga, learning or knowledge, if accompanied by conceit, goes entirely against love. Uproot egoism utterly. This is possible only through love. Whenever desireless love arises in the heart, one feels supreme peace in life. Instead of sup-

pressing the mind, flood it with love. Then you will discover what treasures lie within.

Lead the mind towards the inner Self, not by force,
or suppression of breathing or asceticism, but by gentle
love. Let God be the sole object of enjoyment for all
your senses. Sant Tukaram says that he who is addicted
only to Narayana sees the world brimming with love.

Love is your very nature. Let it be your sadhana as
well as your highest attainment. Love is God. And love
is the universe. The supreme Lord has manifested Himself as this world out of love. Existence is nothing but
the loving throb of divine Shakti. Love is the most
effective means of God-realisation. He cannot be realised
without love. It is your most valuable inner experience.
Seek it within, where you will see the divine Shakti
coursing with lightning speed through your vital fluids,
blood, different forms of prana, in fact, throughout your
entire body. As you experience Her, you will also experience love.

Your inner processes are always active, never stopping.
Your nerves, muscles and blood are constantly performing their functions. Carry out your duties with the same
enthusiasm, steadfastness and love, whether you are at
home, in an ashram or elsewhere.

Man should love his Self, which is all-embracing. He
should have fullest faith in It. Love transfigures a mere
mortal into an ocean of bliss, a haven of peace, a temple
of knowledge. Love is man's very essence. It is his true
beauty. It is the glory of his human form.

Therefore Muktananda says: first love yourself, then
your neighbours and finally let your love embrace the
entire universe. This is true devotion. This is the way
to the bliss of knowledge, to the quiescence of yoga. Love
encompasses all other disciplines. Sri Nityananda is that
love. Approach the Sadguru only with love. Do not
even ask for salvation from him. He is truly supreme
bliss, the noblest goal of all spiritual paths. It is only
by his grace that we become worthy of his love.

# 6

# PLEASING THE GURU
## (The Source of All Attainment)

A student of Siddha Yoga should realise that he cannot attain perfection in the spiritual field by self-effort alone. Even in ordinary mundane matters we seek others' assistance and advice; we learn from others what we are unable to understand ourselves. In Shaktipat or Kriya Yoga, in Siddha Vidya or Kundalini Maha Yoga, the grace of the Guru is the sole determinant. It is well-nigh impossible to reach the highest summit of this path without a Guru's guidance.

The modern attitudes of independent thinking and undisciplined behaviour are the worst obstacles to students of Siddha Yoga. Abusing the word 'freedom,' if a disciple becomes careless or lethargic in obeying the command of the Guru, if he does not have abiding faith in the Guru's words or finds fault with his ways, he will gradually lose the spiritual benefits gained from him. When a king comes to stay in a mansion, he comes in his full glory and lends richness and beauty to it. Its atmosphere exudes joy, charm and splendour. But when he leaves, all the glory departs with him and the mansion is shorn of its sparkle and grandeur. Similarly, the glorious all-knowing divine Shakti, flowing into a seeker from his Guru and working actively within him under the full control of the Guru, leaves the aspirant in a sad plight if he doubts, questions or harbours all sorts of notions about the Guru. On the Siddha Yoga path, the Guru's grace and full obedience to his command are the sole requisites. Muktananda holds with firm conviction that in all knowledge, in all ways of liberation and all inquiries into the nature of Self, the Guru's grace is the principal factor. Your own endeavours, your

practices of *japa*, austerities and various aspects of yoga
will bear fruit only when you are blessed by a Siddha Guru.

Students of Siddha Yoga! Remember that the power
with which a Guru supports you varies in direct proportion to your faith in his greatness, capacity and
perfection of his attainments. The measure of the success
of your efforts, the development of your inner Shakti and
the speed of your progress all depend on the depth of
your devotion for your Guru. The stronger and more
intense your feeling of dedication to your Guru as God
manifest, the quicker your progress; it will not take you
long to reach the goal of perfection. To illustrate this
truth, I will narrate a true story which may deepen your
faith and devotion and thus help you to achieve your goal.

During my recent stay at Mahableshwar, an engineer-
ing student came to meet me. In a few day's time he
obtained my favour and started meditating well. Then
he left for his home in Bombay. His bus was delayed en
route owing to rains. His mother was anxiously awaiting
him, wondering why the bus had not yet arrived. At
about 10 p.m. she gave up hope of his return and started
praying fervently to her Guru, who appeared to her and
said, "Mother, do not worry; your son will reach here
at 12.25 a.m." Hearing this, she gave up all anxiety. The
Guru had appeared in a vision on account of her faith in
him. Once again she became completely engrossed in
meditation, so much so, that she forgot all about her son.
After a while, somebody knocked at the door and called,
"Mother, mother." She got up, opened the door, looked
at her son and then at the clock. It was exactly 12.25 a.m.!
She was overcome by amazement. She later came to
Mahableshwar and recounted the entire episode.

In this context I would quote an *abhanga* composed by
the great saint Tukaram, who dwells in the world of
Siddhas and who is worthy of our daily remembrance.

गुरुचरणी ठेवीता भाव । आपे आप भेटे देव ॥
म्हणुनी गुरुसी भजावे । स्वध्यानासी आणावे ॥
देव गुरुपासी आहे । वारंवार सांगूं काये ॥
तुका म्हणे गुरुभजनी । देव भेटे जनीं वनीं ॥

(God can be easily attained, without any travail of
sadhana, by maintaining deep faith in the Guru's feet;
therefore, worship the Guru and let your thoughts dwell
on him. God is quite close to the Guru. How many times
should I tell you: Tukaram says that by constant remembrance of the Guru, one can meet God anywhere—
in an uninhabited forest or in the midst of multitudes.)

My dear students of Siddha Yoga! Always remember
that it is essential to have such complete faith in and
absolute devotion to your Guru as may serve as an
example for others. The importance of devout feeling
and deep devotion cannot be over-emphasised. Your
attitude should be such as will foster your growth; hence
the importance of a firm attitude of faith. The aspirant
who has once experienced the dynamic force of Chiti
Shakti should always believe fully in the Chiti Shakti
manifesting in him, the greatness of his Gurudev, the
power of his own Self and the universe as a play of the
Divine Will. Then his thoughts will not wander from his
inner Chiti Shakti, his inner Self and his inner feeling
for his Guru. Such a sadhaka does not feel either
pleasure or pain in favourable or unfavourable worldly
conditions which are, after all, fleeting.

To illustrate the faith one should have in the omni-
potence of God and the power of inner consciousness I
will narrate the story of Prahlada, a great devotee who
was born in a family of demons. In spite of the repeated
attempts of his father, Hiranyakashipu, the king of
demons, to dissuade Prahlada from his devotion to
Vishnu and force him to accept demonic values, Prahlada
neither gave up his devotion nor accepted their ways.
Who can frighten him who has had even one direct
experience of the divine power in his own heart? What
can he ever lack if in his inner being Chiti is holding
Her manifest play?

When Hiranyakashipu tired of persuasive methods, he
flared up in anger and shouted, "When I issue a stern
command, the earth bursts and the wind stops; but this
slip of a boy dares to disregard my wishes! How shocking that this stupid little creature should discard his

family traditions and take to contemplation of God instead of emulating his elders who eat, drink, hunt and make merry! This change in him is obviously due to an evil influence. Such a fallen boy is a dark spot on the fair name of our family. How much better it would be to be without issue than to have such a son!" Thus Hiranyakashipu began to roar like an angry lion. He sent for hundreds of frightful demons who came rushing with their weapons flaring. As soon as they arrived, this king commanded them, "Cut Prahlada into pieces!" Hearing this, they rushed towards Prahlada with bare weapons.

Seeing hosts of armed demons approaching to attack him, Prahlada said, without the least fear:

विष्णु: शस्त्रेषु युग्मासु मयि चासौ व्यवस्थित: ।
दैतेयास्तेन सत्येन माक्रमन्त्वायुधानि च ॥

(O demons! Lord Vishnu dwells in your weapons, in you and in me. On account of this truth, your weapons cannot harm me).

Saying this, he stood serenely where he was. As the weapons struck him he did not feel the least pain. The sword strokes were like the soft caress of a garland of roses around his neck. He was not the least affected; nor was his contemplation disturbed; nor did he get perturbed. The firm faith that Lord Vishnu was everywhere and in everything had made Prahlada fearless. He was unmoved because he had given himself over entirely to the keeping of Vishnu. The Lord was the only one who roused him to delight, sorrow, anxiety or grief. He who claims to have surrendered his all to God and yet complains, is a cheat among devotees; he is merely trading in devotion. He is far from Truth; his devotion is a mere show.

It is not at all surprising that God should reveal Himself to one who has the firm faith of Prahlada, in his Guru. That is why Sant Tukaram says that God can be realised without difficulty through unshaking faith in the Guru's holy feet, as God resides with the Guru. As a result of my love for my Guru and his subsequent blessing, realisations sought me—I did not seek them. Various

*bandhas, mudras* and *kriyas* came to me automatically—
I never learned them. My Guru wanted me to establish
an ashram and the different capacities required for its
efficient running pursued me—I never pursued them. I
pursued only my Guru. I was always ready to carry out
his bidding. I followed the path prescribed by him, never
anxious for attainments. I did not even wonder where
the path would lead me. My only concern was to ensure
that I walked unswervingly on whatever path my Guru
pointed out. And as I followed him, I reached where I
ought to have. While I was thus travelling, I did not
allow my attention to roam here and there; nor did I
bother about lesser things. I kept to the straight path
and found what I was to find. What had to happen,
happened. I did not fall short of my destination, even
slightly.

My dear seekers! Thus I have practised what I am
teaching you. A seer has truly said:

श्रीगुरुचरणाम्भोजं सत्यमेव विजानताम् ।
जगत् सत्यमसत्यं वा नेतरेति मतिर्मम ॥

(Knowing the lotus feet of the Guru as the Truth, I have
no other thought of whether the world is real or unreal).
The Guru's feet should, as a matter of fact, be the whole
truth to a student of Siddha Yoga, a seeker of happiness.
Feel certain that they can grant all powers. Sri Jnaneshwar says in this context: "O Sadguru! If an aspirant
worships the Guru's feet representing 'tat' and 'tvam'
with 'asi' (*tat-tvam-asi*—thou art That), there is nothing
else for him to attain."

Dear Siddha students! Honour your Guru with all
your heart. Worship him sincerely. Have true love for
him. All miraculous powers will be ready to serve you.
You will never have to resort to a cheap display of clever
tricks like a magician. The scriptures say:

गुरुसन्तोषमात्रेण सिद्धिर्भवति शाश्वती ।
अन्यथा नैव सिद्धिः स्यादभिचाराय कल्पते ॥

(Everlasting divine power is attained only when the Guru
is pleased. Otherwise there will be no true power but

only a short-lived illusion). You may repeat your mantra indefinitely, practise severe austerities, meditate for long hours, be liberal in charity, perform elaborate sacrifices, or take dips in the Ganges, but you will never attain realisation unless the Guru feels pleased to bless you with his favour.

The various failings which we may observe among the students of Siddha Yoga—weakness, lack of perseverance, lack of inspiration and enthusiasm—are all due to the displeasure of the Guru. It is by the grace of the Guru alone that the mind becomes agile and the intellect sharp, that all suffering ceases and that a genuine interest is developed in sadhana. Only by the Guru's favour does one enjoy repeating God's name and perform yogic exercises spontaneously. Then alone is it possible to attain the *samadhi* state of detachment while engaged in worldly activities, to see God everywhere in the universe. Remember, therefore, the importance of pleasing the Guru. When a tiny spark of the Guru's grace enters into the disciple, it gives rise to a divine feeling. Even *chintamani, parasmani, kalpataru* and *kamdhenu* fade into insignificance compared to the Guru in whom the Universal Consciousness is active. Sunderdas celebrates the glory of such a one in his poetry:

गुरुदेव सर्वोपरि, अधिक विराजमान । गुरुदेव सब्रहि तं, अधिक गरिष्ठ है ॥
गुरुदेव दत्तात्रेय, नारद शुकादि मुनि । गुरुदेव ज्ञानघन, प्रगट वसिष्ठ है ॥
गुरुदेव परम आनन्दमय देखियत । गुरुदेव वर वरि-यान वरिष्ठ है ॥
संुदर कहत कछु महिमा कही न जाये । ऐसे गुरुदेव दादू , मेरे सिर इष्ट हैं ॥

(The Guru is above everyone, he is most brilliant; he is greater than all. The Guru himself is Dattatreya, Narada, Shuka and other seers; he is the treasure of wisdom like the sage Vasishtha. The Guru appears full of divine bliss, he is supreme in all respects. Sunder is unable to sing his glory adequately. Such a Gurudev is Dadu, my most adorable deity).

Whoever has attained spiritual perfection has attained it from a Guru. The favour of a Guru is essential for everlasting liberation. By the Guru's grace the individual soul, bound by *samskaras* reaches supreme freedom. Without a Guru, man remains unhappy; on finding one, he becomes happy. Therefore surrender yourself to the Guru completely and develop *Gurubhava*. Meditating for a few moments and seeing some light is not *Gurubhava*. The deeper your feeling of devotion to your Guru, the higher the level of spiritual enlightenment you will rise to. It is said:

देवे तीर्थे द्विजे मन्त्रे दैवज्ञे भेषजे गुरौ ।
यादृशी भावना यस्य सिद्धिर्भवति तादृशी ॥

(The benefit obtained from deities, holy places, *brahmins*, mantras, astrologers, medicinal herbs and the Guru is directly proportional to the quality of one's feeling for them). Decide yourself what your attitude should be to a Sadguru who lifts people who are sinking into the ocean of worldliness, to his own level; who enters into his disciple's mind and eradicates all doubts from it; who makes Chiti, the Universal Power, active in him; who illuminates his inner being with the light of God and awakens his soul; and who enables him to dwell in the joy of the inner Self just like himself.

The Guru possesses the power of making his disciple realise that this universe is nothing but divine consciousness made visible. As long as man does not perceive the phenomena of the universe as a play of divine consciousness, he cannot obtain lasting peace regardless of his spiritual practices, yogic exercises, sacrifices, *japa*, pilgrimages or fasts. He may observe all the Vedic codes, rules of conduct and behaviour, or visit holy shrines, but he will obtain nothing; he will be spending his time fruitlessly. He may perform different virtuous deeds, acquire supernatural powers, practise severe austerities, or subsist solely on fruit, roots and tubers for his entire life, but he cannot find joy and peace without a direct experience of the play of Chiti, made possible by the Guru's grace. Shri Abhinavagupta Acharya says truly:

स्वतन्त्रः स्वच्छात्मा स्फुरति सततं चेतसि शिवः
पराशक्तिश्रेयं करणसरणिप्रान्तमुदिता ।

तदा भोगैकात्मा स्फुरति च समस्तं जगदिदम्
न जाने कुत्रायं ध्वनिरनुपतेत् संसृतिरिति ॥

(Shiva, the independent and pure Spirit, which always
vibrates in the mind, is this Parashakti which rises as
joy in various sense experiences. Then the experience of
this whole outer world appears as Its Self. I do not know
from where this word *samsara* has come). The supremely
pure Universal Consciousness, called variously God,
Krishna, Rama, Shiva, Divine Mother, Brahman, the One
with or without attributes, Allah, Satnam or Alakh, called
Nityananda by Swami Muktananda, Chiti Shakti in
*Pratyabhijnahrdayam*, and Kundalini by Perfected
Masters, throbs constantly in every mind of Its own free
accord. The same Being, as Parashakti, rises as joy in
the various sense-experiences. The same Universal Spirit,
whose nature comprises Existence, Consciousness and
Bliss, is manifesting Itself as the universe. The same
conscious power or Chiti Shakti dwells in the heart of
every student of Siddha Yoga and experiences the outer
world which is an embodiment of Chiti Herself. Who
but Chiti has the power to appear as the universe? What
can ever sully that absolutely free, supremely pure Chiti
which manifests Herself of Her own free will? The
entire universe is, indeed, a sport of the divine Chiti. To
enable you to comprehend the nature of this game a
little better, I quote some passages of poetry which
describe how the milkmaids of Vraja saw this manifestation of Chiti as the play of Krishna, a sport full of His
glory.

जित देखौं तित स्याममई है ।
स्याम कुंज बन जमुना स्यामा, स्याम गगन घनघटा छई है ॥
सब रंगन में स्याम भरो है, लोग कहत यह बात नई है ॥
मैं बौरी, की लोगन ही की स्याम पुतरिया बदल गई है ॥

(Wherever the eyes may fall, Krishna is all that they
    see,
The bowers, the forests and the river Yamuna,
The sky and the dark clouds, all the different hues,
All, all of them are full of Krishna.

People exclaim what a novel thought!
Whether I am mad or they are blind—I cannot
  decide).

कहि न जाय मुखसौं कछू श्याम-प्रेमकी बात ।
नभ जल थल चर अचर सब स्यामहि स्याम दिखात ॥

ब्रह्म नहीं माया नहीं, नहीं जीव, नहिं काल ।
अपनीहू सुधि ना रही, रह्यो एक नँदलाल ॥
को कासों केहि बिधि कहा, कहै हृदै की बात ।
हरि हेरत हिय हरि, गयो हरि सर्वत्र लखात ॥

(The love of Krishna is beyond words;
I see only Him, Him alone in the sky and waters and
  lands,
In the animate and the inanimate.
Neither Brahman nor *maya* nor time nor the
  individual soul nor I exist;
Krishna alone exists; Krishna, the son of Nanda.
How can I ever express the longing of my heart?
Who can?  In what manner?
I thought I could possess Hari, but He possessess my
  heart.
I see Him everywhere, in all directions).

The entire universe is Chiti's playground; it is God's
visible form; it is the splendour of your Self; it is
pervaded by your revered Guru. That is why I have
emphasised the importance of a Guru and the attitude
with which you should approach him. A student of
Siddha Yoga should be fully vigilant in this matter.
That which is a play of Chiti Shakti is also the universal
form of Sri Gurudev. The same Shakti imparts knowledge
as a Sadguru and receives it as a disciple. She takes
on innumerable forms. The same Sadguru enters into
every being as prana. He assumes the forms of Brahma
(the Creator), Vishnu (the Sustainer) and Rudra (the
Destroyer). It is he again who becomes the celestial
beings, such as Varuna, Indra, and stars and planets like
the sun, moon, Rahu and Ketu, the Pole Star and the
Great Bear constellation, and yet maintains the same
identity without the slightest change. It is also he who

appears as the speaker and what is spoken, as the listener and what is listened to, as the knower and what is known. He is the *Veda* and its knower. He is the Sankhya system of philosophy; he is the science of yoga and the yogic exercises. He is the Lord of yoga. In spite of such multiplicity he remains One. It is the same Sadguru who is the doer, the instruments of action and also the deed performed; he is the experiencer, the objects of experience and also the experience. He is immortality, medicinal herbs and also disease and death. The same One pervades all, from the enlightened to the ignorant, from the discerning to the undiscerning, from gods to human beings. Numerology and mathematics arise from his inner movements. He is the source of all musical compositions, of rhythm and sound. He is the dancer, the singer and also the dance and the song. It is the same perfect Sadguru who is the teacher of pure knowledge and also the founder and exponent of Maha Yoga or Siddha Vidya. The scriptures glorify him: मनुष्य-देहमास्थाय छन्नास्ते परमेश्वरा: । (Almighty God conceals Himself in a human form).

My dear seekers of liberation! This whole universe is the splendour of the Guru. It emanates from the Self dwelling in you all—such is the instruction of the Perfect Ones, the teaching of Vedanta, and the experience of countless saints. If you find duality in this play of Universal Consciousness, you will never be emancipated from the suffering of birth and death.

Shankaracharya says in the *Aparokshanubhuti* :

> स्वल्पमप्यन्तरं कृत्वा जीवात्मपरमात्मनो: ।
> य: संतिष्ठति मूढात्मा भयं तस्याभिभाषितम् ॥

(The ignorant fool, who lives making even the slightest distinction between the Universal Self and his own Self, will always be subject to fear).

The *Upanishads* also declare: द्वितीयाद्वै भयं भवति । (He who sees another will be in fear).

> यथा न्यग्रोधबीजस्थ: शक्तिरूपो महाद्रुम: ।
> तथा हृदयबीजस्थं विश्वमेतच्चराचरम् ॥

(Just as the tiniest banyan seed grows into a strong, huge, sprawling tree, similarly the power of the Soul, embedded in the heart in seed form, expands into a universe consisting of both the animate and the inanimate).

My dear students of Siddha Yoga! Always remember that all attainments including everlasting peace, originate from the Guru's pleasure.

How does the Guru feel pleased? Do not think that you can please him by flattery and lip-service. If you meditate for a short while once a week but waste twenty days seeing silly pictures; or meditate once in a fortnight but loiter around in the streets like a vagabond for a whole month; or meditate once a month but ruin your digestive system by gourmandising all sorts of food for three months; and then offer thanks to the Guru in a mood of self-congratulation, you are only deluding yourself. He feels pleased only when his disciple attains perfection. Just as an artist, a wrestler or a scholar congratulates and blesses his student on having completed his course under his guidance and mastered his subject, similarly the Guru feels pleased only when his disciple, who has received his spiritual power, reaches the highest attainment. You can never please the Guru just by gifts of food, cloth, other materials and insincere praise. The Guru feels gratified when his disciple merges into him and attains Guruhood. That is why Muktananda exhorts you to seek refuge in the Guru and in the yoga of meditation; to attain devotion and love for the Guru; to see the divine in others and to remember the Guru constantly. Let the Guru be the master of your intellect and reason; let him be your supreme goal. Let him be your sole delight, for he is your own Self. This I know to be the Truth, the sole, the final Truth.

# 7

# NATURAL SAMADHI

One aphorism of the *Pratyabhijnahardayam* reads: मध्यविकासात् चिदानन्दलाभ: ।That means that when the Kundalini is raised in *sushumna*, the central nerve, by the Guru's grace, the all-pervasive Chiti illumines a student with Her knowledge. His mind becomes quiescent through meditation and this state also persists in his practical life. He sees Chiti unfolding Herself in all his daily actions and activities, in worship, scriptural study and meditation; in his household, family, servants and the objects of his enjoyments. He then enjoys full peace in meditation and freedom from anxiety in his worldly affairs. As he masters this yogic stage, he spontaneously glides into a permanent imperturbable state. In fact, Chitshakti Herself assumes this state and dwells within such a yogi, thus rewarding him for practising sadhana by the Guru's grace. This is the state of natural *samadhi*. One who achieves this is considered to be a great yogi, a supreme devotee of Shiva, even though he may continue to live in the world.

This yogi perceives only Chiti's ever-lasting sport, within as well as without— सबाह्याभ्यन्तर: अयं नित्योदितसमावेशात्मा । Such an attitude results in perfect equipoise. In this unchangeable state, endowed with the power of the great mantra, one sees his body, prana, senses and their objects as no different from his inner Self, brimming with consciousness. He feels that he may consider them in any manner; it is the supremely glorious Chitshakti that lies at the basis of all of them.

If Chiti did not vibrate, one could not perceive any object. She reveals everything by Her existence. Thus the selfsame Chitshakti plays in all conditions, enters all things and absorbs them all in Her being. She manifests as matter, assuming the distinctions of space, time and form. Every entity in this world is illuminated by Her. In fact, all inner and outer objects are created, sustained or dissolved within Her being. A Siddha student or yogi experiences Godhood by looking upon his psychic functions and outer sense organs as Her rays. As this knowledge dawns, his mind is blessed with peace and equanimity. In this state of natural *samadhi*, he directly perceives the indivisible God, who is the ground of the universe, underlying all forms and movements and every being. He sees the divine influence working continually in his various actions. Just as the characteristics of a fruit, like its shape, juice and smell exist as a simple unity, similarly, external objects, their knowledge and their knower are all one with the omnipresent God—their innermost basis. A Siddha student, by this vision, overcomes the notion "I am imperfect," gaining the knowledge that "I am perfect." This is indeed spontaneous *samadhi*.

In fact, all worldly appearance is nothing but Chiti. For a Siddha student, it does not contain any substance other than Chiti. Sri Shankaracharya says:

रज्ज्वज्ञानात् क्षणेनैव यद्वद्रज्जुर्हि सर्पिणी ।
भाति तद्वच्चिति: साक्षाद्विश्वाकारेण केवला ॥

(*Aparokshanubhuti*, 44)

(As through the ignorance of the real nature of a rope, the same rope may appear in an instant as a snake, so also does pure consciousness appear in the form of the phenomenal universe without undergoing any change). A rope suddenly appears to be a serpent because of one's own delusion. As a result, one may be so frightened that he falls unconscious; another may scream himself out of his wits, shouting, "Run! Run for your life!" These cries may attract the attention of a wise man who knows the rope for what it is. He would remark, "O, you stupid fool! Why are you shouting yourself into such a disconcerted state? This is not a serpent, but a mere rope." These words extinguish the illusion immediately. That

which had earlier appeared to be a snake is seen as a
rope again. In the same manner, the universe appears
in Chiti Herself:

ब्रह्मैव सर्वनामानि रूपाणि विविधानि च ।
कर्माण्यपि समग्राणि बिभर्तीति श्रुतिर्जगौ ॥

(*Aparokshanubhuti*, 50)

(The *Vedas* have clearly declared that Brahman alone is
the substratum of all varieties of names, forms, and
actions).

As a matter of fact, God Himself becomes the various
objects of the external world, assuming their respective
names and functions such as the eye's function of seeing,
the hand's of holding and the tongue's of speaking. Men
are able to conduct their affairs only because the Absolute
exists. No activity can ever take place without It. A
radio functions with electricity, in the absence of which
it goes dead. Similarly, Chiti or the conscious Soul is
behind all the sense functions. Ignorant fools, for lack
of the knowledge imparted by the Guru, believe that the
eyes see, the tongue speaks, the legs walk and all other
senses act independently. As a radio cannot work
without electricity, so the eyes cannot see, or the tongue
speak, without the conscious Soul. For this reason,
Shankaracharya holds that all activities are possible only
because of the existence of consciousness. The same Chiti
speaks with the tongue, sees with the eyes, hears with
the ears and thinks with the mind. The realisation that
one Universal Consciousness revels in the function of
every part of man's being, in every movement of the
inner and outer universe, makes one tranquil, emancipat-
ing him from the distinction of unity and multiplicity.
This is the state of natural *samadhi*.

Meditating Siddha students have experienced that the
mind becomes free from thought in pure meditation. As
the mind converges on the Blue Pearl, it becomes permeated by It. Then, for a short while, it sheds its self-
consciousness, becoming oblivious to the inner as well as
the outer world. Sights are not seen when there is no one

to see them. Sounds are not heard in the absence of a
hearer. In this state neither happiness nor sorrow, the
perceiver nor the perceived exists. However, it is not
a state of blankness. Only pure God, pulsating in His
own Being as pure 'I' remains. This is the imageless,
unchanging, quiescent state—the goal of meditation. One
stays in this state briefly. When meditation ceases, one
comes out of *turiyatita* into *turiya*, in which he perceives
the Transcendent in all. As one passes into deep sleep
from *turiya*, he still possesses higher consciousness and
does not apprehend anything other than his own Self.
As one slips from deep sleep into the dream state, he
becomes his own dream world containing chariots, horses,
elephants or whatever. His discovers that the Witness
of sleep is the same as that of dreams. As one returns
to the waking from the dream state, he realises that the
same transcendental Being also underlies it. Thus the
selfsame Witness passes from *turiyatita* to *turiya*, *turiya*
to deep sleep, deep sleep to dream, dream to waking and
vice versa. These states may differ from one another in
different ways, but their Witness is one and the same.
According to Muktananda, the peace following this
insight constitutes the state of natural *samadhi*.

As long as one is ignorant of Chitshakti, he sees
external objects as distinct from one another and as
falling into innumerable categories according to their
different names, forms, qualities and functions. But
when he becomes aware of Chitshakti through the
awakening caused by the Guru, he realises that Chiti is
one: स चैको द्विरूपस्त्रिमयश्चतुरात्मा सप्तपञ्चकस्वभावः । (*Pratyabhijnahrdayam*, 7). This aphorism means that the One supreme
Shiva becomes the universe by becoming two, three, four
and thirty-five elements. He is the attributeless, formless Satchidananda. He is said to become 'two' as he
expands and also contracts. When he assumes *anaviya*,
*mayiya* and karmic limitations, he becomes 'three.' He
is known as the 'fourfold' Soul when he divides Himself
into *sunya*, *prana*, *puryashtaka* and the physical body.
He becomes thirty-five elements right from Shiva down
to the earth, but He does not lose His identity. None

other than He exists. The *Pratyabhijnahardayam* considers the whole world to be Chiti's sport— चिदात्मा शिवभट्टारक एव एक आत्मा, न तु अन्य: कश्चित् । (There is only one Soul, the Conscious Soul, Lord Shiva; nothing else exists). As this intuition calms the mind's fluctuations, one floats into the state of spontaneity. The *Vijnanabhairava* says:

ग्राह्यग्राहकसंवित्ति: सामान्या सर्वदेहिनाम् ।
योगिनां तु विशेषोऽयं संबन्धे सावधानता ॥

(Knowledge of the perceiver and the perceived is common to all beings. But with yogis it is different. They are aware of them as one). The same Goddess Parashakti Chiti becomes the sensible universe as well as the individual soul, which considers itself to be different from it. The known includes the whole external world with all its objects, while the knower refers to the conscious, individual Self which knows them all. Unenlightened people split the knower and the known into countless divisions. But a yogi, a worshipper of Maha Yoga, blessed by the Guru's grace, having realised Chitshakti, becomes aware that both the perceiver and the perceived have sprung from Her and hence treats them equally. The quiescence attending this vision of equality is the spontaneous state of natural *samadhi*.

The wise regard this universe as a play of Universal Consciousness, a vibration of Chiti. They know that Chiti Herself appears as the world. The universe originating from Chiti is indeed Chiti despite its diverse forms. She underlies all worldly transactions. She Herself takes on myriad forms within Her own being and expands in myriad ways. The supreme peace accompanying this unity-awareness is Muktananda's state of natural *samadhi*.

# BENEDICTION

My dear, my own Siddha students! May you, by the power of the Siddha science and the grace of a Siddha, attain the perfect repose enjoyed by the Perfected Ones, though continually engaged in your various daily activities! This is my blessing to you.

Beloved Siddha students! You belong to the Siddha tradition, having received the grace of a Siddha. Siddhaloka is your true home. Your ultimate destination is the state in which Siddhas are established. The divinest of the divine power of grace of countless great saints, inhabitants of Siddhaloka, is behind you, offering protection. May you be fully protected by it!

Dear Siddha students! Only a few sparks of fire are enough to consume an entire forest. Similarly, may even the tiny ray of Chitshakti of Siddhas, which has entered you, burn all your impurities away! May you achieve full Siddhahood!

You are all rays of Siddha souls. You are all participants in Chitshakti's play. She is active within you. May you achieve true awareness of Her conscious domain and become united with Her! May your mind repose in this universe, which is the restful abode of Goddess Chiti!

My supreme Guru, Sri Nityananda, is also my supreme deity. He is an embodiment of Chiti, abiding in Siddhaloka. By only a small measure of his grace I was able to obliterate my ego and expand with the expanding Chiti Kundalini. He selflessly took away all my suffering and sorrow and transformed me into his own image. In order to protect his Shakti imparted to me, he became Shakti and took seat in me as my innermost Self, the Master of my heart. I am what I am due to him. I belong to him alone. He has transfigured me. May Lord Nityananda, the highest Guru, who, dwelling in all hearts, activates the Shakti, whom I worship constantly, enter

240

all my Siddha students, reside within them as their
inner Self and fill their lives with His supreme bliss!
I bestow my fullest blessings upon you.

Your own,

My worshipful Sri Nityananda's own,

SWAMI MUKTANANDA

APPENDIX

# SOME EXPERIENCES OF SIDDHA STUDENTS

# THE UNFAILING INFLUENCE OF GURUDEV

## NIRMALA THAKKAR

My father has been visiting Ganeshpuri since 1957.
Sometimes I accompanied him. In those days we were
blessed by the physical presence of Bhagawan Nityananda. Then, as our contact with Muktananda Baba, his
greatest disciple, grew, we had many experiences of his
grace, as a result of which my faith in him became firmer.
At that time I was a student in the tenth grade, but little
did I imagine that a new life for me had already
commenced.

During the summer vacation of 1963, I came to the
Gavdevi Ashram to spend four days. Handing me a copy
of *Shiva Sahasra Nama*, Gurudev asked me to chant it
near the statue of Nataraja in the garden. As I was
chanting the hymn, he came there, made a characteristic
sound of 'hum' and went away. After sometime I heard
a sound resembling the roar of a lion and also saw a
bright flame in a vision.

After that I began to see Bhagawan Nityananda and
Gurudev again and again in my dreams. In one dream,
I saw a light emanating from Gurudev's chest and the
figure of Bhagawan Nityananda in that light. I immedi-
ately fell at Bhagawan's feet. In the meanwhile, as
Gurudev touched me near the left ear, an electric current
travelled through me. I heard the buzz of a bee and my
body started trembling. Later and for days together, I
saw Gurudev manifesting everywhere in my college.
Still later, during the Ganesh Yajna being held at the
Ashram, I beheld the form of Ganesh in every direction.
Saints also appeared in my dreams.

Yet the most auspicious day of my life was February 14,
1967. On that day I was summoned by Gurudev to the

* These essays were originally written for the Hindi edition
of *Chitshakti Vilas* in 1969.

245

meditation room. He asked me to sit in the lotus posture and meditate. While moving his hand over my head and back, he said, "Do you want to become a yogini?" Then, imparting a mantra, he asked me to repeat it, which I did and immediately an electrical impulse shot through me. My head felt heavy. Some force appeared to travel upwards from the *muladhar*. I felt a shiver near the throat. My fingers seemed to radiate electric vibrations. In a vision, I saw Gurudev, Bhagawan Nityananda and Ganapati. I saw Lord Vishnu standing near a chariot. An efflulgent ladder also appeared. I thought that Gurudev was showing me a symbol of the way to salvation. And then I saw my own form standing before me.

When I went to meditate the next day, Gurudev asked me, "Do you see any light or hear any sound?" While inquiring thus, he blew into my ear, and I started hearing the rumble of an ocean. Since then, I have always been hearing various divine sounds. At times, I hear the chant of *Om* or *Narayana, Narayana*.

Gradually I started meditating more deeply. As I sat, I would glide into meditation effortlessly. Sometimes I was in a contemplative state the whole day and night. Sometimes the body swayed; sometimes, it trembled; at other times, it became rigid like wood. Sometimes it seemed to shed all its weight and I floated in the air and danced gaily. Afterwards, different postures such as the lotus posture, the posterior stretch and *veerasana* started occurring automatically. Yogic *mudras*, such as *shambhavi, bhujangini,* and *khechari* occurred. Varieties of *kumbhaka* also happened. My eyeballs would either revolve upwards or rotate. I would see a third eye in the forehead. Sometimes I would make different gestures as in a dance. Sometimes the sound of *Om* rose from the navel, while at other times, strange sounds issued from my lips.

In meditation, I beheld the sun, the moon, the stars and planets, mountains, waters, forests, and birds and animals of various kinds. I also inhaled different smells, fair as well as foul. Sour, bitter and sweet juices were secreted in the mouth. Sometimes I felt burning sensations in my hands, feet, back, throat and eyes—so much so, that I felt as though they were smeared with red chillies. Even now I feel such sensations. If I were to compile all my experiences of meditation, they would fill a volume.

In visions, I saw several saints, such as Sri Ramakrishna Paramahansa, Sri Sai Baba of Shirdi, Jalaram Bapa of Veerpur and Sri Anandamayee Ma. I also saw forms of Sri Krishna, Shiva, Dattatreya and goddesses such as Laxmi, Saraswati and Amba. I often beheld the form of Gurudev either inside the figure of *Om* or seated on a flower or inside a temple. Sometimes I saw myself reciting the *Vishnu Sahasra Nama* either with Gurudev or Bhagawan Nityananda. Many times when I visit the latter's shrine, Gurudev appears in a laughing expression. I also see his effulgent lotus feet. I saw Gurudev and Lord Shiva sometimes in the *ajna chakra* and sometimes in the pupils of my eyes.

I have seen lights of different colours. I would see Gurudev's beautiful face irradiated. At times, a blue spot or a radiant strip of *Om* appeared with increasing brilliance. These days even while engaged with teaching or some other work, not in meditation, many different coloured lights appear, shine briefly and then vanish.

Sometimes while I am sitting in meditation, all kinds of thoughts come rushing into my mind. At other times my mind gets so stilled that even loud noises from my neighbourhood are not perceived.

I have many prophetic dreams through which Gurudev conveys the knowledge of future happenings. On several occasions Gurudev would ask me, "Do you know that I visit your house?" My reply is always in the affirmative, which is absolutely true. Many times I perceive his perfume and thus sense his presence. A large portrait of him hangs in our house. In it I can see his different moods reflected, for example, I sometimes see him smiling and sometimes solemn.

Shakti has been flowing out of my hands for some months. One day I was moving my hand on the head of my sick brother who was suffering from smallpox and running high temperature. Gurudev was in Delhi at that time. While moving my hand on his head and remembering Gurudev, I became absorbed in meditation. An electric current kept coursing through my body for five minutes and I felt that Gurudev's divine power was passing into my brother through me; as a result he also started meditating deeply. Many postures, mantras, and other yogic *kriyas* then came to him. His illness vanished soon and he thus escaped death! Similarly, when other aspirants sit with me in meditation, they feel an electric shock, as my forehead or finger happens to touch them.

My mother has been suffering from paralysis for twenty-three years. She was also blessed with the illimitable benevolence of Gurudev; consequently, she started meditating. Now, of course, she is able to meditate deeply. She cannot walk on account of being paralysed, but during meditation, she executes difficult postures. One of which is *ekapadkandharasan*, in which the right leg is raised and brought behind the neck to touch the left shoulder. Sometimes her legs perform vigorous pedalling movements. She also has visions of divine lights, chants mantras spontaneously, and beholds Gurudev in Shiva's form right at home.

One girl from the neighbourhood, who always visits us, had been suffering from migraine headaches for a long time, in spite of having been under the treatment of several doctors. I would always move my hand over her head and console her saying that I would take her to Gurudev Muktananda Baba. But before she could even come to Ganeshpuri, she began to meditate and perform spontaneous yogic movements. And amazingly enough, her headaches vanished soon and she improved in her health.

There is another fourteen-year old girl who used to call on us quite frequently. She also began to meditate and have visions of gods and goddesses. One day she came to our house and sat in meditation. She began to chant mantras loudly. Then she began to spin about and jump up and down. Animal cries came forth from her mouth. She swayed while producing sounds like *hoo, hoo*. Hearing all this, my neighbours gathered in our house and declared that an evil spirit had possessed her. I was in consternation as they could not understand that all those *kriyas* are natural in Siddha Yoga. Meanwhile, that girl embraced me and said, "Why are you feeling scared?" I felt as though Gurudev himself had spoken those words. The girl later told me that she had been commanded in meditation by Gurudev to speak thus. Gurudev appears to her several times during meditation and reveals many things about me.

How can I ever express in words the depth of my gratitude to him! During the past five or six years, I have undergone a complete transformation by his grace. But for his benediction, I would have been entrapped in worldly life, experiencing happiness and misery. But now I float in the waters of bliss. I feel that I am the happiest of all, as I have discovered *kalpavriksha* in the form of my Gurudev. I am marching ahead on the path of Siddha Yoga. Whether or not I reach the final destination depends entirely on him.

My dear Gurudev! My only prayer to you is: May you fill all my thoughts, nay, my entire being.


# ON THE PATH OF SIDDHA YOGA

PANNA NAIK

For the last four years I have been going to Babaji. My father is very devoted to Baba and he has been going to him for nine years. I could not go earlier because I was too young and was studying in my native town. After getting admitted to a school in Bombay, I started going to Baba with my father. I am fifteen years old now and am studying for my final examinations.

In a very natural way, faith and loving devotion towards Baba developed in me. Babaji, too, accepted me and I was blessed. According to Baba's instructions I began to recite the *Gita* and *Vishnu Sahasra Nama* at home. I had not learned Sanskrit, but even so I could read and recite them with ease; now I know *Vishnu Sahasra Nama* by heart.

As I was brought up in a rural village atmosphere, I had not been influenced by luxurious and fashionable city life. Therefore, when I came in contact with Baba my path of devotion to God opened up very easily and I obtained the most valuable thing in life, namely Guru-kripa in the form of Shaktipat. Now, every week-end as well as short and long vacations I go to live in the Ashram.

Last year, during Diwali vacation, Baba advised me to sit for meditation near a girl named Ratna, who was good at meditation. At that time I did not know about meditation or how to practise it. But, as Baba had instructed me, I went to the Dhyan Mandir and sat near Ratna. I asked her what I should do. She told me to do *japa*. For three to four days I went on doing *japa* whenever we sat together for meditation, but nothing happened to me. Baba kept on inquiring if I had had any experiences.

Many students of Siddha Yoga—both boys and girls—sit for meditation in the Ashram's Dhyan Mandir. During vacation it is difficult to find a seat easily and we sit turn by turn. While we are sitting there, quite often Baba pays a visit and goes round to see us. On the fifth day, he suddenly came near me and touched my eyes with his fingers. Next, touching my forehead between my eyebrows he shook my head three times. That very moment my eyes closed and I was drawn into a state of meditation. I did not wish to get up from my seat and my legs were also locked in an *asana*. I experienced unusual divine joy during meditation that day. I feel such joy sometimes even now. I have gone into a similar state of meditation about three times.

One day Baba touched my head again. Thereupon I started having deep meditation. I began to sit in the Dhyan Mandir morning and evening for many hours. On coming out from meditation, other students were telling me that I was going round and round and was also swaying to and fro and that my hands and fingers were moving in various gestures. Later on I came to know that they were yogic *mudras*.

By the practice of meditation, this way, there came a gradual change in my life. I am not even aware how and where all my weaknesses like fear, anger and obstinate nature slowly disappeared. Now my body is always active and alert. My chronic headache was also cured. Formerly, I did not have much interest in my studies but it gradually increased and there was good progress too. My mental capacity also developed and I have become more intelligent.

I continue to practise meditation at home. I see red and white lights. I am unable to describe their beauty. Some time ago, the melodious utterance of *So'ham* mantra was occurring of its own accord and I used to feel great joy within. That mantra was echoing in the entire house and everybody at home was listening to it. This *japa* used to continue for one and a half hours everyday. Those days Baba was in Delhi but I saw him before me in the form of Lord Shiva. His form was very beautiful, sombre and calm. I was blessed by that vision. I bowed down to Baba. My heart was overwhelmed with joy and I began to laugh loudly. Two days later, Baba appeared in a dream and said, "You are having very good meditation." He gave me a bottle of perfume instructing me to apply it on the body. I was having many yogic *kriyas* during that period.

I went to the Ashram to spend my summer vacation. Now I was getting into a good state of meditation. I was able to see a blue spot in vision, which was very bright. It used to shine for a while and then disappear. I was puzzled as to where it came from and where it went.

Three days before examination results were out, I had a vision in which somebody said, "You and your brother will receive the first rank in the exams." Somehow I could not believe this and hence I did not talk about it

to anyone. When it came out to be true I was greatly
astonished. The students of Siddha Yoga in our Ashram
do have such experiences in meditation by which they
know about coming events. Jagruti Trivedi, for instance,
had seen Baba in a yellow silk garment and wearing a
golden crown. Soon on Guru Purnima it actually
occurred. A devotee presented a gold crown and a yellow
silk *lungi* to Baba.

Then I had the rare privilege to accompany Baba and
Amma to Mahableshwar. There I used to sit for meditation with other girls. I was having new types of *mudras*.
One day I had a glimpse of Shiva. Utterances of *So'ham*
mantra would continue for hours during meditation,
accompanied by various types of *mudras*. There would
also be repetition of *Om Gurudev Datta japa*. For two
to three days this *japa* was 'dancing' in my breath and
on my tongue.

One day as I was strolling in the beautiful garden at
Mahableshwar I heard *So'ham* in the cries of birds.
Hearing this I was totally filled with joy and bliss.

Malti Shetty, one of my friends of our meditation group
was spontaneously uttering certain words like *Jyotirmay
Gurudev* (radiant Gurudev), *Sarpavibhushit Gurudev*
(serpent adoring Gurudev), *Atmarupi Gurudev* (the
Absolute Gurudev) and so on. The astonishing thing
about it was that I was visualising all those forms which
she was uttering in meditation. I really enjoyed it and
became deeply drunk in a meditative state. After meditation, in a state of *tandra*, I saw myself performing
various yogic *kriyas*. First I saw myself in a frightful
form and got scared but then I saw my other quiet form.

One day I saw Bhagawan Nityananda, Sai Baba of
Shirdi, Gurudev Muktananda Baba and two other saints
in the blue spot. Sometimes I see lights of different
colours. Once I saw an egg-shaped ball along with white
light. I had the vision of a goddess in meditation and
spontaneously I recited a hymn in Her praise. One time
I saw a chariot, in a flame of fire, in which a celestial
being was sitting. Once I saw a beautiful girl applying
a *tilak* on my forehead.

This is the way in which my sadhana is continuing. My mind is always filled with joy and I never have any worry or anxiety. Even if someone abuses me it has no effect on me. The practice of meditation has never been an obstacle to my academic studies. On the contrary, due to meditation I received a lot of help in my studies— my memory has sharpened, I get inspiration from within while answering questions in examinations and I even secured first place. All this is due to Gurukripa, for which I am deeply indebted to Baba.

# I AM BLESSED

### Malti Shetty

My father has been Baba's devotee for many years. My parents were married by Baba at the holy place of Sri Katil Durga Parmeshwari Kshetra. With Baba's blessings and the grace of Goddess Durga, I was born. I am fourteen years old now and am in the tenth grade at school. Since early childhood I have been going to Ganeshpuri with my parents. Today I am one of the students of Siddha Yoga at Shree Gurudev Ashram.

During one vacation I went to stay in the Ashram. I was looking at one of my friends who was doing *kriyas* in meditation, when Babaji said to me, "You also sit and meditate." Obeying Baba's words I sat for meditation, but could not get into the meditative state. Four or five days later, Baba came to Dhyan Mandir; he touched my eyes and also patted my head softly. That very moment I was drawn into meditation. I did not know what was happening around me. I saw a small black dot and also had some other visions. This state lasted for an hour. At that time I had no knowledge of Shaktipat or Kundalini Shakti. Amma, who lives in the Ashram, looks after the lady disciples staying in the Ashram. She teaches us discipline, talks about the importance of leading a pure life and also gives us good books for reading and study. I talked to her about my experiences and asked her what was happening to me. She explained *dhyan* to me, and said that I had received Shaktipat— that I was fortunate, as Gurudev's divine Shakti had entered into my being.

The next day, I saw a white spot during meditation. Then for three days I could not get into meditation. On the fourth day Baba came into the Dhyan Mandir and applied sacred ashes on my forehead. That very day I visualised a white flame.

I progressed in meditation. Sometimes I would fall into a kind of sleep while meditating in the sitting posture. I always had some visions in that state. I would narrate these experiences to Baba or Amma. The visions at times came true. One day I saw a silver trident in meditation. A few days later, a devotee actually presented such a trident to Baba.

In May 1969, I went to Mahableshwar with Baba and Amma. There, by Gurukripa, my meditation deepened to a great extent. I began to see various colours; I was seeing a saffron light. Also *Shivo'ham* mantra was being spontaneously uttered through my mouth. A white flame was shining between my eyebrows. While talking to Baba about meditation, a small blue dot used to twinkle before my eyes and suddenly disappear. Once I saw a meteor and also the planet Saturn. Sometimes I would feel that someone was throwing light in my eyes, but on opening my eyes I wouldn't find anyone. Then I understood it to be a ray of light. I also heard a sound like that of a *mridang*. At times I would go so deep in meditation that I was unable to find a means of coming out of it. Other times I would repeat *Guru Om* mantra while lying down. Many types of *mudras* began to occur, and I was also moving about a lot in the state of meditation.

While meditating I once saw a small cobra biting the middle finger of my right hand. My hand began to shake with great force and suddenly mantras like—*Om Guru-dev Om, Jyotirmay* (lustrous) *Gurudev, Om Sarpavibhu-shit* (adorned with serpents) *Gurudev* were being uttered from my mouth for three quarters of an hour. My friends said that my voice was very sweet and melodious. That day I experienced the deepest joy. When I narrated this to Baba, he said, "Very good. It is an indication that Lord Shankar is ever with you." The following day in medi-tation, I saw the serpent just touching my palm with its tongue and going away.

One day I saw a circular blue light, then yellow within the blue, and lastly a white circle inside the yellow.

One time, I heard a voice within me saying that one can have *jnana* and *dhyan* through reading the *Bhagavad Gita*.

In this manner, I have been continuing my meditation. In the past, I always used to have pain in my stomach, chest and head—these have disappeared through my practising meditation. My mind has also become more calm than before. If any girl sits by my side for medita-tion, she also gets into that state. The grace of Gurudev is truly immeasurable.

# TWICE BORN

### Noni Patel

One day, while I was sitting outside Dhyan Mandir with my brother, Gurudev suddenly came out, touched my head and gave me a mantra. Before I could realise what had happened he had disappeared. I was told later that that was my initiation, Shaktipat Diksha.

After receiving the initiation, the path was clear and smooth. My bad habits started falling off like autumn leaves. I gave up cigarettes without even shedding a tear.

Alcoholic drinks which I used to consume in large quantities were also given up. A strict non-vegetarian became a strict vegetarian. All these changes came quite naturally to me without any stress or strain. This change in me was noticed by everybody and startled the members of my family and friends.

My long leave of 45 days was due in September, 1968. Normally such vacations in the past were spent in holiday resorts in the Middle East or Europe; but this time, the choice was Ganeshpuri.

I worked in the Ashram ever ready to serve my Master. On October 22, 1968 while cleaning the place where Baba takes his early morning bath, which was part of my daily routine, the Shakti of my Guru descended on me most violently and took full control of me. At first my whole body started to vibrate so strongly that I had to sit down on the floor. Then the mantra started to repeat itself from within automatically and, at times, very loudly. By this time my whole body was sweating profusely.

At first I did not know what was happening to me as wave after wave of Shakti hit me and caused a mental blank; but suddenly the realisation came like a flash that one who had been a sinner all his life had been showered with divine grace by a God-realised saint. The immediate impulse was to rise and rush out of the room in search of Gurudev and to fall at his lotus feet in extreme gratitude and to thank him for his kind grace. "Babaji, Babaji" was all I could utter as I fell at his feet hardly being able to control the tears of joy which were flowing like a river in spate. A smile appeared on the face of the all-knowing and compassionate Gurudev. Babaji's bathroom is one of the places in the Ashram which to my mind is the holiest of the holy, the place where none else is allowed to enter, and is exclusively for Baba. Later, Gurudev explained to me that Shakti is strongest in this room.

With this experience I could say that I was twice born and the truth of the seers dawned on me that a new life is given by a God-realised saint. Meditation, which was a strange thing to me, came automatically. Different types of *kriyas* started. It signified *nadi-shuddhi*, a process which cleans the entire nervous system of all impurities. Different yogic *asanas* and other exercises took place automatically and I did them for hours without feeling tired. At other times I would dance with joy combining laughter with tears. Every time something new would happen to me in *dhyan* and I would be most eager to find time to sit for meditation.

All different types of yogic exercises started during meditation. This took place at my home in Nairobi, in the Dhyan Room at the Ganeshpuri Ashram, in Hong Kong, where I used to spend one week at a time, and also during the weekly satsang at the Rafiya Manzil in Bombay.

These yogic exercises, which I had never practised before, nor was I aware of how they should be done, took place at times for hours together. It caused no fatigue or stress. On the contrary, they proved most refreshing. Accompanying these *kriyas* the *Om* mantra would start on its own from within, very loud and long. At times, instead of the mantra, a sound like that of a flying airplane would start without a break in my breathing.

I had a rather violent and forceful meditation in the Dhyan Room at the Ashram sometime in November, 1968. It began with the wailing sound of an airplane. The sound became very high-pitched, and with it a sort of dazzling light from within also grew in brightness, while my eyes were shut. It soon reached an unbearable degree when Gurudev came quickly inside the room and, taking the peacock broom, started to strike me on my head. This caused extreme joy and I burst into laughter, which continued for a long time, while I was rolling on the floor with divine joy being unable to control myself.

Once I accompanied Baba to Delhi and to Dehra Dun. There, one evening, while sitting in Baba's bedroom the divine Shakti suddenly took over and soon I was crawling and roaring like a lion. This went on for a long time and during that period of meditation I felt as if I was a lion.

At the Rafiya Manzil satsang I have experienced the divine Shakti very strongly and the *kriyas* that take place are also very violent. There, a number of times, the *Om* mantra starts automatically from within, followed by a very vigorous dance using both hands and feet and finally running around the room in circles at a very fast pace—something impossible to be done in normal circumstances.

Lately the yogic exercises have more or less ended, but have been replaced by *mudras* and spells of laughter.

At the time of morning and evening *arati* at the Ashram, the divine Shakti once again takes over and a sort of very graceful type of step ensues causing no fatigue but a very light feeling.

Once at the Rafiya Manzil satsang, at the end of meditation, sudden barking like a dog started and I felt as if I was a dog. Jumping on the floor, standing on my head, shouting the *Om* mantra loudly, dancing like a madman and running around the room have been reducing gradually and a more steady type of meditation, where one loses complete sense of time and place, a sort of complete mental blank appears.

Nairobi being the headquarters of my company, the flat in which I live has been divided and a section converted into a meditation room with photographs of Bhagawan Nityananda, Baba and other saints. Through Baba's grace the small room is so highly charged with his Shakti that friends of mine, who have become very interested in Baba's teachings by reading about him in the various *Shree Gurudev-Vanis* and also through our satsang, now come to me very often and sit in my little Dhyan Room. They have not only had effortless meditation but they have also felt a stronger inner bliss descending on them. This type of experience they have never had before.

The experiences I have had are due entirely to the grace and benevolence of Baba. All I have done is to try to surrender myself as far as possible to him. Sri Gurudev has given me a new life and what a new life! A life now so full of joy, a life so full of meaning, a life now spent in the meditation of Gurudev, in the service of Gurudev, and in prayers to Gurudev.

## SADGURU—THE PROTECTOR

### DILIP PANDIT

When I came to know that my mother goes into deep meditation I was really amused. This was soon after Baba returned from Delhi in March, 1969. Until now, during my visits to the Ashram, I had seen only two persons absorbed in meditation. To me meditation was a new subject. So one night, on March 20, out of fun and curiosity, I sat near my mother to watch her meditate. While I was watching her perform some strange movements, I suddenly slipped into meditation. I experienced tremors in my spine and electric currents passing through my body and pain between my eyebrows. I saw light. My head began to move round and round. I felt very cold. I began to sob and tears rolled down my cheeks. They were neither the tears of joy nor of pain. I myself did not understand why I was weeping. With Baba's grace, my meditation started from that very day. Whenever I sat in meditation all sorts of things happened. Each time I saw different kinds of colours and heard various sounds.

After a week we went to Ganeshpuri. As soon as I set foot in the Ashram I experienced an inexplicable joy. It was a joy such as I would not have experienced had I won the table-tennis match, which I like very much. With Baba's permission I sat for meditation in the Dhyan Room. In my meditation I saw a great saint like Bhagawan Nityananda sitting on a *shivalinga*. I saw only his body. I could not see his face. He wore only a saffron loin-cloth. Seeing him, I felt joy compared to that of a lost calf who finds its mother or to that of one who sees light in the darkness. Since that day I always see him in my meditation. I see myself sitting in meditation near that *shivalinga* and the saint. I feel as if we have been related to each other for aeons.

I developed reverence for him and gradually became fond of him. He, whom I now call *langotidhari* (one with the loin-cloth), told me to do *So'ham japa* and from that day I have started doing it.

One day the *langotidhari* said to me, "Do not sit here for meditation. I will show you another place. From now on you will sit there." Then he took me to a mountain where there were many caves in which many sages were practising penance. He showed me a cave. As I entered it I felt as if from that day I was to start on a great mission. The work for which I had been waiting for 14 years (which is presently my age) was about to begin. I felt as if I knew what that mission was and how it was to be carried out. Only I had not known about it so far. But that day I was, as it were, awakened to it. I was like a person who knew how to drive a car but did not have the key. But now I had found the key. I had only to start the car.

Although I had been talking to the *langotidhari*, so far I had not seen his face. One day I asked him to show it to me. He laughed in his usual style and stood up. At that very moment my eyes were dazzled to see the whole universe in his body. I saw the sun, moon, stars and the milky way. I could see the whole world in him. I realised that He was the universe, and the universe was He. In the meantime I heard his deep voice, "Have you seen me? I am the whole universe! Now why do you want to see my face! If you see me everywhere, it is enough."

Two days later it so happened that when my meditation ended, I was unable to open my eyes and the *jnana mudra* of my hands would not loosen. I asked my mother to touch my eyes. As soon as she did so they opened, but the *jnana mudra* was very tight as if the thumb and the finger had become one. I heard the voice of the *langotidhari*. "Go to your sister who is sitting upstairs." I went upstairs and saw Madhavi, my sister, relating the experiences of her meditation to others. Again I heard the same voice, "Hit her on the back with your *jnana mudra*, so that it will open and she will slip into meditation." I hit her on the back with force, then again on her face according to the instructions of the voice. My sister immediately began to laugh and was absorbed in deep meditation for half an hour.

One night, when I was about to go to bed, I automatically slipped into meditation. It was only for a few minutes, when the *langotidhari* said to me, "I won't let you appear at your examination. I have to tell you so many things. Your right hand will be injured." I related this to my mother. Everyone in the house made fun of me saying that I had found an excuse for not studying.

After two days, on April 7, I met with a motor accident and my right hand was put in a sling. I was happy; not because I was relieved from appearing at the examination but because now I could sit for meditation. However, I was disappointed. My ribs had been hurt in the accident. Therefore, when *So'ham japa* started in meditation I felt as if my chest was being filled up with air and I could not endure the pressure. So I was unable to sit in meditation.

After a few days I went to our farm at Saphala with my two younger brothers, as now I had nothing to do. There we used to play with the airgun and I killed a bird. It was April 15. As I woke up in the morning, and was still feeling drowsy, the *langotidhari* appeared and said, "Your airgun wants the blood of a human being." I asked, "Whose blood?" He replied, "You will soon know. God will decide about it." Though I did not pay much attention to what he said, I wrote it down on a piece of paper. I removed the bandage on my hand and taking the airgun with me I went to the jungle with my brothers. My younger brother fired the gun and the bullet almost hit the ear of a passer-by. At once I remembered the warning of the *langotidhari*. I began to take care of the gun.

At last what was destined to happen did happen. In the evening, while holding the airgun between my legs, I began to open the lock of the room. As I bent down the gun slipped. A young boy who was standing near me tried to hold it. His hand fell on the trigger and the gun went off. A bullet went straight into the right side of my chest. Yet I held the pain firmly and very calmly.

There were no tears in my eyes. I am sure I had got this power of endurance as a result of meditation. I was taken to the doctor who nursed me and I lay down at his place peacefully.

The doctor told us that the bullet had missed the lung very narrowly. Half an hour before the operation I slipped into meditation and the *langotidhari* gave me an important instruction which I immediately wrote down on a piece of paper. He also advised me not to talk about it to anyone. Later, when I went to the Ashram, I handed over that paper to Baba.

After the operation, while in drowsiness, I told my parents that Baba and the *langotidhari* were present there. It was a great comfort to have them near me. The *langotidhari* was really very cunning. Although he knew everything, he was inquiring how it all happened. I explained everything by gestures. When he got up I touched his feet.

I did have pain in my chest but on looking at the photograph of Bhagawan Nityananda, I would be absorbed in meditation. In this condition I would tell my mother that I was paying the penalty of my sin and that I realised what pain must have been felt by the bird I had killed the other day. The *langotidhari* passed his hand on my wound and the pain subsided. My mother told me that I myself was touching the wound.

After the stitches were removed I went to Ganeshpuri. Baba lovingly inquired after me. He asked me about the *langotidhari* and gave me a book* to read, in which similar true experiences of a young boy named Kedar are described.

While in meditation, I am transported to some other world. I experience an unusual bliss. My Sadguru has given me the gift of this sublime happiness. It is he who protected me from a great calamity. All is due to Sadguru's grace.

---

* *Sadhu-darshan va Sat-prasang* by M. M. Pandit Gopinath Kaviraj.

# GLOSSARY

*Abhanga* : devotional verse in the Marathi language.

*Abhaya mudra* : one hand raised with palm outward, meaning, "Do not fear."

*Ajna chakra* : two-petalled lotus between the eyebrows; the seat of the Guru.

*Akasha* : subtle inner space.

*Anaviya–Mayiya–Karmic* : the three limitations (*malas*) which the Supreme Being assumes in order to manifest Himself. By *anaviya mala* the universal becomes individual; by *mayiya mala* the undifferentiated becomes differentiated; by *karmic mala* the non-doer becomes the doer.

*Arati* : waving of lights and/or fragrant incense to an idol or a saint; a ritual of worship.

*Asana* : posture; seat.

*Ashram* : the abode of a Guru or saint; a spiritual community.

*Avadhoot* : a great mystic-renunciate who has risen above body-consciousness, all duality and all conventional standards.

*Ayurvedic* : pertaining to *Ayurveda*, the Indian system of medicine.


*Baba* : term of affection for a saint.

*Bandha* : a Hatha Yoga practice; a muscular lock.

*Bhagawan* : the Lord; a divine saint.

*Bhajiya* : fried vegetable and flour.

*Bhava* : feeling of devotion.

*Bhavasamadhi* : absorption in devotional ecstasy.

*Bhujangini mudra* : puckering the mouth like a serpent.

*Brahmabhava* : identification with the all-pervasive Being.

*Brahmamuhurta* : 3 a.m. to 6 a.m.; the traditional period for meditation and other spiritual practices, invested with spiritual power.

*Brahman* : the Absolute.

*Brahmarandhra* : the crown of the head where the *sahasrar* is located.

*Brahmin* : priest.


Celestial cow : *kamdhenu*; wish-fulfilling cow.

Celestial tree : *kalpavriksha*; wish-fulfilling tree.

*Chaitanya* : consciousness.

*Chakra* : a subtle center of energy in the body.

*Chapati* : a kind of pancake made from wheat flour (Indian bread).

*Chidakash* : subtle space of consciousness in the *sahasrar*.
*Chinmudra* : hand gesture in which the tip of the thumb and index finger touch while the other three fingers are outstretched; practised during meditation to keep spiritual energy from flowing out of the body.
*Chintamani* : a precious mythological stone which appears according to the possessor's wishes.
*Chiti* : *Chitshakti*; *Kundalini*; *Mahamaya*; *Parashakti*; *Shakti*; Divine conscious energy; dynamic aspect of Godhead; referred to as a Goddess.
*Chitshakti* : see *Chiti*.

*Darshan* : seeing a saint or a sacred idol, which bestows blessings.
*Dattatreya* : the Lord.
*Dharma* : righteousness; duty; religion; morality.
*Dhoti* : a common dress for men in north India, worn around the waist.
*Dhyan* : meditation.
*Diksha* : initiation.

Five elements : ether, air, fire, water, earth.
Five sheaths : the five coverings of an embodied soul which determine personality and the nature of the individual consciousness: *annamaya kosha* : composed by food, constitutes the gross body; *pranamaya kosha* : corresponds roughly to the nervous system, vital being; *manomaya kosha* : the mind; *vijnanamaya kosha* : the intellect; *anandamaya kosha* : the blissful sheath.

*Ganapati* : Ganesh, the elephant-faced god; a son of Shiva.
*Gulabjaman* : egg-shaped Indian sweet.
*Gunas* : the three basic qualities of Nature : *sattva* : light, balance, harmony purity; *rajas* : activity, passion; *tamas* : inertia, ignorance.
*Gurubhava* : love for the Guru; identification with the Guru.
*Gurudev* : the Guru who is an embodiment of God.
*Gurukripa* : Guru's grace.
*Gurutattva* : essence of Guruhood; the Supreme Lord.

*Hatha Yoga* : a yogic discipline which involves gaining mastery over the body and its functions.

*Japa* : repetition of a divine name or mantra.
*Jivanmukti* : liberation while still in the body.
*Jnana mudra* : see *chinmudra*.
*Jnani* : an enlightened person; a seeker on the path of knowledge.

*Heena* : an Indian perfume.
*Kailas* : see *Mt. Kailas.*
*Kala* : quality.
*Kalpataru* : the wishing-tree (*kalpavriksha*).
*Kamdhenu* : the celestial wishing-cow.
*Karma* : action; force of one's accumulated past actions.
*Kartikeya* : a son of Shiva.
*Kashi* : Benares, a holy place in India.
*Khechari mudra* : the state in which the tongue rises into the the nasal pharynx, causing the release of nectar.
*Khichari* : an Indian dish prepared from rice and lentil.
*Khus* : an Indian perfume.
*Kinnaras* : celestial beings.
*Kriya* : yogic movement or process.
*Kum-kum* : coloured powder.
*Kumbhaka* : holding of the breath.
*Kundalini* : the Serpent Power; the creative force of the universe which lies coiled at the base of the spine; see *Chiti.*
*Kutir* : hut.

*Lakh* : 100,000.
*Lungi* : common dress for men in south India; cloth worn around the waist.

*Mahadeva* : one of the names of Shiva, meaning "Great God."
*Mahamandaleshwar* : religious head of a region; equivalent to arch-bishop.
*Mandir* : temple.
*Mantra* : sacred words or sounds invested with the power to transform the individual who repeats them; name of God.
*Maya* : illusion; the manifested universe, the dance of atoms, which appears to be real; in contradistinction to the Real, the unchanging Absolute.
*Mayiya* : see *anaviya.*
Milkmaids of Vraja : the lovers of Lord Krishna; *gopis.*
*Mogra* : fragrant flower.
*Mridang* : a kind of drum.
*Mt. Kailas* : a mountain in the Himalayas of Tibet; the abode of Shiva.
*Mudra* : a pose; posture; gesture.
*Muladhar* : the *chakra* at the base of the spine where Kundalini lies dormant.
*Murccha* : a Hatha Yoga practice in which the breath is held until the mind becomes empty of thoughts; this is called the "fainting of the mind."

*Nada* : divine music or sound.
*Nataraja* : name for dancing Lord Shiva.

Nine Openings : eyes, ears, nostrils, mouth, anus and sex organ.

*Nirguna* : without attributes; the formless aspect of God.

*Nirvikalpa* : mentation-free *samadhi*.

*Om Namah Shivaya* : a mantra meaning, "*Om*. I bow to Shiva."

*Parashakti* : see *Chiti*.

*Parashiva* : name of Shiva meaning "Supreme Shiva;" the Absolute.

*Parasmani* : the philosopher's stone.

*Paryushtaka* : lit. City of Eight; subtle body consisting of the essences of the five elements, mind, intellect and ego.

*Pashyanti* : non-verbal, non-conceptual, primal level of sound.

*Prakriti* : force of manifestation.

*Pranava* : *Om*; *Udgitha*.

*Pranayama* : control of *prana*; breathing exercise.

*Prarabdha* : accumulated past karma which determines the present birth.

*Prasad* : food that has been offered to God or the Guru and is then distributed to the devotees, sanctified; a gift from the Guru.

*Purana* : mythological and historical stories; part of the Hindu Scriptures.

*Purusha* : Person; the Lord.

*Raja Yoga* : yoga of concentration.

*Rajasic* : having the qualities of passion, activity.

*Rudraksha* : a dried seed from which prayer beads are made.

Sacred thread : thread worn over one shoulder symbolizing religious initiation.

*Sadguru* : the true Guru.

*Sadhaka* : seeker.

*Sadhana* : spiritual discipline.

*Sadhu* : an ascetic.

*Saguna* : having attributes; the Personal Aspect of God.

*Sahasrar* : the thousand-petalled lotus in the brain, located at the crown of the head; the seat of Shiva.

*Samadhi* : a state of meditative union with the Absolute.

*Samsara* : change; becoming; worldliness.

*Samskara* : past impressions.

*Sannyasi* : one who has taken formal vows of renunciation.

*Satchidananda* : the nature of the Supreme Reality : Existence-Consciousness-Bliss.

*Satsang* : a meeting of devotees to hear Scriptures, chant, or sit in the presence of the Guru.

*Sattvic* : having the qualities of harmony and purity.

GLOSSARY                                              267

*Shabda-Brahman* : God in the form of sound.
*Shaivite* : worshipper of Shiva.
Seed letter : (seed mantra) basic sound which gives rise to an
    object, deity or state.
Seven bodily components : lymphatic fluid, flesh, bone, blood,
    marrow, semen and fat.
Seven sages : Atri, Gautama, Vasishtha, Bharadwaj, Kashyap,
    Vishvamitra and Jamadagni.
*Shakti* : see *Chiti*.
*Shaktipat* : transmission of spiritual power (*Shakti*) from Guru
    to disciple; spiritual awakening.
*Shambhavi mudra* : state of absorption in the inner Self, in
    which the eyes remain half-open; Parashiva.
*Siddha* : Perfected One; one who has attained oneness with God.
*Siddhasana* : the perfect posture.
*Siddhis* : supernatural powers.
Six Schools of Indian Philosophy : Vedanta, Sankhya, Nyaya,
    Vaisheshika, Purva Mimansa, Uttara Mimansa.
*Svadhishthan chakra* : *chakra* at the root of the sex organ.
*Shivalinga* : oval-shaped symbol of Lord Shiva made from stone,
    metal or clay.
Shiva's armour : group of mantras sacred to Lord Shiva which
    secure His protection.
*Sunya* : void.

*Tamasic* : having the qualities of inertia and darkness.
*Tamboura* : a stringed instrument.
*Tantra* : the esoteric, gnostic teachings of Hinduism and Buddh-
    ism.
*Tarpan* : funeral rite in which food is offered to the departed.
Thirty-six constituents : different stages of manifestation accord-
    ing to Shaivite Philosophy.
Three knots : identification with the three bodies : gross, subtle
    and causal.
Three worlds : heaven, earth and hell.
Threefold misery : physical and mental suffering caused by one-
    self, others, or fate and forces of nature.
*Tilak* : sacred mark on the forehead.
*Tonga* : two-wheeled horse-drawn carriage.
*Turiya* : the fourth state, beyond waking, dream and deep sleep;
    the transcendental state.
*Turiyatita* : beyond the fourth state.

*Udgitha* : *Om*; *Pranava*; the primal sound.
*Urdhvareta* : perfect celibate whose seminal fluid flows upwards.

*Vaikuntha* : the abode of Lord Vishnu.
*Vaishnavite* : worshiper of Vishnu.

*Vedanta* : non-dual philosophy of the *Upanishads*
*Veena* : stringed instrument.
*Veerasana* : heroic posture.
*Vishuddha chakra* : *chakra* in the throat.

*Yogini* : female practitioner of yoga.
*Yajna* : ritualistic sacrifice.